The Development of the
Colombian Labor Movement

The Development of the Colombian Labor Movement

by Miguel Urrutia

112235

New Haven and London, Yale University Press, 1969

Preface

This book is not a comprehensive history of the Colombian labor movement. It is an attempt to describe the complex interplay of political and economic forces which has made possible the growth of a labor movement in Colombia.

The emergence of a strong, nonrevolutionary labor movement in an underdeveloped country is somewhat unexpected. The purpose of this book is to give a historical explanation of the rise of such a labor movement in Colombia, emphasizing the necessary preconditions which made this possible and the way in which these preconditions determined the direction and nature of the movement.

My central thesis is that, except within the small group of skilled workers, the labor movement could not develop in a country with as much surplus labor as Colombia, unless it obtained the active support of government. This thesis has made the study as much a political history as a labor history, as its major purpose is to trace the relationships between the labor movement and the government and the way in which government support allowed the labor movement to develop through its various stages.

The first part of the book traces the movement back to the early nineteenth century and the first organizations of artisans in Colombia. This history is relevant to the general understanding of the later growth of the labor movement, since all attempts at labor organization before 1930 failed because of a lack of state protection. In part two, emphasis is placed on the role of organized labor in the transformation of the ideology of the Liberal Party. Thus, although politics have determined the changes of fortune of the Colombian labor movement, organized labor has also helped to bring about political development.

In part three I trace the emergence of political bargaining as a union tactic, and in part four the development of collective bargaining is explained in terms of changes in labor legislation, the growth of modern industry, and the political defeat of Liberalism. Finally, the effectiveness of collective bargaining is evaluated statistically, and the success of the labor movement is demonstrated by showing the rapid increases in the real wages of urban workers in the last decade.

Some of my interpretations are controversial and many Colombians will find them biased. I look forward to other interpretations. Since many of the Colombian leaders who created the Confederación de Trabajadores de Colombia (CTC) and the Unión de Trabajadores de Colombia (UTC) are still alive and active, I hope this history motivates these men to write their own accounts of how the Colombian labor movement became what it is today.

Among those to whom this book and I owe a particular debt are Walter Galeson, Lloyd Ulman, and William McGreevey of the faculty of the University of California at Berkeley, whose constructive criticism was always helpful. I would also like to extend my thanks to the Centro de Estudios sobre Desarrollo Económico of the Universidad de los Andes, where, as a research associate, I was able to write this book.

Miguel Urrutia

Bogotá
May 1, 1968

Contents

CONTENTS

Tables

Part I

Labor in the Nineteenth Century

1

The Organization of the Society of Artisans in 1847

In 1847, when the Sociedad de Artesanos de Bogotá was being organized, Colombia still had the economic organization that it had inherited from Spain. As in most colonial economies, the central government controlled important sectors of the economy. There were government monopolies of salt, tobacco, gunpowder, and liquor production, as well as such restrictions on trade as high import and export duties, a 20 percent tax on the production of gold and silver, and the famous *alcabala*, or cumulative sales tax.

Furthermore, large parts of the national wealth were specifically withdrawn from the market. For example, the institution of the Indian commune, the *resguardo*, had as a major purpose the conservation of Indian territory in Indian hands, and it was against the law to sell such land. The *ejido*, or town common, was another category of land that was outside the free market. These lands were the property of all citizens and were usually kept as pastures for the cattle of the urban dwellers. Finally there were the extremely large landholdings of the Church and the system of *censos* on private land. The latter was a contract between an owner of land and a private individual or community in which the landowner committed himself to give a specified income in perpetuity to the beneficiary of the contract. When such property was sold, the censo was binding on the new owner. Needless to say, this form of contract immobilized these properties by making them unattractive to buy on the free market.

Not only was a large part of the land outside the free market economy, and an important part of the manufacturing activity possible in such a primitive economy monopolized by a non-entrepreneurial state, but the population was also kept immobile and outside the free market. In the first place, the institution of slavery, although not widespread, had survived. Furthermore, since the Indian resguardos were organized on a communal basis, with sharing of work and income, the Indian population was in fact tied to the commune since leaving it meant that the individual lost the income corresponding to his share of resguardo land; and since there were no export crops and no large consumption centers, agriculture on lands outside the resguardo was not productive enough to justify employing workers at wages that were sufficiently above subsistence to entice the Indians to leave the resguardo.

If we consider that the Church may have owned as much as one-third of the cultivable land in the country,[1] that town commons often included, as in the case of Cali, all territory distant one league (three miles) from the center of the town,[2] and that during the early eighteenth century the resguardos included the greater part of cultivable land, it is easy to see that most of the productive capacity of the nation (capital as well as labor) was outside the market economy as late as the middle of the nineteenth century. The effects of this type of productive organization on economic growth were completely negative.

The conservative governments after Bolívar did not use the

1. Indalecio Liévano Aguirre, *El proceso de Mosquera ante el Senado* (Bogotá, Italgraf, 1966), p. 49.

2. *Gaceta Oficial,* year XX, no. 1144 (February 6, 1851). According to colonial law, when a town was founded, sufficient land had to be put aside for common use *(ejidos)* so that "even if the population increases very much, there will always be sufficient area for the recreation of the population and sufficient area to pasture the town's cattle without causing any damage."

power of the state as an engine of economic development because the political leaders of the time were really economic liberals and did not believe in direct state intervention.[3] In spite of this, these governments did not see fit to dismantle the colonial system of restrictions which hindered the entrepreneurial activity of the nation's bourgeoisie. The result was a more complete economic stagnation than had been the case before independence. Scattered wage data dramatically confirm the extent of this stagnation. For example, in 1669 Indian labor earned two *reales* a day, a wage found among unskilled construction workers in Bogotá in 1820 and 1836.[4] In the decade before 1845, members of the republican upper classes attempted to establish a variety of small consumer goods factories, using machinery of the latest European models, but enterprises that did not fail had very modest success due to the limitations of the market, civil wars, and the general stagnation of the economy.

The result of economic stagnation was that between 1842 and 1850, there took place among the leaders of both political parties a gradual shift of opinion toward a dogmatic laissez-faire policy. During this period, in which the economic policy of neocolonialism proved clearly undesirable, the Liberal Party, whose members advocated an extreme form of political liberalism and economic laissez-faire, gathered its forces to take power from the Conservatives.

3. The ruling class after independence had many of the values and beliefs of the European bourgeoisie. In 1810 there was only one nobleman in Nueva Granada, the Marques de San Jorge, and even he had had his title annulled in 1777 because he did not pay the required contributions to the crown. Ten landowners on the Sabana refused to accept titles at the end of the eighteenth century because they were unable or unwilling to pay the requisite contributions (see Frank R. Safford, "Commerce and Enterprise in Central Colombia, 1821–1870" [doctoral dissertation, New York, Columbia University, 1965]).

4. These figures have been kindly made available to me by Dr. Alberto Pardo Pardo. The first comes from convent records found in the Archivo Nacional, and the others from the archives of the Colegio del Rosario.

In April of 1845, General Tomás Cipriano de Mosquera was sworn in as President of Nueva Granada. Although elected by the Conservative Party, he was liberal at heart. It is, therefore, not surprising that he should have initiated the destruction of the colonial economy, and that as a Liberal President in 1861 he should have liquidated the holdings of the Church, the last vestige of the colonial order. Between the two presidencies of Mosquera, however, Colombia[5] lived through various guerrilla uprisings, one revolution with undertones of class war, and one civil war. During the same period the economic organization of the nation was completely overhauled. Very likely the economic change initiated by the Liberal bourgeoisie in 1850 set the foundations for the industrial revolution that occurred in Colombia after the turn of the century, but in the short run it created a growing income inequality and lowered the standard of living of the sizable class of independent artisans and agricultural workers. It was in this context that the first labor organizations in the nation's history emerged.

The Society of Artisans

The first organization of Colombian workers emerged as a reaction against the liberalization of the economy started by President Mosquera, when near the end of his term he decided to take the first steps toward complete free trade. In his report to Congress in 1847, Florentino González, Mosquera's Secretary of the Treasury, the most important follower of the English school of economic laissez-faire, advocated an extreme form of free trade policy. He reasoned that:

> In a country rich in mines and agricultural products, which can sustain a considerable and beneficial export trade, the law should not attempt to encourage industries that distract

5. The name of the country was changed from Nueva Granada to Colombia in the Constitution of 1863.

6

the inhabitants from the agricultural and mining occupations. . . . Europe with an intelligent population, and with the possession of steam power and its applications, educated in the art of manufacturing, fulfills its mission in the industrial world by giving various forms to raw materials. We too should fulfill our mission, and there is no doubt as to what it is, if we consider the profusion of natural resources with which Providence has endowed this land. We should offer Europe raw materials and open our doors to her manufactures, to facilitate trade and the profit it brings, and to provide the consumer, at a reasonable price, with the products of the manufacturing industry.[6]

Free trade, the first step taken by Florentino González, the theoretician of the new liberal economic order, meant the destruction of the Colombian artisan class. At the same time that Florentino González was opening the doors to free trade from the Treasury Department of a Conservative government, the Bogotá artisans spontaneously started to organize themselves in defense of their livelihood, and against economic liberalism.

In October of 1847, scarcely four months after passage of a law that indirectly lowered import duties,[7] Ambrosio López and a small group of Bogotá artisans started to organize a "society to promote the advancement of the arts and other branches of industry that can contribute to our welfare."[8] The bylaws of this society of artisans, approved on November 18, 1847, merit careful

6. Luis Ospina Vásquez, *Industria y protección en Colombia, 1810–1930* (Medellín, E.S.F., 1955), pp. 208–09. This quotation and all other quotations from Spanish-language sources were translated by Miguel Urrutia.

7. This Law of June 19, 1847, allowed the payment of tariff duties with public debt certificates. Since the customs authorities accepted these certificates at par value, and the same certificates could be purchased substantially under par on the free market, the law lowered tariffs.

8. *Reglamento de la Sociedad de Artesanos* (Bogotá, Imprenta de Nicolás Gómez, 1847).

study.[9] Although the initiative for the society seems to have come from the artisans affected by the new foreign trade policy,[10] Article 3 of the bylaws of the society specifically does not require that members be active in any artisan occupation. To enter the society, only the approval of two-thirds of the members present was required. Article 17 helps to make clear Article 3 by showing that the society had been formed more as' a political pressure group than as a trade union interested in any kind of collective bargaining. Paragraph 5 of Article 17 states that "Members should not vote according to the suggestions of strangers, without first letting the society know the name of the person who has tried to influence his vote."

Then, somewhat in contradiction, but probably keeping in mind that a group of liberal artisans was organizing under a Conservative government, Article 45 stated that "it is forbidden for the members to discuss any political, personal, or religious questions in the society." Needless to say, as far as one can tell, the society discussed almost exclusively political, personal, and religious questions.

Although with time the Sociedad de Artesanos became primarily a political club, it did have some of the functions of primitive trade unions when it was founded. One of the major functions of the society was adult education but, as is clear from the Statutes for Instruction of the Bogotá Society of Artisans published in 1849, this activity complemented in part the political functions of the society.[11] These statutes established six classes for the benefit of the members:

1. Reading
2. Arithmetic

9. Ibid.
10. Ambrosio López, *El desengaño o confidencias de Ambrosio López* (Bogotá, Imprenta de Espinosa, 1851), pp. 14–23.
11. *Reglamento para la instrucción de la Sociedad de Artesanos de Bogotá* (Bogotá, Imprenta de Nicolás Gómez, 1849).

3. Writing
4. Grammar
5. Ethics and good manners
6. Explanation of the Constitution of Nueva Granada, and elementary principles of constitutional law

Furthermore, in Article 7 it is stated that a class could be instituted on military ordnance, use of arms, and other knowledge necessary for participating in the national guard. This class and the constitutional law class planned by the society clearly had political undertones. The class on constitutional law was to be a form of agitation in favor of the new constitution planned by the Liberals, and the class preparing the artisans for service in the national guard was part of the Liberal strategy of creating a popular fighting force to counteract the traditionally Conservative regular army.

Although not specified in the statutes, the real purpose of the society was to rally the artisans against the government's free trade policy. In an interesting pamphlet debate which took place in 1851 between two of the founding members of the society,[12] the ultimate purpose of the society was very clearly stated, and both Ambrosio López and Emeterio Heredia agreed that the original purpose of the society was to obtain tariff protection for the products of the Bogotá artisans. Heredia, who was president of the society in 1849, wrote that "we founded the society in order to attempt to have spokesmen who would ask for an increase in tariff protection on manufactured goods that could be produced in the country."[13]

The artisans organized themselves in 1847 in reaction to the

12. López, *El desengaño;* Emeterio Heredia, *Contestación al cuaderno titulado, "El desengaño o confidencias de Ambrosio López, etc." por el presidente que fué de la Sociedad de Artesanos el 7 de Marzo de 1849* (Bogotá, Imprenta de Morales, 1851); Ambrosio López, *El triunfo sobre la serpiente roja cuyo asunto es del dominio de la nación* (Bogotá, Espinosa, 1851).

13. Heredia, p. 9.

competition of foreign manufactured goods. This competition had become more threatening to the artisans because of two factors. First, the Secretary of the Treasury had taken the first steps toward trade liberalization; and second, technological advances in transportation and factory production had lowered the prices of English manufactures on the Colombian market.

As early as 1830 English textiles and other manufactured goods were already competing with the products of local artisans, but in 1846–47 steam navigation was established on the Magdalena River and the competitive position of imports improved rapidly in the Bogotá area. In fact, decreasing transportation costs were a more serious threat to the artisans than the moderate reduction of tariffs proposed by Florentino González.[14]

One of the strategic variables in Colombia's economic development has always been the cost of transport, and in the first half of the nineteenth century customs duties were much less efficient protection for the artisans than was the topography of the country. Augusto Le Moyne's description of his trip from Le Havre to Bogotá in 1828 gives a clear picture of the transportation problem in Nueva Granada.

From Le Havre to Santa Marta, on the north coast of Nueva Granada, the trip took 52 days, but between Santa Marta and Bogotá Le Moyne traveled 73 days in the most intense discomfort. The greater part of the trip was spent on the Magdalena River on primitive sampans, in which the passengers and cargo were exposed to all the humidity, heat, and insects of the tropics.[15]

It is not surprising then that, given the geographic barriers to foreign trade, agitation for higher import duties should have coincided with the establishment of steam navigation on the Magdalena River. Although freight rates were not immediately

14. Customs duties in Nueva Granada before 1848 were moderate. For textiles imported on foreign ships they varied from 17.5 percent ad valorem in 1831 to 20 percent in 1840 (Ospina Vásquez, *Industria,* p. 170).

15. Augusto Le Moyne, *Viajes y estancias en América del Sur* (Bogotá, Biblioteca Popular de Cultura Colombiana, 1945).

and radically lowered, the speed and security of the new method of transportation lowered transport costs substantially.

Since the artisans were threatened by new technology which was beyond their control, and since they could no longer compete with imported manufactures, it was impossible for them to maintain their standard of living as long as the state did not protect them. Faced with the threat of foreign competition they turned to political action in order to obtain state protection. Their first appearance on the political scene was in the presidential election of 1849.

The Artisans Turn to Political Action

According to the Constitution of 1843, the President was to be elected by a majority of the votes of the electors, and if no candidate obtained the majority, Congress was to elect a President from the three candidates who had obtained the most votes in the electoral assemblies.[16] The election of the President was indirect in all cases. In the last days of June 1848, the primary elections for the Presidency took place throughout the republic in complete peace, and in early August there followed the secondary elections in which the electors in the various regions were to choose President, senators, and members of the lower house.[17] The votes cast in these secondary elections did not give any candidate an absolute majority and showed the following distribution:[18] José Hilario López, the Liberal candidate, 735 votes; Rufino José Cuervo, the Conservative candidate who had the sympathy of the government, 304 votes; José Joaquín Gori, a Conservative with some support from more moderate elements,

16. Angel y Rufino José Cuervo, *Vida de Rufino Cuervo y noticias de su epoca* (Bogotá, Biblioteca Popular de Cultura Colombiana, 1946), 2, 22.

17. José Manuel Restrepo, *Historia de la Nueva Granada, 1845–1854* (Bogotá, Editorial El Catolicismo, 1963), pp. 84, 89.

18. José María Cordovéz Moure, *Reminiscencias de Santafé y Bogotá* (Bogotá, Biblioteca Popular de Cultura Colombiana, 1945), 4, 191.

348 votes; various other candidates, 688 votes; blank votes, 1.

It was, therefore, up to Congress to elect the President for the period 1849–52, and in this election the Sociedad de Artesanos could make its wishes known. The election was scheduled for March 7, and in the early days of that month it became generally known in the capital, a town of 30,000, that the artisans had purchased all the pistols, knives, and powder that the Bogotá stores had in stock. Aware of the results of the European revolution of 1848 and of the precedent set in Venezuela the previous year, when the army reserve attacked the Congress in defense of a liberal president and killed four deputies and three other upper class persons,[19] the members of Congress had good reason to be uneasy on the morning of March 7.

Early that day the Church of Santo Domingo, where the election was to take place, was completely filled by artisans presumably there to intimidate the Congress. During the day it was necessary to vote four times to achieve the required majority, and the proceedings took place amid much disorder. Confusion became widespread both within the Church and among the artisans gathered in the square outside after the second vote, when the Conservative candidate obtained 42 votes, the Liberal candidate 40, and 2 votes were left blank. In the general confusion the crowd thought that Cuervo had won, and there was an attempt to invade the area occupied by Congress. In time order was restored, the chamber was cleared, and on the fourth vote José Hilario López, the Liberal candidate, was elected President by a 6-vote majority. Mariano Ospina, Conservative leader and future President, voted for López and wrote on his ballot: "I vote for General José Hilario López so that the Deputies will not be assassinated."

From the historical accounts it is unclear whether the presence of the artisans in fact determined the outcome. On the one hand, Liberal historians point out that López won because of the Con-

19. Restrepo, pp. 70, 102.

servative division. This interpretation is plausible, since the partisans of Gori were in fact moderates, and had more in common with the Liberals than with the Conservatives. Conservative historians, on the other hand, assert that the Liberal victory was achieved by intimidation.

In all fairness it must be admitted that the election was very close, and that if the threatening presence of the sovereign people intimidated even one or two congressmen, the election of López owed much to the Sociedad de Artesanos. Whatever the truth of the matter, the incident changed the future of the Sociedad. Shortly after the election, the society changed its name to Sociedad Democrática, significantly dropping the word artisan from its title. It became a political club dedicated to the defense of the government that it thought it had helped to elect, and soon after even became the armed guard of the new government by becoming integrated with the national guard with which the Liberals tried to replace the traditional army.

The Conservative Artisan Societies

Aware of the importance of having an organization ready to come to its defense in difficult times, the Liberal government decided to encourage societies similar to that of Bogotá all over the country. Many such societies were founded from 1849 to 1852, and these became the primary support of the government. Throughout the period, the government newspaper published the statutes of most of the Sociedades Democráticas founded, and from these it is possible to determine the nature of the societies. In the statutes we still find some reference to the "encouragement of the arts," but more commonly the societies appear to be purely political. A typical case may be that of the Sociedad de Amigos de los Principios Liberales bajo el Sistema Democrático[20] founded in the parish of Micaí. The purpose of the society was to "uphold

20 Society of Friends of Liberal Principles under Democratic Systems.

under all circumstances our present system of government, encourage agriculture and industry, and make known the sacred principles of equality, liberty, and fraternity."[21] The purposes of the Sociedad Democrática de Castrolarma are more bluntly stated as "being the same as those professed by the present administration. . . . [the society] is committed to giving this administration cooperation and a strong arm to realize these beautiful dogmas . . ."[22] But despite the almost exclusively political nature of the societies, they were still composed largely of artisans. Although not strictly trade unions, they were the first attempt by the Colombian working classes to intervene in an organized manner in matters of collective interest. The Sociedades Democráticas spent a great deal of time discussing problems such as the substitution of a single direct tax for the colonial fiscal system,[23] a policy defended by the more radical Liberals, problems of tariff protection, and other matters of collective interest.

Once the political effectiveness of the societies had been demonstrated, Conservative elements in Bogotá and other cities attempted to create their own political clubs. In Bogotá, Conservative politicians founded the Sociedad Popular on December 17, 1849. As with most Conservative enterprises of the period, the new society was heavily permeated by clerical influence. According to Emeterio Heredia, president of the Sociedad de Artesanos, two clerics were president and vice-president of the Sociedad Popular in the artisan quarter of Las Nieves.[24] In Cali the wealthy Conservative leader Julio Arboleda founded the Sociedad de Amigos del Pueblo in 1850 to neutralize the militantly Liberal

21. *Gaceta Oficial,* year XX, no. 1185 (January 5, 1851).
22. Ibid.
23. This was the topic of discussion at a meeting of the Cali society described with some sarcasm in an anonymous pamphlet published in 1856 and entitled *Reseña histórica de los principales acontecimientos políticos de la ciudad de Cali, desde el año de 1848 hasta el de 1855 inclusive* (Bogotá, Imprenta de Echeverri Hermanos, 1856), pp. 52–55.
24. Heredia, p. 56.

Sociedad Democrática of that locality.[25] This society was officially supposed to "protect industry" by holding an exhibition of artifacts made by local artisans and by giving prizes to those who won the competition. The exhibition took place only once, and the new society shortly found itself engaged in open political conflict with the Sociedad Democrática.

Apparently, however, clerically dominated artisan societies with veiled political tendencies were not new in Colombia.[26] There is evidence that in 1838 Monsignor Baluffi, Papal Nuncio in Bogotá, helped to organize the Sociedad Católica, which had as its purpose the propagation of the gospel. This activity soon included attacks on the *filosofismo*,[27] common among Liberal intellectuals, and involved the Sociedad Católica in political questions. The Liberals then decided to create a "democratic society" destined to combat fanaticism, and to plead for religious liberty and political federalism. The Sociedad Católica finally dissolved when the prior of the Dominican convent sent a letter to the newspaper directed by General Santander in which he attributed obvious political purposes to the society.

Some years later the Jesuits, who had been called back to Nueva Granada after the civil war of 1840, attempted to establish workers' congregations (Congregaciones de Obreros). Toward 1849, at the time that the Sociedad de Artesanos was being organized, the Jesuits are said to have had substantial influence over the artisans and the lower classes through these congregaciones, but they lost this influence after the presidential election of 1849.

In general, the Sociedad Popular and the other societies of Conservative artisans created to neutralize the democratic so-

25. *Reseña histórica*, pp. 26–30.

26. The source for the story of these early confessional societies is an unpublished paper by Germán Colmenares based on his research in the archives of the French Foreign Office.

27. This was an intellectual movement based on the writings of the French *philosophes*.

15

cieties were a failure. They did not improve the position of the Conservatives but did create conflict. On January 14, 1850, some Liberal artisans invaded the meeting of the Popular but though there was disorder and some gunfire, no one was hurt. In a similar but less fortunate attack against a meeting of the Popular in March 1851, one Conservative and one member of the Democrática lost their lives.[28] In Cali, on March 10, 1850, a battle between the Conservative Sociedad de Amigos del Pueblo[29] and the Sociedad Democrática was barely avoided.[30]

Some months later, the conflict between the Conservative and Liberal organizations ceased to be important because of a serious crisis within the Sociedades Democráticas which caused a radical confrontation between the artisans and the Liberal bourgeoisie. To understand the source of this conflict, it is necessary to analyze the social and political philosophy of the men who came to power in 1849.

28. Venancio Ortiz, *Historia de la revolución del 17 de abril de 1854* (Bogotá, Imprenta de Francisco Torres Amaya, 1855), p. 13.

29. The Society of Friends of the People, an organization created by Conservative politicians.

30. *Reseña histórica*, pp. 30–32.

2

The Conflict Between Classical Economics and Political Liberalism in Nueva Granada

Between 1848 and 1854 a new generation came to power in Nueva Granada. During that period all the conflicts latent in the society came to the surface, and the nation experienced the effects of a series of radical economic and social reforms.

In a New Year editorial in the official government newspaper, the director asked rhetorically, "What does Nueva Granada hope to achieve in 1851? The answer is reform of the constitution, abolition of slavery and the death penalty, free enterprise in the economic field, organization of national guards in order to achieve the suppression of the permanent army, the emancipation of the Church, popular election of bishops and priests, and adoption of a direct national tax until the abolition of all custom duties is achieved."[1] The editorial does not mention the achievements of the previous year and a half, which included (1) the abolition of the state monopoly on the production and sale of tobacco, which thereby lowered the nation's fiscal income by about one-third, (2) a 50 percent reduction in the standing army because, as President López explained in his inaugural speech, "the army is unnecessary when the government emanates from the will of

1. *Gaceta Oficial*, year XX, no. 1184 (January 2, 1851).

people,"[2] (3) the decentralization of taxation and government investment, a measure which meant abolition of various taxes such as the 20 percent tax on metals mined, (4) the expulsion of the Jesuits, (5) the destruction of the Indian communities, and (6) an educational reform.

By April 1853, when José María Obando was sworn in as President, much of what this extraordinary generation of statesmen and intellectuals who came to power in 1849 had set out to do had been accomplished. In effect, the colonial social organization had been destroyed, while nothing had been created to replace it. To the generation of the 1850s this was exactly as it should be. They seriously believed that in a society completely free from state and church interference, prosperity was inevitable.

When the Sociedad de Artesanos first started to hold meetings, the young Liberal intellectuals attended and made speeches in the latest revolutionary style, imported from the Europe of 1848. There was an air of camaraderie at the meetings of the society, where artisans in *ruanas* (a garment similar to the Mexican poncho) rubbed elbows with Liberal intellectuals in *casacas* (dress coats).[3] But despite the goodwill shown by both sides, it must be assumed that the mixture of *cachacos* and artisans was not altogether comfortable for the parties concerned. On September 25, 1850, a new society, more in the nature of a debating club, was formed and given the name of Sociedad Republicana. It was established largely by university students and young Liberal intellectuals,[4] and became a vehicle for the expression of the liberal economic ideas which the artisans refused to listen to in the Sociedades Democráticas.

2. Restrepo, *Historia, 1845–1854*, p. 199.
3. From this word was derived the generic name of *cachacos* given to the upper-class Bogotanos by the artisans.
4. As usual, the Conservatives followed with the founding of the Sociedad Filotémica in October, in the hope of neutralizing the Republicana, and thus helped to increase political tension by creating two more warring camps.

In the Sociedad Republicana, and sometimes in the Sociedad Democrática, the Liberal intellectuals continued to agitate for reform. Important merchants and their sons[5] made speeches full of radical theories common in Europe, and their frequent references to the equality preached by Him who died the death of a slave on Golgotha earned the more radical wing of the Liberals the name of *Gólgotas*.

The Conservative historians Angel and Rufino José Cuervo recount that during the meetings of the Sociedad Democrática the advantages of association were preached in the language of Saint-Simon and Fourier, and that the artisans were promised the establishment of industrial workshops.[6] In the Sociedad Republicana socialism was also the fad of the moment. In a session on March 7, 1851, in the Republicana, Antonio Ruiz declared, "property is nothing but the abundant happiness of the few at the expense of the excess of work and unhappiness of the many."[7] Another frequent definition of property, that property is theft, clearly echoed Pierre Joseph Proudhon, the barrel maker's son and self-educated printer who popularized that theory in his book *What is Property?* published in 1840.[8] José María Samper, Liberal theoretician, politician, and member of one of Bogotá's foremost merchant families, described the Sociedad Republicana with great accuracy.

---

5. The upper-class Liberals usually practiced one of the professions, journalism, or trade. Interestingly enough, in Bogotá all of these occupations carried high prestige. Frank Safford has gone so far as to say that "social distinction among Bogotanos was determined by wealth, and secondarily by education (thus the prestige of journalists and professionals). Commerce was the favored vocation of the elite, and material consumption its measure of status." (Safford, *Commerce and Enterprise.*)

6. Cuervo, *Vida de Rufino Cuervo*, p. 188.

7. Gustavo Samper Bernal, *Breve historia constitucional y política de Colombia* (Bogotá, Litografía Colombia S.A., 1957).

8. Edmund Wilson, *To the Finland Station* (Garden City, N.Y., Doubleday Anchor Books, 1953), p. 154.

> It can be said that the escuela republicana was the chrysalis of the radical party. . . . In it we were all socialists, without having studied socialism nor understood it, in love with the word, the political novelty and all of the generous extravagances of the French writers. . . . We talked like socialists, with an enthusiasm that much alarmed President López and the old liberals. In one of my speeches at the Republicana, I invoked in favor of the socialist and equalitarian ideals the example of the martyr of Golgotha . . .[9]

The Radical youths seemed to be sincere in their ideals, but the artisans were not interested in freedom and equality if these concepts implied free trade and equal treatment of foreign and national manufactured goods. To the romantic Radicals, who were consistent in their own way, it implied precisely that. But as Samper suggested, not all Liberals were romantic utopians. President López and the professional politicians within the Party were not irrevocably committed to low tariffs, like the members of the Bogotá commercial bourgeoisie, and they were certainly not particularly interested in the withering away of the state and in minimizing the role of government. This faction of the Liberal Party, closely identified with the government and including many government employees, had much more in common with the artisans than did the Gólgotas. In time this wing of the Liberal Party became known as the *Draconianos*.

The intellectual doctrine of the Gólgotas probably went no further than the romantic equalitarianism described by Samper. Both contemporary historians and modern writers of intellectual history agree that the Gólgotas were influenced by Proudhon, Saint-Simon, Fourier, Louis Blanc, and Lamartine,[10] a combination of intellectual influences which could not lead to a well-

9. José María Samper, *Historia de un alma* (Bogotá, Biblioteca Popular de Autores Colombianos, 1946), *2*, 256.

10. Jaime Jaramillo Uribe, *El pensamiento colombiano en el siglo XIX* (Bogotá, Editorial Temis, 1964), p. 175; Cuervo, p. 188.

structured political doctrine. Although the vocabulary was that of the French revolutionaries of 1848, the really lasting intellectual influence on these Liberal intellectuals was that of the English classical economists.

The Influence of the French Revolution of 1848

The influence of the French Revolution of 1848 on the radical generation in Nueva Granada has been the subject of some debate. Contemporary writers of both parties in Nueva Granada always mentioned the events of Paris when they dealt with the change in intellectual opinion which led to the reforms of the 1850s. Luis Eduardo Nieto Arteta, however, has pointed out that the changes wrought in Nueva Granada were brought about by local economic and social conditions and that contemporary writers emphasized the influence of European events simply because of the Latin American custom of interpreting American events in the light of European experience. He blames this custom on the lack of an "American [Latin American] sociology."[11] Nieto Arteta justifies his interpretation by pointing out the difference between the social and economic conditions in France in 1848 and those in Nueva Granada in 1850.

> The revolution of February 1848 in France was an artisan political movement, and the theory of utopian socialism was based on the existence of a vast artisan or semi-artisan class . . . how different is the social background of the anticolonial revolution of 1850 in Nueva Granada! Due to different historical conditions the artisans of Nueva Granada did not constitute a group that was fighting against its imminent disappearance, as was the case in France. On the contrary, they were a dynamic and enterprising group which wanted

11. Luis Eduardo Nieto Arteta, *Economia y cultura en la historia de Colombia* (Bogotá, Tercer Mundo, 1962), pp. 229–32.

to destroy the colonial barriers that impeded the economic development of Nueva Granada. . . .[12]

This interpretation of Nueva Granada's revolution is completely misleading. The parallels between events in France and in Nueva Granada in 1848–49 are surprising. The social causes of class conflict were the same, and in both nations the outcome of class war was also the same—the triumph of reaction.

In the early days of 1848, intellectuals in France and Nueva Granada imagined that the workers would be farsighted and generous about social reorganization, and that they would happily follow the lead of their sincere well-wishers from the upper classes. Incongruous as it may seem, these romantic socialists believed in the fusion of the classes and that all classes could benefit together.[13] These beliefs were based not on personal experience and actual communication between classes in Bogotá or Paris, but on the intellectual theories common at the time in both capitals. Therefore, the first uneasy coalitions of intellectuals and artisans that led to the toppling of the conservative regimes in both countries were inspired by similar intellectual illusions.

The economic conditions underlying these coalitions were also similar. In Nueva Granada, as in France, the bourgeoisie felt constrained under the rule of a closed circle, and desired more commercial and intellectual freedom.[14] There was little censorship in Nueva Granada, but the Church had very close control

12. Ibid., p. 238. The socialist writer Antonio García makes the same error in believing that the artisans were a dynamic element in the society and that the artisans wanted to eliminate privilege. On the contrary, the artisans fought for the survival of their privileged position. (Antonio García, *Gaitán y el problema de la revolución Colombiana* [Bogotá, Cooperativa Nacional de Artes Graficas, 1955], pp. 74–76.)

13. Priscilla Robertson, *Revolutions of 1848—A Social History* (New York, Harper Torchbooks, 1960), p. 607; Nieto Arteta, *Economia,* pp. 169–82.

14. Robertson, p. 24.

over education and public opinion in general, and in both nations the independent entrepreneur was constantly at odds with insignificant bureaucrats who interfered unpleasantly with the business of accumulation. But most of all, the new bourgeoisie wanted to participate in the business of governing. In Nueva Granada the constraints on voting did not keep the Liberal intellectuals and commercial classes from voting, as happened in France, but the Liberals were convinced that electoral reform (universal suffrage) would make a Conservative victory at the polls impossible. Yet since in Nueva Granada even some artisans could vote under the Conservative electoral law, electoral reform was not the major interest of the Liberal bourgeoisie.

The artisans in both nations also wanted economic security. In both Bogotá and Paris their slogan was the same—"the right to work"—and this need for work security sprang from the impact of the European industrial revolution in both cities. In Paris the right to work became a slogan after the crisis of 1846–47 and the urban unemployment it brought about. Some estimates had a third of the population of Paris on relief in 1847.[15] In Bogotá, unemployment was also the catalyst that drove the artisans to political agitation. In 1823 the French traveler Gaspard Mollien had observed that often the prices of foreign textiles were the same as or lower than prices of textiles produced by the artisans of Socorro,[16] and with the technological advances in transportation that had occurred by 1848, artisan producers were having difficulty competing with the Manchester products.

In summary, two factors led the artisans of Nueva Granada to organization and political agitation: the threat of lower tariff protection, and the lowering of transport costs on foreign manufactures. As in France in 1848, the enemy was competition.[17] In

15. Ibid., p. 18.

16. Gaspard T. Mollien, *Voyage dans la republique de Colombie en 1823* (Bogotá, Biblioteca Popular de Cultura Colombiana, 1944), pp 92–93.

17. Priscilla Robertson believes that to Louis Blanc, "competition specially as it developed under the new English theories of free enterprise,

both Bogotá and Paris the free competitive economy led to unemployment, the greatest plague of the urban proletariat, and in both cities the workers demanded government interference with the free market mechanism, and guarantees against unemployment. The artisans of Nueva Granada were fighting against imminent disappearance. They were not "a dynamic and enterprising group which wanted to destroy the colonial barriers that hindered economic development." The artisans did not believe in free competition, since to them freedom in economics favored only the powerful. In fact the artisans wanted to improve the colonial barriers by bringing about true protection through higher tariffs. This was the source of the conflict between the artisans and the bourgeois Liberals. The bourgeoisie wanted absolute liberty, while the artisans wanted security. Since the proletariat was indifferent to liberty without security, and since economic liberty implied insecurity in the nineteenth century, the radical bourgeoisie abandoned the artisans and united with the moderate Conservatives around the ideal of absolute liberty in social and economic relations.

As early as 1851 a few of the artisan leaders had already realized that the interests of the liberal bourgeoisie and those of the workers were incompatible. Ambrosio López was bitter on the subject. In May 1851, he wrote about the Society of Artisans: "We turned aside from our main object (that of obtaining tariff protection) and we became interested in raising to power certain men, believing that they truly loved us . . . but we, in good faith, served only as stepping stones and today these men sacrifice us and destroy the republic."[18]

---

was the source of incredible evil . . . Of the socialist leaders of 1848, Louis Blanc was [therefore] the most popular because he seemed the most practical and was the author of the best liked slogan of the period, 'the right to work . . .' Labor was to be organized, according to Blanc, by setting up 'social work-shops,' essentially producers' cooperatives, with state money."

18. López, *El desengaño,* Dedicatoria.

The Impact of the Liberal Reforms on the Artisan Class

Just as the free trade policy of the Liberals was clearly against the interests of the artisans, so were most of the other reforms carried out after 1849. Among the reforms that affected the economic position of the artisans were the abolition of slavery, the breakup of the resguardos and the fiscal reforms.

The Abolition of Slavery

In 1852 slavery was abolished. According to the 1851 census there were some 17,000 slaves in the republic out of a population of 2,244,000.[19] They were concentrated in the areas where the *latifundia* were most numerous, and where the Conservative Party had its strength. The abolition of slavery hurt the Conservative land and mine owners of the Southwest (the old province of Cauca) but did not affect the Bogotá, Tolima, or Socorro liberal bourgeoisie. On the contrary, the freed slaves in the South left the countryside and flocked to Cali and other cities where they were soon competing with the established urban workers for jobs, and lowering labor costs. Later on these freed slaves became the labor force for the extraction of cinchona bark, the major export crop in the years after the tobacco boom. In any case, the abolition of slavery did not favorably affect the artisans, since it probably led to a decrease in urban wages.

Anticlerical Laws

Probably the most violently opposed measures of the Liberal administration were its anticlerical laws. In addition to the expulsion of the Jesuits, the Liberals declared the separation of church and state (which implied the complete reform of education), the abolition of the tithe, and the popular election of bishops and parish priests.

19 Restrepo, *Historia, 1845–1954*, p. 212.

25

Although it is clear that some artisans were anticlerical, probably the majority of the urban proletariat was not. In Spanish America the Church had been the educator, healer, and protector of the poor, and it had traditionally been the only force effective in opposing the unbounded desire of the *criollo* upper class to exploit the Indian. Anticlerical legislation could not have been the political dream of the lower classes of Nueva Granada. Ambrosio López' reaction was probably typical. He asked: "Was the purpose of the society of artisans, according to its statutes, to get involved in religious questions, and show lack of respect to the dignity of the Pope and the Archbishop? . . . I think not." Heredia's answer to López seems weak. "It is true that we took down the portrait of the Pope after an argument, and I applaud the action . . . since I believe that having taken down the portrait of a reactionary Pope is not an attack on religion . . ."

Fiscal Reform

The Liberal fiscal reform was limited to doing away with taxes. Except for the abolition of the tithe, most of the tax reform favored the wealthier elements in the society. The direct income tax established in many states to replace the colonial taxes was never collected on a large scale and was soon abandoned. Thus the poor were faced with a destitute state incapable of providing the most basic social services. The artisans had nothing to gain from the government described by José María Plata, a Liberal Finance Minister, in 1854: "We are arriving at the inexpensive and simple form of government which appears weak because it does little, but which is truly strong because it prevents all the evils that originate in institutions."[20] The Bogotá artisans could never be convinced that the best government is that which governs least. The lower classes, probably because of historical experience, have usually had a hard time believing that a weak

20. Nieto Arteta, *Economia,* p. 227.

government, competition, and liberty lead to welfare and equality, and in Nueva Granada this belief was even less likely to take hold after more than three centuries of paternalistic and centralized Spanish rule.

Land Reform

Another major reform of the Liberals was the elimination in 1850 of the collective form of land ownership in Nueva Granada. The attack on the resguardos, or Indian lands, had started much earlier, but since the Indians were not allowed to sell their land, the resguardos had survived. By a law of March 1832, the resguardos had been divided up among the Indian families, but a ten-year restriction on sale was passed as part of the law. Law 23 of June 1843 extended for twenty more years the period in which no Indian could sell his land. Then in June of 1850 all restrictions on the sale of resguardo land were eliminated, and the process of enclosure was left to the provincial assemblies, bodies obviously controlled by the local landlords and capitalists. The process of division soon got the Indians into debt, and they transferred their land to usurers.

Colombian historians agree that the proletarianization of the rural worker and the expansion of the *haciendas* and latifundia date in large part from 1850.[21] The analysis of the effects of the legislation of that year by a contemporary Liberal statesman is graphic:

> The poor Indians were induced to sell their parcels, in which they had their own small house, some independence, and a secure subsistence. In a few years that property fell into the hands of a few landlords, the Indian became a tenant,

21. Ospina Vásquez, *Industria,* p. 450; Nieto Arteta, chap. 11. Indalecio Liévano Aguirre first pointed out to me in conversation the importance of this reform. Nieto Arteta mentions the opinions of contemporaries such as Camacho Roldán and Miguel Samper, who also agree with this interpretation.

the land was shifted to grass for cattle raising, and the supply of agricultural goods decreased substantially. All this as the result of a liberty established without previous study of social conditions.

Miguel Samper finishes his analysis in a pathetic way. "Youth and enthusiasm are no excuse and cannot calm the remorse that he who writes these lines suffers and shall suffer for his participation in the passing of this unwise law."[22]

While some Indians became tenants, others supplied the labor for the new tobacco and coffee plantations of the Liberal merchants. The proletarianization of the Indian did not serve to supply industry with cheap labor, but to supply cheap labor to the export crop plantations. Thus exports jumped from P2,393,600 in 1844–45 to P7,064,584 in 1856–57,[23] and much of the increase was due to growth in tobacco production on new lands. The expansion of export crop plantations came in response to the need to balance exports and imports, and the major merchant families understandably invested heavily in the new ventures. The destruction of the resguardos was a necessary precondition for the expansion of trade and of export-oriented agriculture.

It was a measure consistent with the interests of the Bogotá bourgeoisie, but not with those of the artisans. On the one hand, the destruction of the resguardos made possible the growth of exports and therefore of imports that competed with the production of local artisans; on the other hand, some of the Indians displaced from the resguardos entered the urban labor force and caused the level of wages to decrease. Finally, as Miguel Samper pointed out, the land sold by the Indians was taken out of agriculture, a phenomenon which, added to the high demand for food emanating from the export crop plantations, led to a rise in food

22. Nieto Arteta, p. 164.
23. Ibid., p. 331.

prices.[24] This price increase does not seem to have been offset by a wage increase in cities with artisan populations like Bogotá, Cali, and those artisan centers in the Socorro area which were outside the area of influence of the export plantations.

In conclusion, the great reforms of the 1850s were not in the interest of the artisans who made up the urban Sociedades Democráticas. On the contrary, reforms that seemed humanitarian and progressive actually had the immediate effect of destroying the artisan class, without bringing about the industrialization required to transform the artisans into factory workers. The result of the Liberal reforms was therefore to divide the urban population of Nueva Granada into two hostile camps. Under such circumstances, class war became inevitable.

24. The Finance Minister in office in 1851 stated that the prices of food had increased two or three times (Nieto Arteta, p. 179). He holds that wages also rose, but a careful study by Frank Safford does not substantiate this second conclusion. Safford believes that "data on wages and prices suggest that relatively few gained from the tobacco boom . . . In the cold country wages appear not to have increased at all between 1830 and 1873. But between 1848 and 1858 the price of meat doubled. And in the thirty years between 1848 and 1878, the prices of rice, fresh meat, and eggs tripled, while the price of potatoes more than quintupled."

3

Class War

As a rule, Colombian society has not been divided into antagonistic or even well-defined social classes. Fernando Guillén Martínez describes the turbulent history of Spanish America, with special reference to Colombia, in the following terms:

> The history of Spanish America, during the last two and a half centuries, has been a continuous internal war, open or potential, that never takes the form of struggles between castes or between different social strata, but takes the appearance of struggles between factions and heterogeneous groups, that provoke each other until they get involved in the deadly violence that divided the "political parties" of the nineteenth century. These parties did not represent the interests of antagonistic social classes nor were they divided along the lines of rich and poor, indians and whites . . . [they were] two factions in whose ranks were mixed indistinctly exploited and exploiters, peasants and intellectuals, landowner, and rural serfs, all with the hope of obtaining control of the centralized state, to profit from it and to constitute a transitory, insolent, and all powerful lineage.[1]

1. Fernando Guillén Martínez, *Raíz y futuro de la revolución* (Bogotá, Tercer Mundo, 1963), p. 84.

30

Antonio García, the best-known socialist theoretician in Colombia, agrees with this interpretation. He has studied the historical lack of class consciousness in Colombia and has related this to our traditionally amorphous multiclass political parties.[2] But the nature of these political parties as well as the lack of class consciousness in the society is the result of a surprising degree of social mobility. Guillén Martínez is probably the writer who has best understood the problem.

> The answer that always seemed obvious to the "leftists" was that the basic structure of the nation was or should be that of the division by "social class" . . . with more or less sincerity they fought to instill a "class consciousness" in their partisans. Culturally, that consciousness is the only thing that the Colombian rejects, since it prevents personal mobility . . . which has in fact been potentially obtainable since the time that Spain did not produce a closed aristocracy, nor a system of rural serfdom, nor an institutionalized bourgeoisie. This ideal of social mobility is deeply ingrained in the national "value system" of Colombia, where each individual continuously aspires to economic equality in a manner that it is not possible to find in other areas of the world.[3]

Therefore, treating Colombian history as a succession of class conflicts is probably a distortion of reality, with two exceptions. These are the periods 1851–54 and 1945–49. In both cases the urban proletariat attempted to impose its solutions on the nation, and in both cases the bourgeoisie, supported by the rural masses, defeated the urban workers. We propose now to study the dynamics of the first defeat.

2. García, *Gaitán,* pp. 8–9.
3. Guillén Martínez, pp. 211–19. For a short and fascinating treatment of the problem of social mobility in Colombia see Fernando Guillén Martínez, "Hay una Oligarquía Democrática," *Acción Liberal,* no. 3 (February-March 1966), pp. 43–45.

Cachacos versus *Guaches*

By the time of the presidential election of 1853, the break between the artisan class and the Bogotá bourgeoisie had taken place. The published diatribes between Ambrosio López and Emeterio Heredia show that as early as 1851 some artisans had become disillusioned with the Liberals they had helped politically in 1849, but the conflict became more serious in the months preceding the 1853 elections.

The party of the members of the Sociedad Republicana, headed by Murillo Toro and Florentino González, both of whom had defended and furthered the program of free trade and free enterprise from the Finance Ministry, backed Tomás Herrera for the presidency, while the Sociedad Democrática and the government backed the Liberal *caudillo* José María Obando.[4] In the elections General Obando obtained an absolute majority and therefore did not need to be elected by Congress. Unlike Florentino González and the Bogotá liberal bourgeoisie, Obando was democratic in his customs and behavior. Not wealthy, he lived in a humble dwelling in Las Nieves, one of the poorer neighborhoods of Bogotá, and was present regularly at the meetings of the Sociedad Democrática. His social background as well as his personality made him popular with the people. With the help of her lover his grandmother had strangled her husband, and was subsequently sentenced to death. After escaping, she gave birth to the General's mother. It appears furthermore that Obando was also illegitimate.[5] A guerrilla leader, persecuted, illegitimate, and poor, Obando embodied all of the characteristics of the Colombian mestizo.

Shortly after the inauguration of General Obando on April 1, 1853, the Sociedad Democrática once again started agitation in favor of higher tariff protection and against a proposal before

4. Ortiz, *Historia de la revolución,* pp. 17–19.
5. Milton Puentes, *Historia del Partido Liberal colombiano* (2d ed. Bogotá, Prag, 1965), pp. 183–85.

Congress to lower import duties. On May 19, the members of the Sociedad presented a petition for tariff protection to the House of Representatives. Remembering the behavior of the artisans at the time that Congress elected López, a group of Radical activists decided to occupy the visitors' gallery, well armed with clubs and walking sticks.

During the session, the members of the House casually solved the problem of the artisans' petition by transferring it to the Senate for consideration whenever the law on import duties came up for discussion. Needless to say, this did not satisfy the artisans. Twice the people invaded the chamber, but the Radicals came to the defense of the congressmen. At the end of the session, when the house members were leaving the chamber, feeling ran so high that some congressmen were attacked by members of the Democrática. The Radicals retaliated and were getting the best of the fight when the army and President Obando arrived on the scene. As the conservative historians Angel and Rufino José Cuervo describe it, "A serious fray got started, in which the two factions were distinguished by their clothes; one group wore ruanas [ponchos] and the other casacas [coats], in other words, guaches and cachacos. The fight ended with the appearance of President Obando and the guard, leaving behind one unfortunate artisan dead from knife wounds."[6]

In June the artisans prepared to take revenge on the Gólgota youths who had killed one of their number on May 19. During the first week of June the proletarian neighborhood of Las Nieves celebrated a traditional religious holiday with bullfights and processions; the festivities were the scene of various frays between cachacos and guaches. On June 8 the artisans and upper-class youths finally got into an armed conflict. The cachacos were driven back by the artisans until they reached San Francisco Square, where General Melo and his troops were quartered. According to various observers, General Melo did not intervene

6 Cuervo, *Vida de Rufino Cuervo*, p. 256.

until the upper-class youths, who had obtained reinforcements, began to drive back the artisans. At that point the troops fired into the air, causing great fright among the cachacos, who fired back, wounding various artisans and killing a soldier.

That night patrols of soldiers and artisans traversed the city shouting, "Death to the Gólgotas and cachacos," and on his return home, Florentino González, the Liberal theoretician who was responsible for the first free trade law, was beaten up and almost killed by some individuals in ruanas. The people were getting their revenge. It became unsafe for the members of the upper classes to use the streets in the evening, and on June 19, a gentleman by the name of Antonio París was killed by a group of artisans as he returned home after giving his wife a serenade on her birthday. The murderer and his friends were arrested and prosecuted with a speed unusual in the justice of Nueva Granada. After the artisan Palacios had been publicly executed for this crime, an anonymous artisan had a bitter leaflet printed which read in part, "Artisans, it is time to get wise! . . . Yesterday Nepomuceno Palacios still lived, not so today . . . he has been sacrificed: his trial was speedy because he did not have a university degree and was not a gólgota." The author then asks why the man who murdered the artisan in front of Congress on May 19 is not behind bars. He supplies the answer: "Ah! Because he wears a coat and killed an artisan."[7]

The Government-Sponsored Class Conflict in the West

In the Conservative stronghold of the Southwest, class conflict was more violent and the government did less to curb it since it was interested in holding the Conservative landowners constantly on the defensive. The source of class conflict in Cali, as in Bogotá, was an attempt by the urban masses to defend the old economic order. In Cali, however, the problem was not free trade but ownership of the ejidos, or town commons.

7. Ortiz, p. 25.

While in Bogotá the López government tended to some extent to discourage the activity of the Sociedad Democrática, in the Conservative stronghold of the Southwest, and especially in Cali and Palmira, the government encouraged the antagonism between Democráticos and Conservative landlords. Thus, when the Democratic Society recommended Dr. Ramón Mercado, "a plebeian," for governor of the province of Buenaventura, the central government complied.[8] Mercado immediately proceeded to revive the ejido problem of Cali, and not unexpectedly he took the side of the artisans against the Conservative landlords.

According to a report to the central government by the political chief of Cali,[9] the ejido problem had its source in the fact that when Cali was founded, all land within three miles of the central church was put aside as town commons; ever since, the local landowners had been trying to claim and enclose these lands as their own.[10] In 1772 the Viceroy had ordered some of this land returned to the citizens of Cali, but the order was not obeyed. By 1848 the landlords had fenced a large part of these lands, and in that year the people of Cali retaliated by destroying the fences and invading what they claimed were common lands. The problem was left unsolved, among other things because one of the landlords involved was then governor of the province.

Once Ramón Mercado became governor, he attempted to settle the problem in favor of the citizens of Cali. The landlords were naturally reluctant to accept Mercado's solution, and the people of Cali, some think with the approval of the authorities, decided to take matters into their own hands. Fences were again torn down, but this time some houses were burned and patrols of *zurriageros* were created. (The zurriago is a stick with a leather whip often carried by Colombian peasants, and in this case used for beating and whipping enemies of the people of Cali.) Various murders were committed, and an especially notorious one in-

8. *Reseña histórica,* pp. 21, 35–36.
9. The political chief was a municipal officer.
10. *Gaceta Oficial,* year XX, no. 1119 (February 27, 1851).

volved an important Conservative leader. In the previously mentioned report of these events to the central government, the political chief of Cali justified the burning of the farm of Manuel Ibánez on the grounds that this man was a "dangerous Conservative." It is not surprising to find that a month later, this same Ibánez was one of the leaders of the insurrection of 1851.[11]

The attitude of the authorities with respect to these disorders is well illustrated by an incident described in the official newspaper on March 2, 1851.[12] It seems that a mob freed six men who had been arrested for whipping a man. Governor Carlos Gómez of Cauca explained that this incident was caused by the discrimination of the judicial branch of the government against the Liberals. In this case the people did not believe that there was sufficient proof against the six Liberals arrested and decided to take justice into their own hands, a procedure not censured by Gómez.

On April 16, President López made a proclamation to the people of Popayán, Cauca, and Buenaventura, in which he admitted the existence of civil strife, but pointedly defended and congratulated the Sociedades Democráticas. The societies, however, clearly were not innocent. In a letter from the president of the Democratic Society of Buga to all similar societies in the area, there is some indication of guilt. "The Republican Society of Buga is convinced that the violent tactics that have been adopted in some places of this and other Southern provinces are the most terrible weapons that can be given the Conservatives . . . "[13]

One last significant document of the period is a report on the social conflict in the South sent by Carlos Gómez, Governor of Cauca, to the central government.

> The people who have come out of oppression into liberty, who know that the principle of equality reigns and that in a

11. *Gaceta Oficial,* year XX, no. 1228 (May 24, 1851).
12. *Gaceta Oficial,* year XX, no. 1201 (March 2, 1851).
13. Ibid., year XX, no. 1224 (May 16, 1851).

republic only virtue and merit are held in esteem, frolic and amuse themselves, becoming indignant at times against those who believed that they had the power to humiliate them. The people are agitated, it is true, but the government has nothing to fear from this agitation for on the contrary, whenever the people gather they jubilantly applaud the government . . .[14]

It seems that social conflict in the Cauca Valley reached more alarming proportions than in the highlands of Bogotá, and that the Liberal government was less firm in restoring order. The source of conflict in Cauca was the government's attempt to restore the colonial institution of the town common in order to win popularity with the urban masses, the only force capable of offsetting the power of the Conservative landlords of the region. In theory, the Liberals were being inconsistent when they defended the colonial form of economic organization in Cauca, but in practice they were consistent since they only wanted to destroy the colonial institutions that created a barrier to bourgeois accumulation of wealth. The elimination of the town commons of Cali and Palmira,[15] unlike those of the highland resguardos, did not interest the Liberal bourgeoisie since it benefited only the Conservative landlords of the Cauca Valley.

The Coalition Between the Army and the Artisans

To the great surprise of the Liberals, the first elections under universal suffrage gave a clear majority to the Conservative candidates. As usual, the Liberals had learned their rhetoric from the French, but had gained no political insight from the mistakes of their French counterparts. In France the results of universal suffrage had been the same. On March 5, 1848, the provisional government in Paris had declared that in the elections to the na-

14. Ibid., year XX, no. 1217 (April 26, 1851).
15. Ibid., year XX, no. 1236 (June 11, 1851).

37

tional constituent assembly, to be held in April, every French-man over 21 would be entitled to vote. The instinctively conserva-tive mass of small rural proprietors had ample time to be alarmed by news of the disorders in the capital, and they voted against the radicals and socialists. Out of 876 seats, these parties won only 100.[16]

In Nueva Granada, the Liberals blamed electoral fraud and the influence of the Church for the triumph of the Conservatives in 1854. But that triumph had more serious causes, similar to those responsible for the socialists' defeat in France. In Nueva Granada the vast majority of the rural population owned land, even if very small amounts, and very small landowners are just as conservative as larger proprietors. Whatever the cause, how-ever, once the Liberals were defeated at the polls they began to find valid reasons for limiting suffrage. In fact, this became one of the major reforms advocated by the Liberals in June of 1854.[17]

The Conservative victory in the elections of 1853 demon-strated to the Liberals of both the Gólgota and the Draconiano wings of the party that they could not govern by means of elec-toral majorities. This new political reality drove the Draconianos and the artisans into a coalition with the army, and the Gólgotas into a coalition with the Conservatives. The result of this realign-ment of forces was the military-artisan coup of April 1854.

The military coup had the complete support of the artisan class and the national guard, which as we know was made up almost exclusively of artisans and members of the democratic societies. Their support of a coup against the Radicals was understandable, since it was clear that the Gólgotas, not satisfied with having undermined the economic position of the urban independent workers, had made every effort possible to exterminate the demo-cratic societies. The reasons for the participation of the army in

16. David Thompson, *Europe Since Napoleon* (New York, Knopf, 1958), 183–85.

17. *Gaceta Oficial*, year XXIII, nos. 1735 and 1737 (June 4 and 20, 1854).

an alliance with the Democráticas against the Radical-Conservative coalition have, however, not been discussed.

The reasons were simple enough. On the one hand, the Radicals wanted to vote the army out of existence, and on the other hand, they had long shown a complete disdain for the military as a social class. Unfortunately for the Gólgotas, their policy toward the army would have been politically sound only if the national guards, composed of artisans, had remained loyal to the Radical elite and neutralized the threat of a disaffected regular army.

The campaign against the army was further complicated by the fact that General Obando, as President, was naturally inclined to defend the regular army. Not only was he an army man himself, but the Radicals and Conservatives had voted against him in the presidential elections and now formed the opposition in the Congress, where they constituted a majority.[18] Soon after Obando took office, it became clear that the artisans, the army, and the executive were uniting against the Radical program, which in turn was finding acceptance among the members of the old Conservative Party. It seemed that for the first time in the life of Nueva Granada, the lower orders of urban society were uniting against the elite. In this coalition, however, the peasants were not represented.

At the same time, the landlords and the merchants had found that the Radical economic program was mutually beneficial. Both

18. According to the electoral law which regulated elections before 1853, and under which Obando and the members of Congress had been elected, suffrage was limited to those who could read and write, and there was an income limitation as well, thus insuring that only upper-class citizens and some urban workers could vote. Furthermore there was a property restriction on the holding of congressional office, so that Senators had to own twice as much property as House members, who in turn had to have a substantial income from property. Significantly, the President did not have to own property (see *Gaceta Oficial,* year XX, no. 1204 [March 16, 1851]). As a result of elections held under this law, in 1853 the Senate had a Conservative majority, the House a radical majority made up of merchants and intellectuals, and the President was poor and popular.

the landlords and the urban bourgeoisie obtained land from the resguardos and established export crop plantations. The merchants, on the other hand, supplied themselves and the landlords with imported luxury goods and inexpensive English industrial products such as clothing and china, as well as with the foreign exchange necessary for foreign travel and education, the new external symbols of the elite. The first election under universal suffrage, in September and October of 1853, confirmed the new understanding within the upper class. In that election the Conservative candidate for Attorney General was Florentino González, the man who had initiated the Liberal economic reforms in 1847. Thus the mentor of the Radical generation was adopted by the Conservatives. The only explanation is that the Conservative Party of the great landowners and proclerical intellectuals had realized that the economic revolution preached by Florentino González was compatible with the class interests of its most influential members.

On closer analysis, the union of González with the Conservatives seems inevitable. He believed in "a learned democracy, in which intelligence and property direct the destiny of the people," and he rejected "a barbarian democracy in which equalitarianism and ignorance drown the seeds of happiness and bring disorder and confusion to society."[19] It is significant that he expressed these thoughts five years before being attacked and beaten in the streets of Bogotá by members of the proletariat.

The adoption of Florentino González by the Conservatives was most effective and presaged the fruitful military alliance between Conservatives and Radicals against the military-artisan coup of 1854. The results of the 1853 elections with universal suffrage were as follows:[20]

19. Quoted in Germán Colmenares, "Florentino González: El Mentor," *Revista del Colegio Mayor de Nuestra Señora del Rosario, 59,* no. 474 (November-December 1965), 73.
20. Restrepo, *Historia, 1845–1854,* pp. 303–03.

1.	Florentino González	64,491
	Rufino Cuervo	51,997
	José Ignacio Márquez	50,475
	José María Latorre	47,340
	Bernardo Herrera	34,576
	Others	145,188
		394,067

2.	Liberals (partisans of Obando)	25%
	Liberals (Radicals or Gólgotas)	13%
	Conservatives	59%
	Other Liberals	3%
		100%

The Coup d'Etat of 1854

When congressional sessions started in February 1854, there was little hope of cooperation between Congress and President Obando. In March the executive asked for funds to support an army of 1,240 men; both houses rejected Obando's proposal and recommended a peacetime army of 800 men, with no allowance for any generals, a measure that could not have pleased General Melo, head of the Bogotá garrison. But, realizing that the army and the Sociedades Democráticas had reached the point of considering an open insurrection against Congress, where the Conservatives and Radicals were dedicated to neutralizing the popular government of Obando, the Senate asked the executive to hand over to the governor of the province 1,000 guns so that he could arm respectable citizens for the defense of the constitution. The President answered that he had no information as to the threat of an insurrection, and promised that if there was any attempt against the Congress, the national guard would be called out. Far from quieting the fears of the congressmen, this solution made their situation more desperate. Congress then passed a law declaring free commerce in arms, a measure meant to supply arms to those who could afford them, thereby allowing the wealthy upper class to create its own army to defend Congress. President Obando vetoed this law, a tactic which delayed its passage until April 3. In a sense the law was an ultimatum to the artisans and the army. If they were to act against the Radicals and Conservatives who had obtained control of most of the power of the state, they had to act before these forces could arm themselves.

Two weeks later, while the city slept, six hundred artisans of the Sociedad Democrática and the garrison of Bogotá took over the city. First they offered the dictatorship to President Obando,[21] who, after some hesitation, declined the honor. Later that day General Melo was declared supreme director of a new administration.

The quiet coup of April 17 became a bloody war that lasted eight months, and ended with the physical extermination of the Sociedades Democráticas, most of which had declared themselves in favor of the new government. The surprising thing is that an army reduced to a few thousand men and a handful of urban artisans organized into political clubs could have held out as long as they did against a coalition of all elements of the elite and the rural masses which this elite could mobilize.

In Cali, Popayán, and Bogotá the urban artisans were the backbone of the revolution and were the last to surrender to the so-called constitutional troops.[22] In the taking of Bogotá, the bloodiest episode was the siege of the convent of San Diego, where one of those killed by the constitutional armies was Miguel León, the locksmith who had been president of the Sociedad Demo-

21. Obando's participation in the revolution has been the subject of much debate. Once the counterrevolution had succeeded, Obando was tried by the Senate and found guilty of conspiring against the constitution. Since the Radical-Conservative coalition had won a war in defense of the constitution, they were not likely to find their old enemy of 1854 innocent and allow him to continue as constitutional President.

22. Ortiz, pp. 131–34, 336–51.

crática in 1851.[23] The artisans who survived the war were less fortunate than Miguel León. They were tried and sentenced to hard labor in the insalubrious regions of Panama, where the majority died of yellow fever and dysentery.[24]

Thus the first attempt at working class organization in the history of Colombia ended tragically. This was inevitable given the limited economic and political power of the artisan class. The economic base of the members of the democratic societies was narrow and the European industrial revolution threatened the artisans with economic extinction. The artisan organizations were therefore unable to pursue the goal of economic improvement for their members within the framework of collective bargaining. They were not able to use the weapons of economic war to bargain with employers or consumers, since they organized in the face of a radical reduction in the demand for the products of their labor.

When the Sociedad de Artesanos realized the limited benefits of classic trade union tactics, it turned to politics as the best means for improving the economic conditions of its members. In this area, however, the artisans were also doomed to failure, since they came into conflict with the combined forces of the commercial and landed bourgeoisie.

Although the artisan system of production was doomed to disappear, from the point of view of economic development it was unfortunate that it should have been so rapidly destroyed. The systems of town commons and cottage industry are economically absurd once towns grow into cities and industrialization takes place. Productivity on common land is abysmally low, and economic progress made the destruction of the cottage system of production inevitable. It is also probably wrong to think that factory industry could have developed from the artisan base that existed in the nineteenth century. Historically, the experience of most nations has been that in the early stages of development

23. Cordovéz Moure, *Reminiscencias*, 5, 5.
24. *Reseña histórica*, pp. 103–12; Liévano Aguirre, *El proceso*, p. 38.

artisan industry has competed with factory production instead of serving as a base for the growth of the modern sector.[25]

In Colombia, however, cottage industry was destroyed too rapidly, without being replaced by factory production. This meant the pauperization of a large sector of the labor force and a decrease in the level of effective consumer demand due to an increase in the concentration of income. The destruction of cottage industry also changed consumption habits and made Colombians dependent on imports, a factor that made industrialization more difficult. Finally, the destruction of the economic base of whole sectors of the population and of particular areas of the country led to political instability and civil war.

25. In England, the industrial revolution did not take place in the early eighteenth-century centers of cottage industry. Mantoux says of the old form of industry, "The woolen industry was too conservative, too weighted down by privilege and prejudice, to reform itself by a complete change in technique. The industrial revolution had to be brought in from outside" (Paul Mantoux, *The Industrial Revolution in the Eighteenth Century* [New York, Harper Torchbooks, 1962], p. 88). In Colombia also the industrial revolution took place in an area with no artisan tradition: Antioquia. Interestingly enough, the cities of Antioquia were among the last to have Sociedades Democráticas. For example, Medellín, which was to be the city around which grew modern industry, had a Sociedad founded only in October 1851 (*Gaceta Oficial*, year XX, no. 1286 [November 8, 1851]).

Part II

The Birth of the
Industrial Labor Force

4

The Transformation of the Traditional Economy

After the defeat of the artisans in December 1854, Colombia entered a period of almost continuous political chaos. There was a major civil war in 1860, which led to a great economic crisis and, as usual, a new constitution. That constitution, which was the great triumph of the liberal bourgeoisie, institutionalized chaos. It was federalist in the extreme, allowing free traffic in arms and making it possible for each state to create its own private army. Without much exaggeration the period can be described as the era of the warlords. Between 1863 and 1885 there were some fifty armed insurrections and some forty-two state constitutions.[1] Some of the conflicts were major ones, such as that of 1876–77, and all of them were costly.

Economic stagnation was undoubtedly one of the causes of civil war and political chaos, yet civil war made it impossible for the country to develop. This vicious circle lasted more than thirty years. Salvador Camacho Roldán explained the civil war of 1876–77 in terms of the economic crisis of 1875, and Carlos Calderón stated bluntly that "all these civil wars, including the spark of the conflagration of 1884–85, were caused by economic depression, a phenomenon which explains many a political crisis."[2]

1. Nieto Arteta, in *Economia*, quotes Samper on the subject, p. 374.
2. Ibid., p. 369.

As has been pointed out, the economic and social reforms started in 1848 and directed toward eliminating the collectivist and regulated economy of colonial times probably had the effect of lowering the standard of living of large sectors of the lower classes in the country. For example, the valuable statistics assembled by Dr. Alberto Pardo Pardo, as yet unpublished, show real wages in Bogotá in the period 1850–1900 to be below the levels of the eighteenth century. This phenomenon was probably not unrelated to the endemic state of civil war in the second half of the nineteenth century. The basis for economic development was laid only when the state was reorganized on a centralized pattern in the 1880s. Banks organized by Colombians began to thrive, and after the last and bloodiest major civil war of the nation's history in 1899–1902, manufacturing industry finally acclimatized itself to the Colombian environment. Parallel to the development of the modern textile, tobacco, beer, and cement industries, the nation's railroad and road transportation networks began to grow. Slowly and with virtually no foreign help, the nation started on the path of economic development.

But clearly political stability was not a sufficient condition for growth. In the 1880s, a crucial change was introduced into the Colombian economy: the rapid expansion of coffee cultivation.[3] This phenomenon transformed the economic and social structure of the country and made possible the emergence of modern manufacturing industry.

The success of coffee stemmed from the fact that it was well suited to cultivation on sloping land, an advantage since most of inhabited Colombia is mountainous. Coffee therefore became the first export and commercial crop that could be produced in various areas of the country. Furthermore, it was well suited to cultivation on the uninhabited lands of Caldas and Valle del Cauca, where colonizers grew it on family-size farms. Tobacco cultiva-

---

3. The average annual rate of expansion of coffee exports in 1887–97 was 18.5 percent. William P. McGreevey, "Economic Development of Colombia" (doctoral dissertation, Cambridge, Mass., M.I.T., 1965), p. 65.

tion, in contrast, was limited to soils with special characteristics and became concentrated in the area of volcanic soils around Ambalema.

Coffee therefore had two crucial functions. The first was to create an internal market. In western Colombia, coffee cultivation created a large mass of small independent farmers who demanded textiles and other mass-consumption goods. The response to this demand was the creation of the consumer-oriented industry of Antioquia starting in the first decade of the century. At the same time, the need to transport coffee to the ports led to the development of railroads and the transportation industry.

Although in the West coffee cultivation led to a production structure dominated by the family farms of the new colonizers of Caldas and Valle, in the eastern area of traditional settlements, coffee was grown on large estates with the old hacienda methods of labor recruitment. The landowner gave the peasant land in return for labor services or for work at nominal wages. In order to guarantee a labor supply at harvest time, the peasant was forbidden to plant coffee trees on his land. In the East coffee cultivation did not create a class of independent farmers and, not surprisingly, manufacturing industry, lacking a mass market, did not prosper there. Given the nature of the internal transportation problem in Colombia, a national market was too much to hope for, but a regional market for cheap mass-produced industrial goods was necessary before modern industry could successfully emerge. A further problem in the East was that the artisan textile industry could compete with factory production, a problem not present in the West where there had been no artisan tradition, and where transportation costs to some extent protected the new manufacturers from eastern artisan production.

Although many economic and sociological factors, including the high level of liquid assets among Antioqueño gold miners, favored the establishment of modern manufacturing industry in Antioquia, development of a mass market for consumer goods to the west of the Magdalena River must be considered one of the determinants of the geographic localization of modern factory production in the first stage of Colombian economic development.

The second contribution of coffee to industrialization was its impact on the social and political structure of the country, since one of the major sources of instability throughout the nineteenth century was geographically unbalanced growth. While in the 1850s the tobacco boom led to the rapid enrichment of certain groups and geographical areas, economic expansion lowered the income of large sectors of the population. Prosperity did not spread outside the limited area of tobacco cultivation and did not benefit any of the classes except the new merchant upper class and tobacco workers and farmers. The results of this unbalanced growth were the artisan-led revolts previously described and civil war. Nieto Arteta argues convincingly that before the expansion of coffee cultivation "the great civil wars, with some exception, start[ed] in poor regions. Economic stagnation caused political anarchy which spread to the islands of economic prosperity."[4]

The prosperity caused by coffee cultivation spread to most of the centers of population in the nation, and thus the political instability caused by regional economic imbalance was reduced. Even where coffee was not grown, as on the Caribbean coast, the demand for transportation services created by coffee exports generated local prosperity.

The impact of coffee on the country's social structure was also important. As has been explained, it made possible the creation of a large class of small independent farmers producing a cash crop in western Colombia. This class of rural proprietors gave the nation political stability. Many of these small property owners joined the Liberal Party, which had once drawn most of its support from merchants and the urban masses. On the other hand, the manufacturers of Antioquia, prosperous due to coffee-generated consumer demand, were Conservatives. Thus Colombia embarked on industrialization with multiclass political parties.

4. Luis Eduardo Nieto Arteta, *El café en la sociedad colombiana* (Bogotá, Breviarios de Orientatión en Colombia, 1958), pp. 34–45.

50

Although the Liberal Party still had its strength in the cities, it had the support of a substantial rural electorate, in addition to the urban workers, bankers, merchants, and large coffee plantation owners. The Conservative Party, on the other hand, could count on the support of the Medellín industrialists, in addition to the conservative rural masses and landlords. Thus, as industrialization proceeded, Colombia did not become politically divided along class or urban-rural lines. This made economic development politically feasible.

The Mutual Benefit Societies

Between 1850 and 1900 labor did very little in the way of organization. The artisan class was in decline and no factory industry had replaced it.[5] Agricultural production on the large estates did not involve large concentrations of landless peasants, since the tenant system was common. A peasant received land in return for a number of labor hours to be supplied weekly or monthly and with the exception of a few large coffee plantations, the Colombian latifundia were used for cattle raising, an activity that requires little labor.

Although numerically and politically weak, workers did make a few attempts at organization, mostly in the form of creating mutual benefit societies. For example, records have survived of an artisan society founded in 1910 for the purchase and upkeep of a funeral wagon.[6] In its statutes is found the usual prohibition against "treating at its meetings political, religious, or any other subjects that are not directly related to the purposes of the society." An older society founded in Manizales in 1889 was more ambitious. It had a weekly ten-cent fee and gave aid to those who

5. Even construction activity declined. The stonecutters and roofmakers of colonial times had disappeared with the introduction from Europe of plaster molds for wall decorations. Construction activity did not revive until after 1910.

6. *Estatutos de la Sociedad de Artesanos de Manizales* (Manizales, Imprenta "El Remacimiento," 1911).

51

fell sick or were thrown into prison or exiled, and paid the funeral expenses of members.[7] Significantly, however, the society's constitution explicitly stated that all could belong without any distinction of nationality, political opinion, social condition, or profession. It was therefore not a craft society.

The history of the mutual benefit society of Bucaramanga illustrates some of the problems faced by these societies during the politically turbulent second half of the century. Founded in June 1892, it was approved by the governor of the state and the parish priest of San Caureano. The society accepted members irrespective of political opinion, religion, nationality, or profession, and was more a white-collar than a proletarian organization. Its purpose was to insure its members against sickness, and it had an arrangement with a similar society in Cúcuta according to which each society took on the responsibility of assisting traveling members of the other society.[8]

This society replaced the Sociedad de Socorros Mutuos, which in 1890 was forced to disband by order of the governor of the province. It seems that the governor became convinced that the society had become a political club, and, keeping in mind the activities of the famous Sociedades Democráticas, immediately ordered its dissolution on the scantiest evidence of political involvement.[9] The Governor felt that according to Article 47 of the Constitution, which prohibited the meetings of popular political clubs, he could force the society to disband. This constitutional prohibition threatened any workers' organization, since it was difficult to assemble any group of Colombians, who when together would not discuss politics. Worst of all, urban workers (white and blue collar) were Liberals, and the government had

7. *Estatutos de la Sociedad de Socorros Mutuos de Manizales* (Bogotá, Imprenta de Zalamea Hnos, 1889).

8. *Estatutos de la Sociedad de Mutuo Auxilio de Bucaramanga* (December 1892).

9. *Sociedad de Socorros Mutuos, acta de la sesión solemne verificada el 6 de agosto de 1890* (Bucaramanga, Imprenta de Silva y Plata, 1890).

TABLE 1

Legally Recognized Associations,[a] 1909–65

1909	1	1921	4	1933	20	1945	453	1957	129
1910	4	1922	3	1934	64	1946	121	1958	157
1911	3	1923	5	1935	84	1947	48	1959	244
1912	1	1924	9	1936	38	1948	102	1960	329
1913	2	1925	7	1937	159	1949	112	1961	180
1914	3	1926	5	1938	95	1950	59	1962	244
1915	1	1927	8	1939	57	1951	41	1963	251
1916	4	1928	9	1940	71	1952	40	1964	163
1917	8	1929	8	1941	54	1953	43	1965	195
1918	4	1930[b]	14	1942	39	1954	60		
1919	1	1931	16	1943	79	1955	68		
1920	5	1932	17	1944	180	1956	86		

a. According to the Labor Code, Article 368, the legal recognition of the union must be published in the *Diario Oficial* and a copy of the *Diario* must be sent to the Department of Union Supervision. Article 372 of the code further states that "no union can act as such, or fulfill the functions that the law and its statutes establish, or make use of the corresponding rights, until the union is legally recognized (given legal personality)." Since 1931 the law has given unions some legal protection, so it is in the interests of the union to obtain legal recognition in order to be eligible for such protection. For this reason the statistics on the number of unions legally recognized probably reflect accurately the growth of the labor movement after 1931, but probably underestimate its growth before that date.

b. In the 1947 union census, it is stated that up to 1930 there had been 99 legally recognized unions. Thus presumably 10 of the associations recognized before 1931 were not worker associations. By looking at the names of these early associations, we gathered that 6 were not worker or employee associations. Since there is no evidence of how the 1947 estimates were arrived at, the difference of four cannot be explained.

Sources: República de Colombia, *Anexos a la memoria del ministro de Trabajo, Higiene y Previsión Social, 1944–1945, 2,* 403–40; República de Colombia, Contraloría General de la República, *Primer censo sindical de Colombia, 1947* (Bogotá, Editorial Minerva 1949); for 1947–65, República de Colombia, *Diario Oficial* (January 1947–March 1966).

been Conservative since 1886. Although the president of the Bucaramanga benefit society was a Conservative, probably in order to please the authorities, only 33 of the society's 189 members were Conservatives.

Also interesting are the statutes of the Sociedad de Mutuo Auxilio y Beneficencia founded in Girardot in 1906. This society seems to have been organized by members of the working class, and it specifically excluded the unemployed from its assistance programs. The other mutual benefit societies for which records exist seem to be similar to that of Bucaramanga.

In 1909 the government legally recognized the first trade union organized in this century, the Sociedad de Artesanos de Sonsón. Sonsón is a relatively small town in Antioquia, and the union in question was established by tailors, shoemakers, carpenters, and other independent craftsmen,[10] probably on the initiative of the clergy.[11] Later several other craft unions were formed in various cities, but many lasted only a short time or limited their functions to mutual aid activities. Most of these early associations were organized under Church auspices, and their purpose was not so much the economic as the moral improvement of their members. These societies, however, introduced the workers to the mechanics of organization and created self-confident labor leaders from the ranks of the working class itself. Table 1 gives the number of legally recognized associations in the country, and may serve as an index of the development of the labor movement. Before 1931 the advantages of being legally recognized were not as clear as after that date, and therefore the statistics of the earlier period unquestionably underestimate the early growth of the labor movement. But it is still likely that many labor unions organized on a permanent basis would have attempted to obtain legal recognition even before 1931.

10. Horacio Yepes Zuluaga, "El Movimiento Sindical Colombiano," *Estudios de Derecho,* no. 55 (February–March 1959).

11. Suggested by the fact that the Sociedad was one of the first unions to join the Catholic UTC in the 1940s (Archives of the UTC).

5

The Emergence of Craft Unions

The first strikes in Colombia were not carried out by permanent worker organizations. They were spontaneous and short-lived. Unlike the experience of other countries in Latin America, however, the unions organized in the second decade of this century were not controlled by the anarchists, probably because there were few immigrants from southern Europe in the country.

While in Argentina, Chile, and Brazil, Spanish and Italian workers introduced anarcho-syndicalism into the early trade unions, the lack of immigrant workers in Colombia meant that labor unions from the start developed autonomously and did not adopt foreign ideologies. However, the unions in the ports of the Caribbean and on the Magdalena River, whose members had greater contact with the outside world, did tend to be more receptive to foreign ideologies, and in particular to communism.

Significantly, the first strikes in Colombia were among port and transportation workers. In 1918 industrial establishments were still small, and the textile mills, which employed the largest number of industrial workers, had a predominantly female labor force. This was not fertile ground for labor organization. Furthermore, in the larger establishments, such as Fenicia, a glass factory in Bogotá which employed 224 workers,[1] work conditions were sufficiently superior to those in other enterprises that there was little incentive for organization.

1. *El Espectador* (March 29, 1918).

But in the ports and in river transport, work conditions were less attractive, pay was not high, and, probably most significantly, the workers had access to the socialist and anarchist ideas that arrived with the foreign crews. In addition, coastal workers in Colombia have always been more receptive to change than the highland inhabitants, as is easily seen from the rapidity with which they adopt foreign vocabulary and customs. This may explain why one of the first recorded large-scale strikes in Colombian history was limited to the ports of Cartagena, Barranquilla, and Santa Marta. On January 3, 1918, reports of a strike among water-transport workers in the port of Barranquilla reached Bogotá.[2] It was reported that the strikers intimidated the workers who did not join the walkout, removed railroad rails, and did not allow water to be taken to the port of Puerto Colombia. The envoys of the workers and the employers reached an agreement, but the workers did not recognize it. After that, a civic guard of youths "of all social classes" was formed to keep order in the city, and at one point the army had to fire over the heads of the strikers to disperse them. But despite these incidents, when a settlement was reached, employers raised daily wages by 50 percent.[3]

The wage gain in Barranquilla was a tremendous incentive for port workers elsewhere. On January 8, teamsters and port workers in the port of Cartagena went on strike.[4] The movement was organized by the Sociedad de Artesanos y Obreros, which was not officially recognized and probably was not a permanent organization.[5] A tentative agreement was reached with the employers,

2. *El Espectador* (January 3, 1918). There is evidence of a smaller, peaceful strike among workers of the Dorada Railway which took place sometime before.

3. *El Tiempo* (January 5, 1918).

4. *El Tiempo* (January 11, 1918).

5. Colombia, Ministerio de Gobierno, Departamento de Justicia, *Reseña del movimiento sindical, 1909–1937* (Bogotá, Imprenta Nacional, 1937).

but the Sociedad, not satisfied, changed the conditions, claimed that employers threatened not to abide by the agreement, and organized a mass demonstration which soon deteriorated into a riot. More than a thousand workers overflowed into the streets, stores were sacked, and the police were forced to fire on the workers, killing at least two persons.[6]

Public opinion, as expressed in the newspaper editorials of the time, was surprised by the magnitude of the workers' protest. Even the leftist columnists of the Liberal newspapers condemned the disorders in Cartagena. Thus when the government declared the public peace disturbed on the Caribbean coast, public opinion in both traditional parties approved of the action, and a dangerous precedent was set.

By declaring a state of siege due to a threat to the internal peace of the nation, the government was able, among other things, to "prohibit the meeting of permanent strike committees." Decree 2 of 1918 further established that workers could not be represented by any person who did not belong to the craft or enterprise of the workers concerned, and that those participating in the strike movement who did not meet these conditions would be jailed. Furthermore, it was explicitly stated that any foreigners who participated in strikes would be deported and that the only right the workers had was to stop work.[7]

The government decree passed to deal with the Cartagena strike reveals quite a bit about the nature of what seems to have been the first large-scale worker protest in Colombian history. First, it would seem that foreign workers and agitators were present on the scene, judging by the deportation provisions. And second, it appears that the strike leaders did not belong to the working class. Judging by the nature of the strike, which was an attempt at a city-wide general strike, probably not planned by any well-established organization, it seems to have been anarcho-syndical-

6. *El Espectador* (January 15, 1918). There was also one police casualty.

7. *El Tiempo* (January 13, 1918).

ist in origin and, once in progress, was probably directed by foreigners.

The last provision of the government decree was probably the most important. By limiting the right to strike to work stoppage, the government made picketing, demonstrations, and permanent workers (strike) organizations illegal. Since in the future the response of the government to any serious strike would be to declare a stage of siege, stable trade unions did not develop, and worker protests tended to be improvised and short-lived. These were ideal institutional conditions for the development of anarcho-syndicalism, but this ideology did not prosper. As has been suggested, the absence of any substantial groups of immigrants from southern Europe probably accounted for the weakness of anarcho-syndicalism in Colombia.

The government measures taken to restore order in Cartagena were effective, and the strike movement was broken. But the strike wave spread to Santa Marta, the third Caribbean port. There the port workers walked out on January 11 in sympathy with the employees of the Santa Marta Railway Company. Almost immediately the strike degenerated into a riot; parts of the railway and telegraph lines between Santa Marta and Ciénaga were destroyed, and shops in the city were looted. As in Barranquilla, however, the workers were successful. They obtained a 25 percent daily wage increase after four days of strike.[8]

By January 24, order had been restored along the whole Atlantic coast, but the repercussions of this strike wave were to last for some time. Seeing property threatened in Cartagena and Santa Marta, the Liberal Party leaders condemned the strike movement, an attitude which the Liberal Party was to maintain consistently throughout the next ten years and one which separated the party from the more militant labor leaders.

The nation was jolted by the appearance of violent class conflict, and workers became acquainted with the possibility of ob-

8. *El Tiempo* (January 19, 1918); *El Espectador* (January 12, 1918).

taining benefits through strike action. At about the time of the Santa Marta strike, workers and police clashed after a political conference in Medellín and a hundred workers were jailed. Two weeks after that, the banana workers were demanding better conditions from the United Fruit Company,[9] but a decade went by before they went on strike in order to force the company to consider the same demands.

The Creation of a Socialist Labor Movement

Throughout 1918 trade unions began to organize, and at the end of the year, the Confederación de Acción Social was founded to improve the situation of the working class. The stated purposes of the confederation were compatible with the Colombian President's conservative and Catholic ideology, and he was flattered to accept the post of honorary president of the society.[10] A few weeks later, probably to the President's surprise, the moderate newspaper *Gaceta Republicana* abandoned the "Republican Union," a coalition of moderate forces that included both Liberals and Conservatives, and became the mouthpiece of a "Democratic Party,"[11] which was to be a new political organization closely related to the working class movement and to the Confederación de Acción Social in particular.

The new movement was directed by the intellectuals Eduardo Carvajal, Manrique Páramo, and O. Bello. The last two were the director and editor of the *Gaceta Republicana,* a paper that had been founded by Olaya Herrera, a well-known Liberal politician. The ideology of the new movement was confusing, and the only thing clear from the start was that the movement was not associated with the two traditional political parties. Its slogan was "war on politics and professional politicians."[12]

9. *El Tiempo* (January 19, 1918); *El Espectador* (January 28, 1919).
10. *El Espectador* (March 22, 1918).
11. *Gaceta Republicana* (January 13, 1919).
12. Ibid.

The movement was officially launched by Eduardo Carvajal, president of the Confederación de Acción Social, in a speech in which he proposed (1) the constitution of a labor and professional federation; (2) the organization of the professions into unions; and (3) the achievement of worker representation in city councils, state assemblies, and Congress.

The Confederación de Acción Social was not a grass roots movement. Carvajal became interested in the proletariat after his experiences in the assistance committee (Junta de Socorro) set up at the time of the great typhoid epidemic. He had, therefore, what could be called a social worker mentality, heavily permeated by the radical liberalism often found among Colombian intellectuals. In his speech launching the new political workers' movement, he made frequent reference to the Gospels, in a manner reminiscent of the Gólgota speeches of 1851–52. For example, part of his speech ran as follows: "The gospel and the French Revolution left to us as mandates of honor and conscience, of charity and of necessity . . . the fulfillment of their sacred codes."[13]

Although middle class in origin and ideologically confused, the new political movement, still nameless at this stage, effectively encouraged worker organization. On January 21, 1919, the Sindicato Central Obrero (Central Labor Union), in conjunction with the Confederación de Acción Social, called together a workers' congress. By this time more than twenty labor organizations functioned in Bogotá,[14] and more than five hundred workers were present at the congress.

In the labor congress of January 1919, José D. Celis, representative of the Mutual Benefit Society, declared that "when the hour arrives for electing the members of this labor confederation, we should look toward the truly socialist workers; those who

13. Ibid.
14. According to the official statistics used in Table 1, only seven organizations had been recognized by this time, and the *Sindicato Obrero* was not one of them. Thus Table 1 clearly underestimates the growth of the labor movement in these early years.

desire the expansion and triumph of socialism. To this new society we should not admit any one who favors or is an agent of political ideas other than ours. We shall try to save the labor movement from professional politicians . . ."[15] An editorial of January 25, 1919, in the *Gaceta* further reported that the labor congress officially rejected a proposal from the Liberals asking for support in the forthcoming elections, in spite of the fact that to obtain such support, the Liberal Party offered a position on the party's slate for city council to a representative of the workers. The congress preferred to recommend abstention from voting until the workers could go to the elections with their own candidates.

A politically independent labor movement was beginning to emerge, and it predictably called itself socialist, although it was clearly a local brand of socialism. According to an editorial in the *Gaceta,* "Socialism is a tendency toward justice inspired in the true doctrine of Christ, apostle of socialism."[16] The Catholic unions apparently did not take that definition seriously and refused to participate in the labor congress.[17] In the preliminary platform of the Socialist Party published in February 1919, anarchist and "extreme socialist" doctrines were also rejected.[18] These doctrines were rejected because "we do not favor the hegemony of the proletariat over the other classes," an original statement considering it came from a socialist labor congress in 1919. In fact, the platform specifically favored a native brand of socialism: "Given the various tendencies of socialism, each country needs a special type of socialism according to the intellectual state of the people, the development of industry, etc. The new political party shall be called the 'Socialist Party,' but as has been said, a special socialism tailored to our people, that is to say, Christian." The platform further declared that the party did not condemn the institution of private property, and that only members of the

15. *Gaceta Republicana* (January 13, 1919).
16. *Gaceta Republicana* (February 6, 1919).
17. Ibid. (February 5, 1919).
18. Ibid. (February 15, 1919).

working classes should be accepted into the new organization. This last proposition was consistent with the fact that the platform was drafted by two workers—Manuel Antonio Reyes and José D. Celís.

During the following months the labor movement prospered. A union of tailors was formed in Bogotá with two hundred members, the shoemakers organized around the Sociedad Industrial de Zapateros, two hundred carpenters and cabinetmakers attended an organizational meeting of their trade, and builders also organized a trade union.[19] The organizational drive was also successful in Girardot and other cities, and by March 7, twelve newspapers in the provinces were supporting the attempts at union organization.

The trade unions affiliated with the new Socialist Party, however, were not interested in collective bargaining. In the general organizational plan drafted in accordance with Agreement No. 3 of the Labor Congress of Bogotá, the purpose of unions was declared to be:

1. The establishment of savings associations, consumer cooperatives, and death benefit plans, health and life insurance, and popular education.
2. In the political field, the unions shall attempt to obtain the representation of the workers in the legislative bodies and shall present to the state the grievances of the trades.[20]

In 1919, as in 1850, the urban proletariat was still largely made up of independent craftsmen, and therefore collective bargaining could not be one of the major purposes of organization. The trades that organized in 1919 were tailors, shoemakers, cabinetmakers, and builders, and as in 1850, the new unions soon turned to politics in order to obtain protection from foreign competition.

19. Ibid. (February 5–14, 1919).
20. Ibid. (March 12, 1919).

In early March of 1919 President Suárez signed a decree by which he authorized the purchase of uniforms and other military supplies abroad. Immediately the officers of the *Gaceta Republicana* started to organize a protest rally for Sunday, March 18. On March 15, the walls of the city were papered with notices printed by the *Gaceta* inviting workers of all classes to a protest march on the presidential palace. As a prelude to the march, violent articles opposing the government appeared in the *Gaceta* throughout that week.

A day before the rally, the government annulled the decree appointing a commission to buy army uniforms. The tragicomic aspect of the whole incident is that the uniforms were not needed for any more important reason than the celebration of the centennial of the battle for independence at Boyacá. In the Conservative peace of the first decades of the twentieth century the most important events in Bogotá were the crowning of national poets and parades celebrating various national or religious dates.

Quiet clearly, the Socialist intellectuals of the *Gaceta* needed an excuse for a show of force. When on Sunday more than three thousand workers and students arrived before the presidential palace, the excuse for the rally was no longer valid. With characteristic irresponsibility, the speakers acted as if the decree had not been annulled. When President Suárez went out on the balcony to talk to the rally, the crowd had become enraged. They did not allow the President to speak and shouted down the leaders of the rally when they tried to establish order. Stones were thrown and shouts of "Long Live Socialism" interrupted the conference that the President was trying to hold with the leaders of the protest. When Manrique Páramo was unable to explain to the multitude that the presidential decree had already been annulled, the President got very excited and threatened to investigate his behavior. Manrique Páramo ran out of the palace, and it seems he further incited the crowd. After this, as was so often to be the case with street demonstrations in Bogotá, the crowd got out of hand. Whether or not seriously threatened, the presidential guard fired into the crowd, and gave Colombian Socialists their first martyrs.[21] The fighting soon spread, and the cavalry was called in to disperse the rioters, but only after some stores had been looted, public buildings stoned, and detachments of the army attacked. The final death toll was seven, none of whom were soldiers, and about fifteen persons were wounded. After the event both the President and the War Minister claimed they had not given the order to fire, declarations which did nothing to improve the government's prestige. The Socialist leaders were not blameless either; they recklessly sacrificed seven lives for no reason at all.

The Emergence of the Craft Unions

In contrast to the March events, the railroad strike of November 1919 illustrates the rationale and effectiveness of serious trade union action. On November 18, 1919, the workers of the Girardot Railway presented a demand for a 40 percent wage increase. It was argued that inflation made such an increase necessary if the standard of living of the workers was to be maintained. The effectiveness of the petition hinged on the fact that the National Railroad Society, founded shortly before on the initiative of the workers on the Southern, Sabana, and Northern railways and on the Bogotá streetcar lines, supported the Girardot railroad workers. The real threat, as *El Espectador* explained, was the possibility of a general strike. "If the workers of the Girardot line do not get what they demand, the other railroads are paralyzed in sympathy. If they do obtain their demands, the others are going to ask for the same."[22] This, in a nutshell, is the bargaining tactic of any national union.

The next day, the National Railroad Society announced that it

21. For differing accounts of these events, including the official interpretation and those of various shades of opposition to the government, see *El Espectador, El Tiempo,* and *Gaceta Republicana* (March 13–22, 1919).

22. *El Espectador* (November 18, 1919).

would present to the other railroads a petition similar to that of the Girardot Railway workers. At the same time, the director of the Girardot Railway announced that since a wage increase had been granted to most workers a few months before, the company would not accept the workers' demands. The director further declared publicly that he did not believe that the threatened stoppage would be carried out.

At seven A.M. on November 20, to everyone's great surprise, an effective walkout took place, and the National Railway Society presented demands to three other railroads and to the Bogotá streetcar company. The first reaction of the government was to send a hundred policemen to Facatativá, where the strikers were strongest. But since the railroad workers monopolized a scarce skill and no strikebreakers could be found, their walkout was effective and violence was not needed to make the strike effective. Public opinion was pleasantly surprised by the peacefulness of the labor protest, and both Liberal and Conservative newspapers sided with the workers.[23] As the *Espectador* editorial expressed it: "The workers are in the right as long as they behave with moderation and do not threaten destruction of property or disturbance of the peace."[24] In an *El Tiempo* account of a meeting of the National Railway Society, the observer noted great maturity and moderation during the debates and the absence of anarchist or bolshevik tendencies. The latter was probably true, since the organizations involved seemed to be truly proletarian in origin, and were led by semieducated Colombian workers.

By November 22, the strike had spread not only to the workers of the other central Colombian railroads, but also to most of the manufacturing establishments of Bogotá. Beer, textile, flour, and smelting factories were paralyzed, and workers on the streetcars declared they would not return to work until the demands of the

23. *El Espectador* (November 25, 1919). In Cali, on November 23, Pedro Lozano, parish priest, gave a pro-union conference, thus showing the approval of the Church.

24. *El Espectador* (November 20, 1919).

other groups were met. The National Socialist Committee supported the strikers, but it is hard to say whether it organized any walkouts. Its influence on the Girardot Railway workers was probably substantial, but the subsequent walkouts seem to have been spontaneous.

While the strike spread, the Minister of the Interior declared in the House of Representatives that the right to strike is one which no one can take from the workers, and he ordered the prefect of Girardot to be absolutely neutral in the conflict between the workers and the company as long as the strike maintained its peaceful character. Clearly the Conservative government accepted the right of workers to strike peacefully. But given the nature of Colombian industry and of the labor skills it required, this did not ensure the growth of the labor movement.

Most of Colombian industry was primitive and required low labor skills. This meant that most strikes could be broken with cheap unskilled labor, and therefore a peaceful strike could be successful only in the few industries where unskilled strikebreakers were useless. In the early stages of Colombian development skilled labor was essential only in railroads, shipping, and a few other industries. In other sectors of the economy, a strike could be effective only if strikebreakers and new workers were kept out through violence.

On November 24, masons and bakers joined the general strike. At a meeting of 5,000 construction workers, a masons' union was formed, but the trade was unable to organize an effective strike. By contrast, that same morning the railroads signed agreements with their workers. Girardot railroad workers obtained a 40 percent wage increase, Sabana workers 20 percent, and Southern Railway workers 30 percent, as well as a half-hour reduction in the work load. The other railways also gave increases. The strikes triggered by the railway workers did not fare as well. Bakers in Bogotá struck again on December 4. The workers insisted that the demands drafted by the National Socialist Committee be met. By December 6, the strikers started stoning bakeries, and on the 9th, employers announced that production would resume with workers who did not want to strike. During the walkout the city was supplied via the railroads by bakeries in the surrounding cities of Facatativá, Zipaquirá, Nemocón, and Soacha. Not being organized even on a regional basis, the bakers resorted to violence to keep bread baked outside Bogotá from being imported. One morning they detained some women bringing bread from Zipaquirá and distributed it among the assembled crowd. Four bakers were sentenced to thirty days in prison for this. Under these conditions, the strike was broken. The bakers had been unable to organize completely in the city, and were not organized at all in the areas of potential supply of bread. Faced with failure, they resorted to violence, but this mechanism was not effective in a dispersed industry like baking.

Another trade that was able to organize an effective union was that of the river workers. One of the reasons for this was that their strikes did not have to last long to be effective. Since even a short strike is costly to the shipping companies, they tend to settle with the dock workers instead of incurring the cost of a strike.

In addition to having a high cost per hour, dock strikes are also effective due to the characteristics of the occupation. On the docks of the Magdalena River, just as in Manhattan, labor violence can effectively keep strikebreakers at bay in the short run and can thus make short strikes effective despite the easy substitutability of dock workers. When on April 8, 1919, crews went on strike at the Pineda López Company, the walkout was effective. The firm claimed that strikers kept nonstrikers from working, and in response the government sent troops to restore order in Girardot. Nevertheless, the company raised daily wages to end the strike.[25]

In the case of the more skilled workers in river transport, such as machinists and engineers, their bargaining position was naturally strong. Riverboat workers, like railroad workers, had the first

25. *Gaceta Republicana* (April 8, 1919).

craft unions with a strong bargaining position. The supply of labor in these occupations was inelastic in the short run, and it was hard to find strikebreakers—conditions that made possible the emergence of strong unions in the period before unionism was given legal protection.

Socialist Ideology and Union Tactics

Generally, in Colombia as in other nations, the first labor organizations effective in carrying out strikes and obtaining improved working conditions were those in the skilled trades. But because of the historical development of the economy, the construction trades were not among this group, since construction workers have tended to have low levels of skill. The first labor organizations to function effectively were in transport, where modern technology requiring new and scarce skills was first adopted.

But, unfortunately for the Colombian labor movement, some of the craft unions that could have developed a strong bargaining position wasted their energies in political agitation and brought upon themselves the opposition of the authorities without having first obtained the strength to withstand that opposition. This was the case of the Union of Dorada Railroad Workers.

When that union held its first meeting it committed itself to the socialist creed and sent a letter to the Socialist executive committee declaring that it had the same ideals and aspirations as the party. The relationship between the new union and the Socialists was probably quite harmful. In contrast to the rational and well-thought-out petitions of the railroad workers which culminated in the successful strike of November 1919, the Dorada Railroad workers demanded a 258 percent wage increase in January 1920. A strike ensued, and very soon violence erupted. A train on which General Gamboa, the police chief sent to the scene by the government, was traveling was attacked and a policeman was mortally wounded. The army then intervened, and soldiers drove the trains until a settlement was reached.

Public opinion and the press soon disapproved of the strike. An editorial in *El Espectador,* a Liberal newspaper always sympathetic to labor, stated: "The strike on the Dorada railway is probably the first example in Colombia of a disagreeable strike. They ask for too much . . . And now the workers adopt violent tactics! The government should take steps so that the general public is not harmed . . ."[26]

After nine days of strike and agitation, the workers reduced their demands to a 30 percent wage increase, but since the representatives of the workers were not employees of the railroad, the company refused to bargain.[27] The agitators who kept the conflict alive were a colorful group. They were Isaias Díaz Quevedo, a former cleric from the city of Honda who had abandoned the robe to dedicate himself to the defense of the workers, Carlos Rueda, a carpenter, and Felix Mora.[28] On the tenth day of the strike eighty workers at the Beltrán station returned to work and Carlos Rueda was jailed.

At this point the workers rejected the conditions for settlement formulated by the Socialist Directorate of Honda and reached an agreement with the company. After an eleven-day strike, they obtained a 10 percent wage increase for office employees, a 40 percent increase for machinists, and a 30 percent increase for manual workers. The workers did not gain from their association with socialism. On the contrary, they obtained an agreement only after they rejected the Socialist leadership.

Although the experience of the Dorada Railroad Workers and other unions with Socialist tactics was not a positive one, the popularity of the Socialist creed among organized workers in general had the useful effect of modernizing the ideology of the Liberal Party. This was probably the major contribution of socialism to Colombian social and economic development.

26. *El Espectador* (January 7, 1920).
27. Ibid. (January 8, 1920).
28. Ibid. (January 9, 1920).

6

Socialism and Liberalism Bid
for Labor's Political Support

Throughout the first three decades of this century, the Colombian Liberals constituted a minority party. Although strong in some rural areas, such as those of coffee cultivation and certain regions of Cundinamarca, their real strength was in the cities. In this respect, Colombian political history is similar to that of Europe and the United States, where liberalism was also an urban phenomenon.

Throughout its history, the Colombian Liberal Party has had to depend on the urban vote, and therefore on Labor's support. The problem for the party has thus always been that of reconciling the liberalism of the urban and rural bourgeoisie with the political attitudes and demands of the organized and unorganized urban proletariat. For example, as soon as an industrial labor force came into being, the Liberal Party made it clear that it could not support the more extreme forms of labor protest, and any strike that threatened private property was immediately criticized by the party press. Since in the first stages of labor organization the very weakness of the labor unions led them to adopt violent tactics and to organize solidarity strikes, which often deteriorated into riots, relations between the party and the more militant labor leaders were strained. As a result, when labor organization began in Colombia, the labor movement refused to support the Liberal Party, and in 1919, when the nation was living through its first strikes, trade union leaders participated actively in the creation of the Socialist Party.

As in other two-party systems, however, the importance of a third party in Colombia did not depend on the strength it achieved, but on the influence it had on the two great mass parties. When faced by the threat of losing some of its urban strength to the Socialists, the Liberal Party decided to reform.

As has already been mentioned, in the first congress of the Socialist Party it was decided not to support the candidates of the traditional political groups. In May 1919, the Republican Directorate (a coalition of Liberals and moderate Conservatives) published a list of candidates for the elections to the House of Representatives which included the following names: Eduardo Santos, director of the newspaper *El Tiempo* and Liberal President from 1938 to 1942; Diego Mendoza Pérez; Laureano Gómez, Conservative President from 1950 to 1953; and Marco T. Amorocho, Socialist and president of the Asamblea Obrera. In spite of the inclusion of a representative of the workers, the Socialist Party did not yield and refrained from endorsing any list of candidates. On May 20, 1919, it went even further; the first paragraph of the officially adopted platform of the party stated: "The workers' congress declares that the present labor movement is independent of the established political parties and of religious sects."[1]

This platform followed closely the preliminary program of the party drafted at the labor congress in February of 1919 and was influenced by the viewpoints of the Asamblea Obrera y Profesional (Assembly of Workers and Professionals) and the Sindicato Central Obrero (Central Labor Union), the most influential organizations within the party. The Sindicato Central Obrero was founded in 1917 by five individuals belonging to various trades and having different political opinions. The purpose of the organization was "to form a collective fund for the benefit of its mem-

1. *Gaceta Republicana* (May 30, 1919).

bers and to provide the means to defend the rights of those members." To fulfill these obligations the union established saving deposits, health insurance, consumer cooperatives, death benefit plans, and a credit cooperative. In early 1919, probably influenced by the intellectuals in the Social Action Confederation, the Central Labor Union invited various labor organizations to Colombia's first labor congress. The congress in turn created the Socialist Party and elected its first executive committee. Thus direct control of the party was in the hands of labor unions or mutual benefit societies.

In order to understand the makeup of the Socialist Party it may be of interest to list the names of the organizations that were represented in the labor congress that continued to function after the February meeting.[2]

1. La Propagadora de la Luz No. 53 (The Spreader of Light No. 53)
2. Unión Obrera de Colombia (Laborers' Union of Colombia)
3. Sociedad de Mutuo Auxilio (Mutual Help Society)
4. Centro de Contabilidad (Accounting Center)
5. Sociedad Unión de Barberos (Barbers' Union)
6. Sindicato Central Obrero (Central Labor Union)
7. Centro la Inmensidad
8. Gremio de Sastres (Tailors' Union)
9. Sociedad de Seguros de Muerte (Death Insurance Society)

At a later time, the following organizations also joined:

10. Sociedad Tipográfica (Typographical Society)
11. Gremio de Ebanistas y Carpinteros (Union of Carpenters and Cabinetmakers)

2. *Gaceta Republicana* (May 6, 1919).

12. Gremio de Litógrafos (Union of Lithographers)
13. Sindicato del Comercio (Union of Commerce)
14. Gremio de Herreros y Mecánicos (Union of Blacksmiths and Mechanics)

It appears that most of these organizations were truly proletarian in character and that within the Socialist Party the intellectuals were sometimes on the defensive. For example, an editorial in the *Gaceta Republicana* of May 7, 1919, argued that although unions should not admit anyone who did not belong to the working class, militant intellectuals should be allowed to join the Socialist Party. Clearly the intellectuals were then under attack within the party.

Given the proletarian nature of the Socialist Party, its strength was concentrated in cities where railroad and port workers made up a large proportion of the labor force. In the elections for the House of Representatives in February 1921, the Socialists presented their own lists and obtained a substantial number of votes in these cities. In Medellín, the cradle of industrialization and, paradoxically, the most strongly Conservative of the larger cities, the Socialists obtained 23 percent of the vote in comparison with 15 percent obtained by the Liberals,[3] and in Bucaramanga the Liberals claimed they lost the elections because the Socialists in that locality asked their electorate to abstain.[4]

The Socialization of the Liberal Party

The elections of 1921 convinced the Liberals that the Socialists threatened their electoral majority in the cities. The problem is well illustrated by an editorial in *El Espectador:*

It is necessary that the Socialists understand that since the Conservative Party is presently the only obstacle to the

3. *El Espectador* (February 7, 1921).
4. Ibid. (February 8, 1921).

initiation of social reform, only by helping to defeat it through a successful campaign by a unified Liberalism, is one really working to further the interests of the people.[5]

In an editorial on May 1, *El Espectador* again discussed the relationship between the workers and the Liberal Party:

> The workers should start on the road to their autonomous organization. But gradually and with prudence. Today, the most rational attitude and, therefore, the most effective would be that of enthusiastically backing the new policies of Liberalism. Why? It is very clear: because it is the only party sufficiently numerous and militant to push through the reforms that are needed . . .

Apparently, however, the ideology of the Liberal Party was not sufficiently progressive to suit the Socialists, and in the city council elections of October 1921, the Socialists again voted independently. Although the Liberals obtained a majority in all of the major cities of Colombia except Medellín, Ibagué, and Manizales, the competition from the Socialists was sufficient to cause a radical change in the ideology of the Liberal Party at the party convention in the latter part of the month. According to José Mar, writing at the time:

> In its convention the Liberal Party adopted the moderate and viable socialist ideas . . . In view of this fact, the modest reforms for which our serious socialist groups have been aspiring come under the most efficient sponsorship—that of the Liberal Party, which advocates a new ideology and has abandoned the old individualist doctrines . . . In view of this new attitude, completely new, and logically divorced from ineffective individualism, the Liberal forces shall be strength-

5. Ibid. (March 31, 1921).

ened on the one hand, and on the other hand will be forced to advocate the reforms for which the small and enthusiastic socialist groups have valiantly fought.[6]

Toward the end of 1921, after having abandoned part of its individualistic ideology, the Liberal Party decided to present its own candidate for the presidential elections of the following year. This was a radical departure from the traditional Liberal tactic of backing a moderate Conservative. Clearly the Liberals were convinced that they had gained sufficient strength to win a national election.

Two weeks after having been designated Liberal candidate, Benjamín Herrera wrote a letter to the executive committee for organization of the Socialist Party stating that "it is within the Liberal Party that the groups which favor socialist organization can work with the greatest hope of success and achieve the reforms which would improve the living standard of the masses."[7] After the influential Sindicato Central Obrero declared its support for Benjamín Herrera, the Socialists of Girardot and Medellín soon followed. It appears that the Liberal Party, in order to ensure for itself the vote of the growing mass of industrial workers, adopted the reformist ideals of the Colombian Socialist Party. Thus, the historic function of the Socialist Party was to make the Liberals abandon their individualistic free enterprise and free trade ideology. In other words, it helped to bring Colombian Liberalism into the ideological stream of the twentieth century.

As was to be expected, Benjamín Herrera won large majorities in the major urban centers. Socialist support was probably significant in the cities, since in Ibagué, Bucaramanga, and Medellín the Liberals obtained a majority, while in the October 1921 elections they had been defeated in those cities.[8] Of the growing departmental capitals only Manizales remained Conservative. In the

6. Ibid. (October 24, 1921).
7. Ibid. (December 31, 1921).
8. Ibid. (February 13, 1922).

historic but stagnating cities of Tunja and Popayán the Conservative triumph was inevitable. But since Colombia was still largely rural and backward, the Conservative candidate Pedro Nel Ospina won the election. The Liberals, however, have always claimed that the Conservative victory was fraudulent. Although there was fraud in many areas, it seems implausible that even in a fair election the Liberals could have won the Presidency in 1922. The Liberals could only have won the election if the urban masses and the workers in modern industry had been a larger proportion of the population than they were in 1922.

On the one hand, the Liberal doctrine was essentially an urban ideology, and on the other, clean elections were an urban phenomenon. With respect to the honesty of elections, it must be kept in mind that the Conservatives had been in power for decades, and the authorities were all members of the Conservative Party. The Conservative machinery for rigging elections was, therefore, much more efficient than that of the Liberals. Clean elections were then a prerequisite for a Liberal triumph. Since it was generally agreed that the degree of dishonesty in elections varied proportionally to the distance from the urban areas, urbanization weakened the power of the Conservatives to rig elections in their favor and gave the Liberals the possibility of an electoral victory. Urbanization thus favored the Liberals in two ways. The Liberal creed became relevant to an ever larger proportion of the population, and election ethics improved. Both of these processes made possible the Liberal electoral victories of the following decade.

The New Liberal Generation

The adoption by the Liberal Party of a moderate reform platform similar to that sponsored by the Colombian Socialists was more than a simple electoral tactic. The leadership of the party sincerely adopted the new ideology, and, more important still, the party admitted into its ranks the young Socialist intellectuals. A case in point is that of the young law student Jorge Eliécer Gaitán. One year before he presented his dissertation, entitled

"Las ideas socialistas en Colombia,"[9] he was already active in Liberal politics. In the Liberal state assembly of Cundinamarca in April 1924, he presented a proposition, which was unanimously approved; in it he asked congressmen "to direct their congressional activities toward a vigorous, daring, and efficient fight to solve social problems. Not through shallow reforms but by achieving through cooperative institutions, in production, distribution and consumption, a degree of equality among the social classes."[10] Commenting on this event in his editorial column in *El Espectador,* Luis Tejada, one of the founders of the Communist Party in Colombia,[11] had this to say:

> Not only among the young militants of the party, but also among its leadership (see the declarations of the Liberal leaders in the Apulo agreement), there exists an ever greater and more obvious sympathy with what has been called the socialization of liberalism, that is to say, the adoption of the collectivist forms of organization. And this had to occur. It was unlikely that the foreign environment, agitated by social revolution, should not influence our Liberal thinkers to also desire the adoption of different administrative methods, more equitable and efficient than those that have been acceptable until now.[12]

Gaitán was not the only leftist to enter Liberal politics at this time. Another student who was attracted by socialism was Gabriel Turbay,[13] although unlike Gaitán he was not initially convinced

9. Later published as Jorge Eliécer Gaitán, *Las ideas socialistas en Colombia* (Bogotá, Editorial América Libre, 1963).

10. *El Espectador* (April 22, 1923).

11. Comisión del Comité Central, *Treinto años de lucha del Partido Comunista de Colombia* (Bogotá, Ediciones Paz y Socialismo, 1960), p. 12.

12. *El Espectador* (April 22, 1923).

13. Gaitán and Turbay were the two Liberal presidential candidates in the 1946 elections.

that socialism could be best served from within the ranks of the Liberal Party. The ideology adopted in the twenties by the future leadership of the Liberal Party was not, however, that of orthodox socialism. For example, Turbay joined a Marxist study group led by the Russian Silvestre Savitski in 1923.[14] The biography of Savitski suggests the nature of the socialist activity of those years. A university student sent to China to purchase wheat for the revolution, Savitski met and fell in love with a Russian girl, the daughter of a former tsarist provincial governor. He gambled the funds of the revolution at the roulette table, lost them, and fled to Tokyo. From there he traveled to Panama and then established himself as a laundry worker in Bogotá. Before being deported in 1928, Savitski dedicated himself to gaining adherents to the principles of the Soviet revolution among the young intellectuals of the capital, and his study group included among others Luis Tejada and José Mar, both of whom wrote for the important Liberal daily *El Espectador,* Diego Mejía, Alejandro Vallejo, Moisés Prieto, and Roberto García Peña, present director of the nation's largest daily, *El Tiempo.*[15]

At the time that Savitski founded his Marxist study group in 1923, the Colombian Socialist Party was still militant but as ideologically confused as ever. It was directed by Francisco Heredia (club man), Tomás Uribe Márquez (intellectual), and the artisans Juan C. Dávila, Jacinto Albarracín, and Juan de Dios Romero. Romero directed the paper *El Socialista* and was imprisoned in April 1923 because he advocated political assassination and military revolt from the columns of his paper.[16] The new liberalism also weakened socialism electorally, and in the by-election of January 1922, the Socialists even lost in Girardot, their former stronghold.

14. Comisión del Comité Central, p. 12.
15. Diego Montaña Cuéllar, *Colombia, país formal y país real* (Buenos Aires, Editorial Platina, 1963), p. 131.
16. *El Espectador* (April 27, 1923).

Jorge Eliécer Gaitán saw no future in either the orthodox Marxist group of Savitski or the somewhat anarchistic Socialist Party. In his university dissertation (1924) he clearly stated that he did not belong to any socialist party,

> because although in Colombia there are valuable groups that profess these ideals, they have not understood the characteristics of our political life, and, therefore, have not interpreted events correctly and have followed the wrong tactics . . . We profess with conviction and enthusiasm the [socialist] ideas discussed in these pages, but we cannot consider ourselves militants of a socialist party in our country because, among other things, no such party exists.[17]

Except for a short time in the thirties when he formed the independent movement called UNIR, Gaitán always believed that the transformation of Colombian society could best be carried out from within the Liberal Party. In 1924 he stated:

> It is not by destroying the political tendency that in Colombia represents the opposition and progressive party that one works best for the triumph of the reforms that the people wish; we believe that it is better to fight so that the progressive forces of Colombia inscribe on their banners the new ideas, and so that they make their own the battle for the welfare of the proletariat and for the necessary vindication of the serfs of capital.[18]

By working for reform, for the legal protection of workers, and for labor organization, Gaitán believed that he was preparing the ground for the Socialist transformation of society. His ideology was very consistent throughout his political life, and,

17. Gaitán, p. 11.
18. Ibid.

despite variations in political tactics, he remained faithful to the Marxist dogmas and superstitions of his youth.[19] His knowledge of economics was limited and he was never a Marxist or Socialist theoretician, but he did believe in the socialization of the means of production and the elimination of the individualist structure of Colombian society.[20] He even questioned the major postulate of liberalism. In his dissertation he asked, "To the man who is dying of hunger, what does it matter if he has liberty?"[21]

In time, however, when Liberalism started to become electorally strong, the intellectuals who had been members of the socialist and communist organizations in the early twenties joined the Liberal bandwagon. Characteristically, Gaitán remained the most independent man of that generation, leaving the party for a short time when the others joined it.

From 1925 on, the old reformist socialist groups lost ground to the Communists and the Liberals, and the Colombian labor movement began to be dominated by communist groups influenced and sometimes directed by the international communist movement. But by then, socialism had played the historical role of forcing the modernization of the Liberal Party.

19. García, *Gaitán,* pp. 4, 96.
20. Gaitán, pp. 39–40.
21. Ibid., p. 97.

7

The Period of the Great Strikes

By the year 1924, the communist movement in Colombia had gained some strength among intellectuals and radical politicians. Various young Colombians had returned from the Soviet Union where they had studied and become partisans of the revolution. From the start, these intellectuals tried to infiltrate the labor movement, and they had close relations with María Cano, the communist labor leader of Girardot.

In November 1923, Luis Tejada, the most famous communist writer of his time, started to agitate from the editorial pages of *El Espectador* for the meeting of a labor congress. He saw the labor congress more as the basis for a political party than as a business meeting of trade union leaders, and considered that its function should be that of

creating a strong, stable, and powerful organization of unions in order to start the battle to obtain certain political guarantees which organized labor does not at present have. For example it is necessary to obtain an electoral law sufficiently broad and elastic so that it records the will of the workers who are independent of the traditional political parties. It is necessary that the workers elect to the representative bodies of the nation their own candidates; since it has been shown it is impossible to obtain adequate labor legislation through indirect representatives . . . The latter are ignorant of proletarian problems, or if they understand them, it is not in their class interest to solve them.[1]

In March 1924, the Sindicato Central Obrero, which had called together the first labor congress in 1919, invited various labor organizations to a new congress.[2] The new congress opened on May 1 with delegates of worker organizations from all sections of the nation. The committee on credentials was controlled by the Sindicato Central Obrero, but despite the efforts of the committee, the congress was clearly divided into four distinct groups: bread-and-butter unionists, socialists, communists, and anarcho-syndicalists.[3] By 1924, the Sindicato Central seems to have been in the camp of the moderates who obtained control of the congress, but the triumph of the moderates was not easy. During the first working session on May 3, the division among the delegates crystallized over a proposition prohibiting political discussion at the congress. The socalists opposed the proposition and order was restored only when the police dragged away the Socialist delegate Juan de Dios Romero.

Since the division between the socialists and the economically oriented unionists was sharp and permanent, a Socialist congress began to meet parallel to the labor congress. This Socialist congress soon became divided also, but from the start it had one characteristic that made it different from the labor congress: it was dominated by young leftist intellectuals. The list of delegates to the Socialist congress included Luis Tejada, Armando Solano, and José Mar, all writers for *El Espectador,* the poet León de Greiff, communist labor leader Raúl Eduardo Mahecha, Juan de Dios Romero and Francisco Heredia, both Socialists, Dionisio Arango Vélez, and César Julio Rodriguez.[4]

1. *El Espectador* (November 23, 1923).
2. Ibid. (March 13, 1924).
3. Ibid. (April 30, 1924).
4. Ibid., Segunda Edición (April 30, 1924).

While intellectuals dominated the Socialist camp, in the labor congress the leadership of the intellectuals was specifically rejected. Thus, as in 1919, there was a strong labor group ready to reject the intellectuals, and to create a labor movement led by genuine members of the proletariat.

While the labor congress met during the day, the Socialists aired their division during the evening. In the latter group it soon became clear that the intellectuals would disown the old Socialist Party. They declared themselves to be the First Communist Congress of Colombia, and adopted the twenty-one conditions required by the Communist International of those parties that wanted to affiliate themselves with the organization. The break with the old party was dramatic. The communist intellectuals such as José Mar and Gabriel Turbay, who were later to be the epitome of liberal moderation, dominated the proceedings. José Mar answered a socialist labor leader as follows:[5]

> We are going to conquer the positions of power by coercion, with the violence of right . . . The delegate who preceded me at the podium mentioned that yesterday's Socialists did not stuff themselves with European theories; this is true: these Socialists were good and candid people who did not understand European theories.

A week later, the Socialist congress dissolved because the socialists and communists were unable to reach an agreement. On May 21, the labor congress also adjourned without having achieved anything lasting. But the events of May 1924 were crucial because they determined the eclipse of the national and pragmatic socialist movement. From then on, the Colombian labor movement was to be largely under the control of the Communists, and the three great strikes of the twenties were to be led by the Communist Raúl Eduardo Mahecha, vice-president of the Socialist congress of 1924.

5. Ibid. (May 6, 1924).

Economic Prosperity

In 1923, the United States paid the Colombian government the first installment of the 25-million-dollar indemnity for the American intervention in the separation of Panama from Colombia.[6] In addition, Colombia began to profit from world prosperity, and was able to place loans on the American and European markets. Between 1923 and 1928, almost 200 million dollars entered the country in the form of loans and the indemnity for Panama; and from 1920 to 1929, the investment of American citizens in Colombia increased from 30 million to 280 million dollars.[7]

TABLE 2

Colombian Trade Statistics, 1919–32

Year	Imports	Exports	Difference
1919	P 47,451,724	P 79,010,983	P + 31,559,259
1920	101,397,906	71,017,729	− 30,380,177
1921	33,078,317	63,042,132	+ 29,963,815
1922	44,148,024	52,731,477	+ 8,583,453
1923	67,207,725	56,044,456	− 11,203,269
1924	62,251,228	84,247,819	+ 21,996,591
1925	97,208,000	88,214,350	+ 8,993,650
1926	123,973,505	110,195,521	− 13,777,984
1927	139,165,525	107,622,092	− 31,543,433
1928	162,380,690	132,502,134	− 29,878,556
1929	141,540,853	121,677,241	− 19,863,612
1930	70,381,811	104,224,969	+ 33,843,158
1931	45,971,119	80,449,592	+ 34,478,473
1932	34,327,091	67,108,723	+ 32,781,632

Source: Guillermo Torres García, *Historia de la moneda en Colombia* (Bogotá, Imprenta del Banco de la República, 1945), 369–85.

6. Guillermo Torres García, *Historia de la moneda en Colombia* (Bogotá, Imprenta del Banco de la República, 1945), p. 353.
7. J. Fred Rippy, *The Capitalists and Colombia* (New York, Vanguard Press, 1931), p. 152.

Parallel to the inflow of capital, world demand for Colombian products increased, and Colombian producers responded by almost tripling exports between 1923 and 1928. Table 2 shows the imports and exports of Colombia in the years immediately before the rise of the modern labor movement, and may serve as a rough index of changing economic conditions.

A great proportion of the foreign capital coming into the country at the time was spent by the state in creating the infrastructure needed for the consolidation of economic development, and this, in turn, stimulated private investment and economic activity. Between 1925 and 1929, 26 percent of Colombia's gross national product was invested, and it has been estimated that the per capita gross national product increased at the rapid rate of 5.2 percent per year during the period.[8] Despite the strategic role of foreign capital, it must be kept in mind that at the time no more than 15 percent of the capital available in the nation was in foreign hands.[9] In fact, in 1913 there was probably less American capital in Colombia than in any other Latin American country.[10]

The sudden spurt of economic activity plus the inflow of foreign capital soon caused serious bottlenecks in the economy, and a rapid price rise began to affect the salaried classes. For example, between 1923 and 1929, the prices of a group of income-elastic products such as meat and dairy products in-

8. Naciones Unidas, CEPAL, *Análisis y proyecciones del desarrollo económico—el desarrollo económico en Colombia* (Mexico City, Naciones Unidas, 1957), pp. 10–11.

9. Ibid.

10. The relatively small importance of foreign capital in Colombia must be kept in mind in any discussion of the historical development of trade unionism. The first and most violent strikes took place against American companies, and communist unions were most effective in those companies. If foreign enterprises had been more common, it is very likely that labor-management relations in Colombia would have developed along more violent lines, and that the labor movement today would be more radical in ideology.

85

TABLE 3

Price Index for Three Groups of Foodstuffs in Six Major Cities

(1923 = 100)

City	Groups of Food-stuffs*	1924	1925	1926	1927	1928	1929	1930	1931	1932	1933	1934
Bogotá	1	104	122	158	138	121	127	116	107	75	82	113
	2	109	115	143	185	169	180	162	127	98	103	114
	3	126	140	149	131	140	190	143	133	88	84	115
Barranquilla	1	118	121	121	91	123	109	92	82	81	93	113
	2	109	125	120	110	127	134	104	88	71	68	90
	3	134	121	168	148	136	113	83	69	52	55	74
Cali	1	113	121	158	120	132	107	89	69	67	72	—
	2	90	79	98	107	101	104	68	57	49	50	—
	3	101	101	85	105	86	71	52	48	26	31	—
Ibagué	1	99	119	210	138	150	144	134	111	81	80	137
	2	101	115	145	144	144	139	105	85	72	76	88
	3	128	173	251	170	245	205	130	123	87	103	157

Medellín	1	112	125	163	112	131	106	87	76	62	70	94
	2	113	103	140	147	149	131	91	80	68	69	71
	3	108	85	80	80	75	72	50	41	26	26	48
Santa Marta	1	104	104	104	85	113	100	84	83	77	80	—
	2	115	118	122	113	146	119	108	88	88	80	—
	3	129	112	162	134	139	126	92	86	58	55	—

*The groups of foodstuffs contained the following goods:

Group 1	Group 2	Group 3
1 arroba rice	1 arroba beef	1 arroba unrefined brown sugar
1 arroba frijoles	1 arroba pork	1 arroba sugar
1 arroba wheat flour	1 arroba lard	1 arroba bananas
1 arroba corn	25 bottles of milk	1 arroba potatoes
1 arroba coffee	100 eggs	1 arroba yucca

It appears that within the groups a simple average was calculated, without giving weights to the various products.

Source: Torres García, pp. 357–411.

creased by 90 percent in Bogotá. Table 3 shows a price index for foodstuffs in the major industrial cities. Table 4 shows the tonnage mobilized by riverboats and by railroads, and is also a good index of the state of the economy.

TABLE 4

Freight Moved by the Railroads and Riverboats (in tons)

Year	Freight Moved on the Magdalena River	Freight Moved on the Railroads and Air Cables
1923	582,000	1,582,000
1924	663,000	1,820,000
1925	776,000	2,101,000
1926	779,000	2,650,000
1927	1,197,000	3,068,000
1928	1,521,000	3,315,000
1929	1,307,000	3,134,000
1930	902,000	2,197,000
1931	677,000	1,917,000
1932	763,000	2,128,000
1933	934,000	2,340,000

Source: Torres García, pp. 355 and 385.

The Level of Employment and Labor Organization

For the study of the development of unionism it is of the utmost importance to determine the employment situation in the nation, since the possibility of organizing laborers into unions depends to a large extent on whether at any given point in time there is a tight or a loose labor market. Unfortunately, before 1962 there have never been any unemployment statistics in Colombia. It is therefore necessary to attempt to determine the unemployment situation by indirect methods such as literary and newspaper accounts, supplemented every so often by official government estimates of unemployment and official statistics on the growth of employment in manufacturing industry.

Previous chapters have analyzed the emergence of unionism in 1918–19. It appears that this was a period of relative prosperity and rising prices, and that urban unemployment was not widespread.[11] By the end of 1920, however, unemployment was beginning to be a serious problem. In Medellín it was estimated that 3,000 workers were unemployed, and firms started to lay off workers and reduce wages.[12] In March 1921 cables from Barranquilla also recorded serious unemployment in the city,[13] and in June the unemployed demanded work from the government in Bogotá.[14] It seems that the growing unemployment was caused by a paralysis of public works projects, a decrease in coffee prices on the world market, and a general decrease in private investment.

Because of growing unemployment, there were no strikes of any importance after April 1920, and the labor movement began to lose strength. Even railway workers were affected by the growth of unemployment and the decreasing demand for labor, and a railway workers' strike in May 1920 was unsuccessful.[15] The unemployment situation did not improve substantially until the latter part of 1924. In March of that year, unemployed workers in Bogotá again petitioned the President for employment, and an attempt was made to form a league of the unemployed. This initiative was backed by the Directorio Central Obrero de Bogotá, and one of its requests was that the government should establish rural colonies to employ those urban workers who could not find jobs.[16] At the time it was estimated that 4,000 workers were un-

11. *El Espectador* (November and December, 1919).
12. Ibid. (November 9, 1920).
13. Ibid. (March 7, 1921).
14. Ibid. (April 2 and 5, June 8, 1921). The petition was signed by some 1,200 workers, whose names appeared in *El Espectador*. Among the signers were officers of the Patronato Obrero de Cundinamarca, officials of the carpenters' union, and the presidents of various mutual benefit societies.
15. Ibid. (May 11, 1920).
16. Ibid. (March 25, 1924).

employed in Bogotá and 3,000 in the Socialist stronghold of Girardot.[17] But by the end of 1924, it was clear that the labor market situation was improving; President Ospina told the unemployed workers that there were already 14,000 workers employed in the government's public works projects, and price increases also signaled an economic upturn.

Nevertheless, the government ordered the Ministry of Industry to carry out a census of the unemployed and instituted a system by which unemployed workers who registered would be transported free on state railroads to areas where there was a high demand for labor. Table 5 gives statistics on the number of unemployed workers who were relocated under this government program. In the census of the unemployed carried out in 1924

TABLE 5

Number of Unemployed Workers Who Used Railroad Passes to Travel to Areas of Employment Opportunity, 1924–30

April–July 1924	900
July–December 1924	202
January–May 1925	466
January–December 1927	246
July 1928–June 1929	234
August 1929–June 1930	1,699

Source: Ministerio de Industrias, *Memorias del Ministro de Industrias al Congreso* for 1924, 1925, 1928, 1929, 1930.

the state governors informed the government that the demand for workers was greater than the supply in all states except Santander and Atlántico, where there were still groups of unemployed workers.[18] This survey shows that by the end of that year unemployment had ceased to be a serious problem.

By the time the government was starting its census of the unemployed, it was becoming clear that employment opportunities

17. Ibid. (April 7, 1924).
18. Ministerio de Industrias, *Memoria presentada al Congreso de 1924.*

were increasing in some branches of industry and in some sectors of the nation, and a new strike wave swept the country. First, a strike took place among streetcar workers in Bogotá; it was soon followed by labor conflicts in a match factory, the telephone company of Bogotá, a textile factory, and the mines of Valle.[19] Parallel to the revival of labor-management conflict and bargaining, new unions were organized and old unions were revived. In June 1924 the majority of Bogotá's unions held a meeting to discuss an organization drive,[20] and in the same month the workers of the Sabana Railroad again organized themselves.[21]

In the early years of the development of the Colombian labor movement, it is clear that there was a positive correlation between union growth and economic prosperity. Furthermore, union militancy and strikes were closely and positively correlated with increases in the cost of living. The lack of strikes between 1921 and 1924, a period of relative economic stagnation, confirms this relationship.

Table 6, which shows the wages of unskilled construction workers employed by the Public Works Ministry, also reflects the changes in the employment situation. Wages improved slightly in 1918 and 1919, and toward the end of the post-war boom, in 1920, they increased 14 percent. By the end of that year, unemployment was beginning to grow; wages stagnated in 1921 and dropped very substantially in 1922. Since in 1923 unemployment was still high, wages stagnated at a level 20 percent below that of 1921. In 1924 investment in public works revived and wages began to increase again. By 1925 prosperity was well established and wages started an upward swing that would only be checked by the great crash of 1929. Thus, although throughout this period there was probably underemployment in the agricultural sector, prosperity in the limited modern sector of the economy had an important impact on wages in the modern sector. It seems that

19. *El Espectador* (April 21, June 6, June 7, and August 22, 1924).
20. Ibid. (June 3, 1924).
21. Ibid. (June 27, 1924).

the labor market serving the small modern sector was limited, and increases in demand did raise the supply price of labor.

Table 6 also shows the trend of real wages from 1923 to 1932. The important thing to notice is that real wages increased most when prices decreased most. This was certainly the case between 1931 and 1932. Since unions usually disappeared during de-

TABLE 6

Average Daily Wage of Unskilled Construction Workers in
Bogotá, 1914–32

Year	Nominal Wage (pesos)	Year	Nominal Wage (pesos)	Index of Real Wages*
1914	0.41	1923	0.53	100
1915	0.44	1924	0.64	104
1916	0.48	1925	0.67	100
1917	0.46	1926	0.83	105
1918	0.49	1927	1.04	123
1919	0.50	1928	1.05	126
1920	0.61	1929	1.04	112
1921	0.67	1930	1.00	128
1922	0.51	1931	1.06	157
		1932	1.07	220

*The real wage was calculated by deflating the nominal wage by a price index derived from Table 3. The three groups of goods in that table were given weights derived from the consumer budget study of 1953–54, and the resulting averages for the three groups were used to make the following price index for Bogotá:

Year	Index	Year	Index	Year	Index
1923	100	1927	158	1931	126
1924	114	1928	156	1932	91
1925	125	1929	175	1933	93
1926	148	1930	147	1934	114

Source: Wage data obtained from the payroll lists in the archives of the Public Works Ministry.

pressions, they cannot be given credit for maintaining the level of wages at those times. Cyclical factors, therefore, had a much more important effect on real wages than strikes or growing labor organization. Although not effective during the depression, it is possible that at this early stage of economic development the unions did keep real wages in some sectors of the economy from falling during periods of inflation. Although nothing definite can be said on this score, there is little doubt that the labor movement prospered only during periods of high employment and inflation.

The Strikes Against the Tropical Oil Company

As in the case of the United Fruit Company, the first major industrial relations conflict at Tropical Oil was the culmination of a long period of frustration and injustice. In April 1922 the workers at Tropical's camps were already complaining about working conditions. There were few hospitals in the oil region despite extremely unhealthy conditions, and while Colombians earned P1.50 a day without room or board, foreign workers in the same jobs earned P3.50 plus room and board.[22] Throughout the next few years conditions did not improve, and tension between foreign and national workers increased.

By March 1924 the conflict between the company and its workers was so explosive that the Minister of Industry traveled to Barrancabermeja to attempt to mediate between the parties. A pact was signed in which the company promised to improve health facilities and to supply better food. The pathetic conditions of the oil workers, however, can be illustrated by some health statistics published by the government oil inspector in September 1924. The statistics were meant to show an improvement in the conditions of the laborers, but serve only to underline the causes of the coming strike. In the first quarter of 1924, 1,023 out of 2,838 Colombian workers fell sick, and 5 died. This meant that 36 per-

22 Ibid. (April 27, 1922).

93

cent of the workers fell sick; although in the previous year 40.8 percent of the workers employed fell sick, the improved conditions of 1924 still showed a depressing situation.[23] These unhealthy conditions, coupled with the fact that despite inflation, wages in 1924 were still at the 1922 level, P1.50 a day, go a long way toward explaining the events of October.

On October 8, 1924, more than five hundred workers went on strike, and two days later the strike was total.[24] The strike was organized by Raúl Eduardo Mahecha in the name of the Sociedad Obrera de Barrancabermeja (Society of Workers of Barrancabermeja), which probably had very few members. Mahecha circulated a leaflet in which he demanded a wage increase and fulfillment of the pact signed by the company in March; but his most effective argument for the strike was his assertion that in the nearby Puerto Wilches area the railroad needed workers and was willing to pay more than the P1.50 wage paid by Tropical Oil. The desperate working conditions, plus the possibility of finding alternative employment, made the employees of Tropical Oil receptive to Mahecha's propaganda.

At first the strike was peaceful, but in a matter of hours the strikers were trying to keep the laborers who wanted to work from entering the company installations. The company, however, refused to bargain. Its rationale was that the strike had been declared without warning and that the delegates of the Sociedad Obrera were not employees of the company. Although strictly speaking the strike was illegal for these reasons, the government clearly wanted the parties to bargain, and the Minister of Industry flew to Barranca to attempt to obtain a settlement.

By the time the Minister arrived at Barranca, the company's unwillingness to bargain had caused the strikers to turn to violence. They destroyed the tracks of the company's railroad, paralyzed the company's vehicles, forced unwilling workers to

23. Ibid. (September 8, 1924).
24. This strike is described in *El Espectador* (October 8, 1928), and in Ministerio de Industrias, *Memoria presentada al Congreso de 1925*.

join the walkout, and organized a popular army. The city was in the hands of Mahecha, and crowds paraded through the streets firing revolvers in the air and carrying a red flag decorated with three 8's. The 8's symbolized the worker's demands: eight-hour work day, eight hours of rest, and eight hours of education. On October 13, after six days of strike, Mahecha delivered an ultimatum to the company in which he demanded that it fire two of its executives or else he would have the oil installations attacked and reduced to cinders.

The next day the Minister of Industry and the company reached an agreement which did not include a wage increase. According to the government, wages at the Tropical Oil camps were similar to those in other industries, and therefore no wage increase was justified. The pact limited itself to vague promises by the company to improve sanitary conditions.

Needless to say, Mahecha was not satisfied with the solution proposed. In response to Mahecha's arguments, the Minister replied that wages could not be dealt with because the workers were outside the law and because the manager of Tropical Oil was not authorized by the company's home office to give wage increases. The Minister also refused to consider the demand that workers who had committed punishable acts during the last few days not be prosecuted. He believed that accepting that demand would be a threat and an affront to society. Since the strike was technically illegal, this left the company in complete freedom to persecute the strikers.

In the face of the intransigence of the government and the company, Mahecha refused to accept their conditions. When he was forced to present the pact to the masses in the square he simply said: "I will not be made responsible if tonight the Minister of Industry is assassinated."[25] This proved to be an empty threat. The workers, who were ignorant of trade union activity, accepted the government-sponsored agreement. A few days later Mahecha

25. *El Espectador* (October 15, 1924).

was jailed and the government took all the steps necessary to disarm the population of Barranca. With Mahecha in jail and then deported from Barranca with the other leaders of the strike, the company proceeded to carry out a massive campaign of union persecution. By October 28, twenty days after the strike began, the company had fired 1,200 workers. Threatened by a serious problem of peace-keeping, the government transported these workers to other labor markets at its own expense.

The solution given by Tropical Oil Company to its labor problems was typical but not effective. About two years later, Tropical Oil was again faced by a major strike, one which lasted longer and cost numerous lives.[26] As in 1924, the strike that started on January 5, 1927, was not organized by an established trade union with a large membership. The labor legislation of 1927 made it possible for firms to fire any employees involved in union activity, a procedure apparently supported indirectly by the government, as was shown at the time of the 1924 oil strike. This made the establishment and subsistence of any well-organized and permanent trade union very difficult, and determined that most of the strikes of the twenties took place without any previous planning. The lack of strike funds and a well-thought-out strategy meant that these strikes easily fell under the influence of political radicals. This is exactly what happened in the case of the second oil strike.

On January 3 the company gave a 6 percent wage increase to the workers earning the common P1.50 wage. Since that wage had been in force since 1922, and there had been substantial inflation in the intervening years,[27] the oil workers were understandably dissatisfied. A group of them gathered at the entrance to the com-

26. In addition to the usual newspaper sources and the *Memoria of 1927* of the Minister of Industry, the autobiography of one of the leaders of the strike has been consulted. See Isaac Gutiérrez Navarro, *La luz de una vida* (Bogotá, Editorial ABC, 1949).

27. According to Table 6, between 1923 and 1927 prices rose by 58 percent in Bogotá.

pany installations at Barranca on the morning of the 5th, and convinced some of their colleagues to join in a walkout. The next day these workers appointed Isaac Gutiérrez, Rafael Tobón, and Isidoro Mena as their delegates, and made the following demands: (1) a salary increase of 25 percent; (2) job security, i.e. no layoffs without just cause; (3) Sunday rest; (4) an eight-hour day; (5) better food and health conditions; (6) screens on the windows of company housing. Since the cost of living had probably increased substantially more than 25 percent since the date when the P1.50 wage was instituted, the demands of the workers seem justified. As usual, however, the company did not yield and refused to bargain.

Since the company would not deal with the workers even though the strike was legal, the strikers soon turned to Raúl Eduardo Mahecha, at that time editor of a communist newspaper in Barranca. He organized a mass strike which started in earnest on January 8. The strike had definite political undertones, and Mahecha was able to again threaten the government with a mass uprising in Barrancabermeja.

As an organizer, Mahecha proved extraordinary. The strike lasted twenty days, during which time as many as five thousand workers were fed in Barranca. Mahecha obtained food directly from nearby farmers, and kept up morale. Both María Cano and Torres Giraldo, Communist leaders of the time, traveled to Barranca. María Cano, a dynamic Communist orator nicknamed the "red flower of Colombian communism," demanded from the strikers a "Russian style revolution in Colombia."[28] She then went on, to the delight of the crowds, to attack the rich, the government, religion, and the clergy.

By the 21st it was clear that the company would not bargain and that the government would not force it to bargain. That night the police fired on the workers. The casualty toll for the evening was two dead and more than eight wounded, some of them police-

28 Gutiérrez Navarro, p. 210.

men. The government declared a state of siege, and Mahecha, Gutiérrez, and the other strike leaders were jailed and later deported. Once again, the Tropical Oil Company solved its labor–management problems with violence and the police, and the Conservative government lost more prestige among the urban masses.

Not all labor–management conflicts in the prosperous period of the twenties were as dramatic and violent as those of foreign companies like Tropical or the Colombian Mining and Exploration Company. In fact, Colombian-owned companies were usually ready to bargain with their workers, and the few strikes that actually occurred against these companies were relatively free from violence. Among Magdalena River workers there were frequent conflicts, but they had sufficiently scarce skills and controlled the supply of labor to such an extent that the companies could not openly persecute union members and organizers. More often than not, the river workers, well organized by their communist leaders, obtained improved working conditions after bargaining or after short strikes.[29] The railroad workers also obtained wage increases and improved working conditions through bargaining.[30] By 1927, while Tropical had given its workers a ten-cent wage increase, Girardot sailors had obtained a wage increase of twenty cents above the 1924 level, and other Girardot port workers (firemen, foremen, etc.) had received even better wage increases.[31]

29. In 1924, the river workers of Girardot signed a pact in which the minimum wage established for sailors was P1.30 a day, and for firemen 20 percent more. (Since food was included, the real wage was substantially higher than that paid by Tropical Oil.) Furthermore, there was dismissal or layoff pay of three days, and paid holidays were recognized.

30. In 1924, the workers of the Dorada Railway obtained one paid day of rest a week, a 20 percent wage increase for the lower paid workers, and a 10 percent increase for the higher paid, plus health benefits and dismissal pay.

31. Ministerio de Industrias, *Anexos a la memoria presentada al Congreso de 1926.*

In 1925, there were seven major labor–management conflicts. Although as a rule they were not completely peaceful, none presented the spectacle of intransigence found in strikes against foreign companies. In 1928–29, thirty-three major labor–management conflicts were solved without recourse to strikes.[32]

The Strike Against the United Fruit Company

Probably one of the turning points in Colombian history was the strike against the United Fruit Company in 1928. In addition to costing a great many human lives, this strike seriously undermined the Conservative government and paved the way for the return to power of the Liberals.

In Colombia, as in other Latin American republics, the United Fruit Company was a state within a state. It owned its own railroad, telegraph network, and retail stores. In addition, as had happened in the territory of the Tropical Oil Company, it had purchased the local administration, and was the defacto government of the "banana zone." The company's monopoly of the irrigation network of the zone, plus its monopoly of transport, gave it complete control over the national producers, and made it possible for the company to force local producers to sell all of their produce to its agents at low prices.[33] The various monopolies of the United Fruit Company and the blatant use of that monopoly power resulted in constant conflict between Colombian producers and the company.[34]

The conflict between the company and the local traders was even older. The company made a practice of paying part of the wages of its workers in certificates valid only at company stores.[35]

32. Ministerio de Industrias, *Memoria de 1927,* pp. 73–75; and *Memoria de 1929,* pp. 164–72.

33. Ministerio de Industrias, *Memoria de 1928,* pp. 120–22.

34. *El Espectador* (August 30–September 14, 1920).

35. The goods in company stores were relatively cheap since they were carried to Santa Marta on the empty banana ships at very small cost to the company.

Since in many regions the company was the only employer, the trade monopoly of the company was complete. The active support given to the strikers by the local tradesmen was, therefore, self-interested.

Labor–management conflict was also of long standing in the banana zone. As has been mentioned in a previous chapter, in the first strike wave of 1918 the workers on the United Fruit Company railroad had carried out a violent strike, and banana workers had presented a series of demands to the company. When in 1928 the laborers on company land again presented the demands of 1918, the company's response was the same: refusal to bargain.

To understand the bitterness of the strike and the attitude of the workers, it must be remembered that in 1918 the company had promised to consult the Boston home office on the questions of wage increases and eliminating payment by coupon. When during the strike ten years later the company again refused to bargain and merely promised to consult the home office concerning the demands of the workers, the strikers would not accept such a solution. Characteristically, however, the settlement seemed acceptable to the government representatives who tried to settle the strike.

Unlike the other major strikes of the period, the strike against the United Fruit Company was planned and organized in advance. In 1925, a group of foreign workers arrived in Santa Marta and organized a congress of workers in the *corregimiento* of Guacamajal, the union headquarters of the banana zone. This group, led by the Spaniards Elías Castellanos, Abad and Mariano Lacambra, and the Italian Jenaro Toroní, had an anarchist orientation.[36] The communists, however, also had an organization in the banana zone, similar to the Savitsky group in Bogotá, and led

---

36. Carlos Cortés Vargas, *Los sucesos de las bananeras* (Bogotá, Imprenta de la luz," 1929), pp. 8–11; Robert J. Alexander, *Organized Labor in Latin America* (New York, The Free Press, 1965), p. 134; José María Nieto Rojas, *La batalla contra el comunismo en Colombia* (Bogotá, 1956), pp. 11–12.

by José Russo.[37] But the real organizer of the strike was again Raúl Eduardo Mahecha, who although ideologically a communist did not seem to be among the active leadership of the Partido Socialista Revolucionario. When the Marxist faction within the Partido Socialista Revolucionario, a party controlled by the communists and established at the Third Workers Congress, found out about Mahecha's organizational activities among the banana workers, it decided to send Torres Giraldo and María Cano to Barranquilla to help organize a solidarity committee among the local unions and members of the Partido Socialista Revolucionario. Once the strike was under way, the Partido Socialista also sent Alberto Castrillón, who had been in the Soviet Union, into the area to strengthen the resistance of the strikers. According to Robert J. Alexander, two other communists, the Frenchman Rabate and the American Joseph Zack Kornfedder, were also on the spot as agents of the Comintern.[38]

The organization of the strike against the United Fruit Company started on October 6, 1928, when a plenary meeting of the workers' delegates met to draft a set of demands to present to the company. As usual, the company refused to bargain despite having been pressured to do so by the governor of the state. At a meeting of the Unión Sindical de Trabajadores del Magdalena on November 11, it was decided, in the face of the attitude of the company, to declare a general strike in the zone.[39] A few days later thousands of workers (30,000 according to *El Espectador*[40]), went on strike against the company and against national growers in the banana zone.

37. Robert J. Alexander, *Communism in Latin America* (New Brunswick, N.J., Rutgers University Press, 1957), pp. 243–44.

38. Ibid., pp. 245–46.

39. Alberto Castrillón, *Ciento veinte dias bajo el terror militar o la huelga de las bananeras* (Bogotá, Talleres de la Revista Universidad, 1929), pp. 14–27.

40. Like most newspaper statistics, this one is probably inflated, but according to Rippy, there were at least 18,000 workers laboring for the

The petition of the workers consisted of nine demands, the principal one being the recognition by the company that it had employees. In order to evade all of the existing labor legislation, the company did not contract directly with the workers but went through labor contractors. This meant that it did not have to pay for collective insurance nor did it have to meet the housing standards required by legislation. The subcontractors, because they had no capital, were not required to provide these benefits. Thus when the workers demanded collective insurance, payment for work accidents, Sunday rest, housing facilities, and hospital facilities, they were simply demanding that the company keep the spirit of the labor legislation on the books at the time.[41]

The company, however, refused to bargain on these points since it considered that they referred to existing legislation, and that only a legal process or the government could determine whether the company was within the law or not. Since the Ministry of Industry had already established in November 1925, after being consulted by the United Fruit Company, that the obligation to insure workers (Law 37 of 1921) referred only to workers who were hired directly by the company and with whom the company had a work contract,[42] it was clear that the firm's refusal to bargain on these points constituted a rejection of the workers' demands.

The other two major demands of the workers were wage increases and a collective contract instead of individual contracts. If accepted, the latter demand would have implied recognition of the union. The last demand of the workers was the elimination of the company store. This demand was not important in itself,

---

United Fruit Company in 1927 (p. 181). So the workers on strike probably numbered more than 20,000, since those picking fruit for national growers also went on strike.

41. Laws 57 of 1915, 46 of 1916, 37 of 1921, 32 of 1922, 15 of 1925, 57 of 1926, etc.

42. Ministerio de Industrias, *Memoria de 1932.*

but obtained the support of the shop owners in the region who financed the first days of the strike and fed the workers. The support of the shop owners demonstrated that the strike was well thought out and organized.

Surprisingly enough, the strike was being carried out in accordance with legislation on the subject; but in spite of this, by the end of November, the military forces sent to deal with the strike had jailed more than four hundred strikers and had also arrested the local labor inspector because he had declared the strike legal and the workers' petitions reasonable. With the labor inspector in jail, mediation was left to General Cortés Vargas, who from the start favored the company position. On November 15, for example, Cortés had wired the governor explaining his mass arrests on the grounds that he was trying to obtain a settlement from the workers by trading the liberty of hundreds of laborers now in jail for concessions on their part.[43] General Cortés never saw anything one-sided about this mediation method.

In view of the position of the army, which among other things gave total protection to strikebreakers and helped to load fruit on the company trains, the strikers had lost patience by the end of the month and were using any tactics available to keep the walkout effective. This attitude was reinforced by the fact that the company refused to sign an agreement reached on November 24, in which it promised to institute collective insurance once the strike was over and conceded other minor points. It was only willing to sign a letter including these concessions which it would send to the Ministry.

When the striking workers were consulted on this settlement, they turned it down. They wanted higher wages, and, furthermore, a pact between the government and the company was not likely to be effective. This attitude toward the government seems justified in light of a speech made by a member of the commission sent by the Ministry of Industry to settle the strike. This repre-

43. Cortés Vargas, p. 17.

sentative of the government, who was also head of the labor office, said in part:

> The rural salaries in the banana zone are the highest in the republic, and the lack of organization and morality among workers in this region makes any wage increase useless in this zone, since any surplus over a subsistence wage will be spent by the workers on vices which are harmful to their health, and the wage increase will therefore not be translated into results truly beneficial to the working classes.[44]

In his report to Congress he went on to state that he was convinced that the strike could have been settled immediately if an agreement on wages had been reached, but that he did not insist on this point because he was convinced that "obtaining a wage increase was not an urgent necessity of the workers and that on the contrary, such an increase could create greater problems."[45]

Serious violence against property started when the company, realizing that the government and the army were on its side, decided to start work again on December 4. That day, many strikebreakers cut fruit, and as a result the strike became more violent and radical. An army patrol was disarmed by the workers, and the strike leaders decided to call a mass meeting on December 6 to demand a settlement from the governor and the head of the labor office. By this time the strike had entered its fifth week, the workers had lost the support of the shop owners, and consequently were getting desperate. They decided to block the rail lines, and women and children sat down on the tracks to keep the trains loaded with fruit from reaching the port. On December 4, threatened by a mob, General Cortés Vargas abandoned a trainload of prisoners who were then promptly set free by the strikers. The next day, he ordered three hundred men to abandon the square of

44. Ministerio de Industrias, *Memoria de 1929,* p. 190.
45. Ibid., pp. 191–93.

Ciénaga for tactical reasons, since it had been invaded by hundreds of strikers and their families. That night, after receiving a telegram informing him that a state of siege had been declared by the government, General Cortés issued a decree prohibiting all meetings of more than three persons, and ordered the army "to enforce this order by firing upon the multitude if necessary."[46]

On December 6, at 1:30 A.M., an army detachment entered the Ciénaga square; a copy of the declaration of the state of siege was read, and the hundreds of people gathered there were given five minutes to disperse. The noisy crowd, many of them unable to hear the decree, simply stared back at the troops. After the allotted time, General Cortés Vargas ordered his troops to fire into the crowd, and according to his own account, 13 defenseless and peaceful people were killed and 19 wounded.

After this the reign of terror began. The fleeing strikers burned and pillaged, and a siege of the Sevilla company compound took place. The company store and other buildings were burned to the ground, and the strikers attempted to burn out the American and Colombian employees who were holding out in the only house left standing. Before this could happen the army arrived, and in the ensuing battle 29 persons were killed, including Erasmo Coronel, the most active of the workers' delegates in the negotiations of the previous weeks.[47]

As a result of these events, General Cortés Vargas officially declared the strikers a gang of malefactors, and persecuted them as common thieves. There is obviously no agreement on the total number of victims, but what appears to be a serious estimate by a correspondent of *El Espectador*[48] listed 100 dead and 238

46. Adán Arriaga Andrade, "El Liberalismo y los derechos del Trabajador," in Plinio Mendoza Neira and Alberto Camacho Angarita, eds., *El liberalismo en el gobierno* (Bogotá, Prag, 1946), 2, 248.

47. Cortés Vargas, pp. 61–92.

48. *El Espectador* (December 13, 1928). Cortés Vargas gives the figures of 40 dead and 100 wounded, while Alberto Castrillón, the Communist agitator, wrote that there were 1,500 dead for the whole incident.

wounded by December 13, 1928. Fifty-four participants in the strike were tried by court martial, and 31 of them received prison sentences. Castrillón was sentenced to twenty-four years imprisonment, and 14 others were sentenced to more than five years.

The unheard of violence and the arbitrary legal procedures used to convict the strike leaders seriously undermined the prestige of the Conservative government. In the first months of 1929, communist groups all over the nation organized uprisings, and the government carried out mass arrests of communists and other extremists. Caches of arms and bombs were found everywhere,[49] and in June there were serious mass uprisings organized by the communists in Santander, Tolima, and Valle.[50] The uprisings in Libano, Tolima, and San Vicente, Santander, were particularly bloody, and were put down only at some cost to human life. In most cases these uprisings were led by communists and carried out by workers. For example, railroad workers were responsible for the violence in San Vicente, Santander.

The young progressive intellectuals in the Liberal Party found it useful to channel labor discontent into support for their party. In the middle of July, Jorge Eliécer Gaitán, by then a member of the House of Representatives, traveled to the banana zone to investigate the behavior of the army during the strike. He held mass interrogations, spoke before vast crowds, and on July 19, 1929, declared to the press, "If I continue here in the face of so many horrors, I shall end up in an insane asylum."[51] After ten days in the area of the strike, Gaitán returned to Bogotá to prepare a sensational debate against the government.

This was to be one of the most famous debates in Colombian parliamentary history because it brought Jorge Eliécer Gaitán into the political limelight. The debate convinced Gaitán that his

49. *El Espectador* (February 18–23, 1929).
50. Ibid. (July 24–31, 1929).
51. Ibid. (July 19, 1929).

future electorate was to be found among the wage-earning class, and that his popularity depended on his ability to defend the workers' efforts to organize. At the same time, the proletarian masses became convinced that they had found in Gaitán their spokesman and advocate. Before the debate on the massacre in the banana zone, Gaitán had already helped organized workers, as in the case of the collective bargaining conflict between the Bavaria beer company and its workers on July 23, 1928,[52] but the debate that started in September 1929 gave Gaitán publicity, and made him the best-known spokesman for the labor movement.

Given the fact that he was going to be the most important popular leader of the first half of the century, Gaitán's style is well worth analysis. It reflects, among other things, the level of culture of the working classes of Colombia. The most striking characteristic of Gaitán's oratorical style was his mixture of sensationalism and moral righteousness. He began the debate by reading a letter from the parish priest of Aracataca in which the cruelties and orgies of the army were described. He told of a mentally retarded girl being raped by soldiers, of bribes received by the army and civil authorities, and of army threats to witnesses during the court martials.

He described the arbitrary imposition of fines on the population to finance the orgies of the soldiers, and ended this part of the debate with the following phrase: "In those glasses of champagne bubbled the blood and tears of the people."[53]

To demonstrate that even children had been killed during the massacre of the banana workers, Gaitán produced before a session of the House of Representatives the skull of a child which

52. On that occasion the workers named Gaitán as their lawyer and gave him full bargaining authority "because he is completely trusted by the 750 workers concerned" (See Convención Colectiva between Cervecería Bavaria and its workers, July 23, in the archives of the Ministry of Labor).

53. El Espectador (September 5, 1929).

he claimed to have disinterred in the banana zone. The helpless Minister of Education, a physician by profession, was then asked to verify whether it was indeed the skull of a child.

During the whole debate the visitors' gallery was filled to capacity, and Gaitán's oratory had tremendous impact. To a historian, however, the veracity of his assertions is questionable in view of his request, in his last speech, that the evidence he presented not be used to prosecute those responsible for the official violence in the zone. The rationale he gave for this request was that "under a Conservative government, all guilty parties are rewarded instead of punished!"[54]

The Fall of the Conservative Government

The government's handling of the United Fruit Company strike determined its downfall. In September 1929 there was a scandal concerning the use of government funds by the War Minister Rengifo, the man ultimately responsible for the handling of the banana strike by General Cortés Vargas. On June 8, 1929, a student was killed during a mass student demonstration against corruption in the municipal government of Bogotá, and the government officials under attack had to resign.

In addition to these political problems, the Conservatives had to face the world economic crisis. In September 1929, the government reduced salaries among its employees, and in October the governor of Antioquia declared that all workers employed in road construction would have to be laid off. By that time, the labor inspectors were turning in the following unemployment reports: 4,176 unemployed in Antioquia; 5,171 in Bolivar; 5,000 in Caldas; 4,879 in Cundinamarca; 1,000 in Magdalena; 6,000 in Valle; and 500 in Chocó.[55] At the same time the wages of unskilled laborers in public works were reduced from P1.50 a day

54. Ibid. (September 7, 1929).
55. Ibid. (October 10, 1929).

in 1928 to 90 centavos in September 1929, and there was a panic in the Bogotá stock exchange during the week of October 21. The fall in prices on the stock exchange caused a loss of P10,000,000, and between 1929 and 1930 more than forty-four manufacturing enterprises closed down in Bogotá alone.[56]

The unemployment situation was sufficiently desperate to cause armed clashes between the unemployed and the police. In October 1929 unemployed workers attacked the national guard in Puerto Liévano; the casualty toll was one dead and five wounded. Clashes between the unemployed and the police continued through the next few months, as did reductions in wages.[57] The result could only be the crumbling of the existing political system.

To make matters worse, the Conservative Party faced the presidential elections of 1930 divided, with two roughly equally strong factions each backing a different candidate. Divided and unpopular, the Conservative Party lost the presidential elections to a young, dynamic, and reform-minded Liberalism. The new government had the support of labor and, in turn, wanted to encourage the labor movement. With the coming to power of the Liberals, the Colombian labor movement obtained the protection it required to become a major economic and political force in the nation. The period of the twenties did not witness the emergence of a strong labor movement, but the battles waged by the working classes in that period helped to change the political structure of the nation, and the men who came to power with the support of labor in 1930 created the conditions necessary for the development of a strong labor movement.

56. Ministerio de Industrias, *Memoria de 1931, 1.*
57. *El Espectador* (October 24, 1929; January 2, 7, 15, 1930).

Part III

The Era of Political Bargaining

8

The Liberal State
and Labor

Because of the nature of economic organization and the structure of the labor market before 1930, Colombian unions could not prosper in the face of official antagonism. Since the majority of Colombian workers were relatively unskilled, the labor movement could become strong only with the emergence of unions not divided along craft or skill lines. The skilled workers might have had a sufficiently strong bargaining position to organize and bargain successfully in spite of government antagonism and unfavorable labor legislation, but there were so few workers in this position that labor organization would have remained an unimportant and isolated phenomenon if it had only prospered among skilled workers.

The Liberal Party, however, having won the election of 1930 with the support of labor, was interested for political reasons in the emergence of a strong and large labor movement. Therefore, as soon as it came to power it set out to create the legal and institutional conditions necessary for the emergence of a mass labor movement made up of the unskilled and semiskilled workers who were its potential electoral base.

The Presidential Elections of 1930

In January 1930, weeks before the presidential election, the Conservative Party was faced with the following problems:

1. Mass unemployment caused by the world depression
2. Declining wages and salaries
3. Government deficits
4. Proven dishonesty among some of the highest officials of the administration
5. The antagonism of the laboring masses, made more radical by the massacre of the banana workers
6. Two Conservative candidates for the 1930 presidential election

As it turned out, the last problem outweighed the others. The division within the party had various causes, but the one most publicized by the Liberals was the apparent division within the Church concerning the presidential candidates. Several months before the election, the choice of the Conservative candidate began to hinge upon the approval of the Archbishop of Bogotá, Monsignor Perdomo. This prelate gave out confusing statements during the following weeks which made it possible for each side to claim Church support, until the Church itself became hopelessly divided. The Bishop of Ibagué claimed that Valencia had the support of the Freemasons, and Monsignor Builes of Antioquia publicly attacked Vasquez Cobo.[1] In the end, the Conservative Party went to the polls divided, and although it obtained a majority of the votes, the Liberal candidate Enrique Olaya Herrera was elected.

The Conservative division was what convinced the Liberals to enter the presidential race at the last moment. A group of Liberals offered Olaya Herrera, who was then in Washington, the candidacy on December 14, 1929, and some forty days later he had unexpectedly won the presidential elections.[2] The Liberals soon

1. *El Espectador* (January 6 and 9, 1930).
2. For a brilliant and humorous description of the political events that led to the fall of the Conservatives from power, see Alfonso López, "Conferencia en el Teatro Municipal, Noviembre 30, 1936," *Acción Liberal* (December 1936). A more complete account can be found in Mendoza Neira and Camacho Angarita, *El liberalismo*.

114

realized, however, that labor's support had been crucial. They carried all the major industrial cities, including the Conservative strongholds of Medellín and Manizales. The Liberals also carried those rural areas such as Viotá, Fusagasugá, and El Colegio where there was conflict between landlords and tenants, and where there were organizations of rural laborers.

In view of the crucial role of labor in the presidential election, it was in the interest of the Liberal Party to further industrialization and the growth of a labor movement. But, in addition, the Liberals were ideologically committed to labor. Throughout the twenties, their major criticism of the Conservative government focused on its reactionary labor policy. Many of the young men in the party, like Gaitán, Turbay, and Adán Arriaga had been working in support of the proletariat for some time. The support of labor by the Liberals was therefore both tactically important and sincere.

The very rapid economic development that began in 1923 disrupted the traditional economic order and particularly the labor market. The large-scale public works projects required large masses of labor, for at that time construction was still labor intensive. The capital goods imported for these projects consisted of picks, shovels, wheelbarrows, and other such implements, and both roads and railroads were constructed with virtually no machinery.

The necessity of recruiting large masses of workers and attracting them to often unhealthy areas meant that the government had to pay high wages. This was also the case in the new industries established by foreign capital. Both oil and banana production had to be located in hot, unhealthy, sparsely populated areas, and most of the labor force was therefore made up of immigrants from other parts of the country. To attract these workers, it was obviously necessary to pay high wages.

This of course hurt the *hacienda* owners and all those who had to pay higher wages in agriculture, since in that sector labor productivity remained the same. The coffee growers were particularly

115

affected by the immigration of labor to the cities and the public works projects. Faced with a deficient labor supply, they decided to change the contracts of their tenants. To guarantee the availability of labor during the period of harvest, growers began to insist that their tenants could not grow coffee on their own plots.[3] This led to serious conflicts between the growers and the tenants, with the result that in some areas the rural workers organized into peasant leagues, often under communist direction, to demand more favorable contracts. Faced with this transformation in the labor market, the Conservative government sided with the landowners.[4]

We have seen how during the strikes against the Tropical Oil Company and the United Fruit Company, the Conservative government officially recommended, through the Ministry of Industry, that wages not be raised since this would upset the wage structure in other sectors. These were not isolated instances. Within the Public Works Ministry there was a debate on whether to attempt to utilize more capital-intensive technology in order to limit the demand for workers, and therefore to keep the cost of labor to the landowners at a lower level.

At the end of 1929, when the world depression was beginning to cause unemployment, the head of the labor office, Hoyos Becerra, went so far as to make the following statement:

> The introduction of foreign labor for the public works is unpostponable and should be in the future an obligation for contractors of railroad and road construction . . . It is also urgent that machines should be substituted for labor when-

3. In 1928, the Minister of Industry described the problem between landowners and tenants in terms very similar to these. He explained that because of the high labor demand created by the public works projects, the landowner tried to convert his tenant into a full-time wage laborer, while the tenant wanted to be more independent because of the increasing prices of the products he could grow himself (see Ministerio de Industrias, *Memoria presentada al Congreso de 1928,* pp. 146–47).

4. *El Espectador* (December 28, 1929).

ever possible . . . The army should also contribute to the public works, so as to help solve the problem of the supply of labor.[5]

The Liberal policy on wages was vastly different. Since the landlords were Liberalism's major opponents, the problem of maintaining low labor costs for landowners never arose. On the contrary, the Liberals supported the demands of the tenants against the landowners. In an *Acción Liberal* editorial on the outgoing regime, in August 1938, Armando Solano described the López wage policy in the following terms:

> He promoted without rest a rise in wages in all regions, not only by favoring labor organizations, but also by paying wages in the public works which would break the exploitation wage rates common in the countryside, thus forcing the rich farmer to raise wages to defend himself from this competition.

This is a far cry from the Conservative wage policy of the previous decade. In general, the Liberal government followed a classical wage policy. It believed that laborers could attempt to gain wage increases through collective bargaining, but it supported the companies when such wage increases or the lack of wage reductions threatened to bring about unemployment. This wage policy was not incompatible with the strengthening of labor unions and collective bargaining, as the Conservative wage policy clearly had been.

The Labor Movement Obtains Government Support

In 1931, three strikes took place without violence, arrests, or the declaration of a state of siege. The relations between the government and labor were beginning to change, and labor protest

5. Ibid. (January 10, 1929).

was institutionalized instead of forbidden. This process culminated in the passage of Law 83 of 1931.

In addition to explicitly recognizing the workers' right to union organization, Law 83 established fines to be collected from any person or organization that threatened the right of association by preventing any person from joining or belonging to a union. It also prohibited unions from taking any action which would threaten the right-to-work provisions of the constitution, established fines for unions that declared strikes in violation of existing legal provisions, and gave power to the government to declare the dissolution of any union that persisted in a de facto illegal action. Finally, Article 33 made it illegal for unions to participate in politics and allowed the labor office to dissolve any union that so acted.

Thus for the first time Colombian law recognized the existence of unions and the right of workers to organize. In the remaining years of the Olaya administration more legislation in defense of the wage-earning class was passed. This legislation included (1) the obligation to provide paid vacations; (2) the responsibility of the owner of the enterprise to pay the legally enacted benefits, thus eliminating the possibility of getting around the law by subcontracting; (3) the eight-hour day.[6]

Nevertheless, the legal protection of unionism established by Law 83 was not extensive. Article 12 of the law established fines from 20 to 200 pesos for union persecution, a price that any company would gladly pay for destroying a union. Furthermore, the law explicitly forbade unions to behave in any way which might limit the rights of others to work, thus officially protecting strikebreakers.

Therefore, the growth of unionism after 1931 (recorded in Table 1) is not the result of legislative recognition of the right of laborers to organize in Colombia. Rather, the development of the labor movement in this period can be accredited, in large measure,

6. Adán Arriaga Andrade, "El Liberalismo," pp. 253–56.

to the informal support which the executive branch of the government gave unionism and to the manner in which that executive interpreted the law.

In fact, during the period in which Alfonso López was President (1934–38), there was relatively little new labor legislation, but a tremendous growth in the labor movement. This was due to the fact that the "Revolution on the March" of Alfonso López favored the laboring masses in many informal ways. For example, the government mediation of labor–management disputes often consisted of executive pressure on companies to bargain and give concessions, and the initiative for the creation of unions often came directly from the labor office. This was so in the case of the union of the Fenicia glass workers in Bogotá, created in 1933 in the offices of the Ministry of Labor. The labor inspector, Francisco Posada Zarate, called together a group of glass workers and persuaded them to form a union under the protection of Law 83. The officers of the union were then elected, statutes were approved, and the workers left the Ministry after thanking "the labor inspector for his beneficial initiative."[7]

Finally, a further proof that the growth of unionism depended to a large extent on the support of the executive branch is the fact that the unions which grew most rapidly in the thirties were those in the public services. In Law 21 of 1920 it had been established that strikes would be illegal in all enterprises which were judged to provide a public service, and that labor–management differences had to be settled by arbitration in those enterprises.

The list of economic activities in which strikes were forbidden coincides perfectly with the sectors of the economy in which strikes were most frequent during the thirties, and in which unions were strongest. This was because instead of persecuting workers who broke the law by striking, the government always tried to

7. *Estatutos de la Sociedad Obrera de Fenicia,* "acta de fundación" (Bogotá, 1934). Peasant Leagues, such as that of Quipile, were founded by the Casa Liberal, an organization of the Liberal Party (see *Acción Liberal* [June 1935], p. 1199).

TABLE 7

Urban Labor-Management Conflicts, June 1935 to June 1937[a]

	Resulted in Strike	Resolved by Agreement Between the Parties Without Government Intervention	Resolved by Government Conciliation	Resolved by Arbitration
Public Services[b]				
Railroads	2	1	3	—
Streetcars and urban transport	1	—	2	1
Ship and port workers	4	—	—	1
Aqueducts, electricity	—	2	—	—
Hospitals, city cleaning, etc.	1	—	—	—
National mines	—	—	—	—
Other Enterprises				
Textiles	6	—	3	—
Oil	1	—	—	1
Food and drink	1	1	1	—
Tailors	2	—	4	—
Typography	—	1	8	—
Others	12	5	12	—
Total	30	10	33	3

a. The data for 1935 and 1937 are incomplete and only six months of those years are covered.
b. According to Law 21 of 1920, these activities were defined as a Public Service, and strikes were illegal in enterprises that fell within this definition.

Source: Ministerio de Industrias, *Memorias del Ministro de Industrias y Trabajo al Congreso* for 1936 and 1937.

pressure employers to reach a settlement. Furthermore, when arbitration was used, the government also favored the point of view of the workers, and therefore the unions in the public services obtained favorable settlements throughout the period. Table 7 demonstrates that strikes were frequent in the public services, where they were forbidden by law, and that very few agreements between labor and management were signed without the active intervention of the government. In the twenty-four months covered by the table it appears that of 76 settlements reached, only 10 did not require government intervention of any kind.

The Labor Movement Enters Partisan Politics

The government helped the labor movement in its day-to-day dealings with employers because the executive needed the constant support of labor in order to remain in power. Alfonso López, the major figure in the Liberal Party in the thirties, was a politician of the democratic left. He came to the Presidency in 1934 for the purpose of bringing about a radical change in Colombian society. A great admirer of Franklin D. Roosevelt, he wanted to channel the national energies into industrialization and economic growth, but was committed to obtaining an ever larger share of the benefits of such growth for the lower classes.

To this end, he conceived a complete program of economic and social reform and brought to his government a new group of intellectuals and administrators to carry it out. His first cabinet did not include any of the great leaders of the Liberal Party. It was made up of young progressive intellectuals like Alberto Lleras, who was twenty-eight years old, and Plinio Mendoza Neira, Antonio Rocha, Jorge Soto del Corral, and Darío Echandía, all of whom were under thirty-eight; these men were to dominate Colombian politics for the next thirty years.

During the four years after Alfonso López was sworn in as President for his first term, Colombian society was radically but peacefully transformed. Three measures symbolized the Revolution on the March of Alfonso López: tax reform, land reform, and the democratization of education. The government of Olaya Herrera had already taken the first steps toward transformation of the Colombian economy. The Agricultural Credit Bank and the Central Mortgage Bank, which promoted construction, had been founded, and a tariff reform had been carried out, giving the infant industry of Colombia effective and beneficial protection. López carried out the reforms which gave the laboring masses a share in the upturn in economic conditions brought about by the imaginative financial and economic policies of Olaya Herrera and his Finance Minister, Esteban Jaramillo.[8]

López' program of reform and his support of labor made it possible for him to win the presidential elections, but when he came to power Congress remained under the control of the Conservatives, and the Supreme Court was a rightist stronghold.[9] Thus López had programs similar to those of F. D. Roosevelt, and shared many of the same problems, but these were set in the context of a society accustomed to violence, not to political compromise.

Soon after taking office on August 7, 1934, López asked the Congress for progressive income tax laws, but once these were pushed through, they were declared unconstitutional by the Supreme Court. The López land partitioning plan was rejected by Congress.[10] As in the 1850s, Colombian society was again becoming divided along class lines; also, as a century before,

8. The economic policies of Esteban Jaramillo and Olaya were unorthodox for their time, but in the light of modern economics, they seem fortunate indeed. These policies plus the short war with Peru over Leticia got the country moving again at a time when the United States was still deep in the depression (see Torres García, *Historia de la moneda,* pp. 387–414).

9. Alberto Galindo, "La República Liberal," in Mendoza Neira and Camacho Angarita, *1,* 74.

10. Vernon Lee Fluharty, *Dance of the Millions: Military Rule and the Social Revolution in Colombia, 1930–1956* (Pittsburgh, University of Pittsburgh Press, 1957) pp. 51–52.

the executive was the spokesman for the masses, and Congress the voice of reaction. Even the names of the leading actors were the same. Alfonso López, usually considered a patrician or "charter member of the oligarchy,"[11] was the grandson of Ambrosio López, the tailor who had helped to organize the Sociedad de Artesanos in 1847.

The official break between the landlords and López came over the indirect support given by the government to the landless peasants of Cundinamarca and Tolima. Shortly after López came to the Presidency, a group of powerful landowners wrote to him to demand that the government establish law and order in the countryside by driving squatters out of uncultivated land by force of arms. To their indignation, López replied that his policy was

> that the law cannot be put to the unconditional service of injustice, and that although the country's legal institutions were made to defend the owner of property and to maintain the level of misery of the rural wage earners, the government, without ignoring its duty to protect the landowners whose land was cultivated against squatters, preferred to wait until the constitutional reforms it had proposed gave it better instruments for intervention in the social problems of agriculture. [López] further stated that the government's purpose was to improve the standard of living of the peasants, and to condition the right to property to its rational economic use.[12]

López' attitude made moderate Liberals attack the government as communist, and made the Conservative Party mount a violent opposition campaign. A political party of property owners was formed, which went by the name of APEN, and whose slogan was "to fight against the Bolsheviki entrenched in power."[13]

11. Ibid., p. 46.
12. Galindo, p. 79.
13. Ibid., p. 80.

While the property-owning classes were gathering their forces to topple the government, by force if need be,[14] the laboring masses rallied around Alfonso López. On May 1, 1936, thousands of workers paraded in front of the presidential palace to give López their unconditional support. Among the speakers who followed López at the Labor Day rally was Gilberto Vieira, a communist labor leader of the time and secretary general of the Communist Party since the late forties.

During the presidential election the Communists had been opposed to López and had run their own candidate, the Indian leader Eutiguio Timoté;[15] as late as September 28, 1935, the Comintern's International Press Correspondence reported that López "no longer enjoys the slightest sympathy among the masses."[16] But in the middle of 1935 the Comintern made things easier for the Colombian Communists by establishing the popular front against fascism at its Seventh Congress. Although the Colombian Communists took some time to change over to the new orthodoxy, by May 1936 they were the most vocal supporters of López. The local Communists were even able to talk against fascism and be understood since the Conservative Party of Laureano Gómez was under the influence of European Fascism.

Thus in 1936 all sectors of the labor movement and the more sophisticated members of the proletariat were behind López— pragmatic unionists because he offered labor organizations support, the Communists because the international movement had entered into a period of cooperation with the democratic left, and the impoverished masses in general because he offered them equal opportunity through free state education, and economic equality through progressive taxation and land reform.

By 1936 the López program was a reality. In 1935 the Conservatives had decided to keep away from the polls, and López

14. The Conservative leader Laureano Gómez justified plots to kill the President and labeled these extremist tactics "Acción Intrépida."

15. Montaña Cuéllar, *Colombia, país formal*, p. 144.

16. Alexander, *Communism*, p. 247.

had obtained a Liberal majority in Congress. Even though the Liberal majority was to the right of López, his legislative program began to prosper. Law 200 of 1936 was the first land reform in republican times to attempt to give land to the landless. Although its intentions were frustrated by reality, López' popularity among the masses increased. His progressive income tax also allowed him to promise the proletariat both greater equality and an increase in government expenditures on social welfare.

Needless to say, López gained prestige among the lower classes of society at the expense of the hostility of those who owned land and had taxable income. So by May 1938 López had antagonized that sector of the society that had up to then monopolized all power in the nation. To counterbalance this formidable opposition, López needed the support of the weak. He had to frighten and subdue the economic elite by bringing out into the streets thousands of workers committed to upholding the democratic left at all cost. The mass rally of May 1, 1936, was organized as a threat to the disaffected oligarchy. López himself explained to Congress the significance of the rally of May 1 in the following terms:

> The first of May some labor organizations, whose members belong in a great majority to the party in power, in conjunction with the political organizations of the far left, carried out a mass demonstration in support of the political and social orientation of the government. Before the demonstrators, who had also come to make an exhibition of force meant to intimidate the Conservatives and the high authorities of the Catholic Church who threatened to disregard the law and democratic institutions . . . I had to explain that I believe I was faithfully interpreting the program of Liberalism in power.[17]

17. Message of President Alfonso López to Congress in 1936, *Acción Liberal* (August 1936), pp. 48–49.

Thus it is clear that in order to survive, the progressive Liberals, and Alfonso López in particular, needed to confront the forces of reaction with a militant labor movement ready to defend the regime. In a sense, it was a revival of the Sociedades Democráticas of the 1850s, and although in this case the labor organizations were not transformed into national guards, it was clear to all that the labor movement was the potential army of the regime.

126

9

The Tactics of
Structured Violence

Individuals use violence to settle their differences only when there is no institutionalized nonviolent method for achieving a compromise. Before the state and the owners of property in Colombia recognized that workers had a right to demand better working conditions collectively, violence between property owners, the state, and wage laborers was therefore inevitable. Those who had the economic and political power in the society refused to compromise. The only alternative left to the workers was to threaten or force these two powers into considering the possibility of bargaining over economic conditions. Organized labor spent the first four decades in the history of the Colombian labor movement convincing the state and the owners of property that workers had some right to the benefits of capitalist development; since the country was only starting to industrialize, organized labor was not strong enough to do this job through collective bargaining or through the democratic process of bringing about changes in legislation by mobilizing a large mass of electors. Very often, organized labor could win a victory for its cause only through organized violence.

This is a very common phenomenon in the history of the international labor movement. As a general rule, the labor movement begins and has its strength in the manufacturing, mining, and transport sectors, since agricultural and service workers are dispersed and hard to organize. Therefore, the labor movement can become an important electoral force only in economically advanced nations, even if there is unrestricted universal suffrage. If women, who are usually not in the labor force, have the vote, as in many of the newly developing nations, the possibility of a large labor vote is even smaller.

In most developing nations, labor also lacks economic strength, the other major tool of any pressure group. In any struggle with employers or with the state, the labor movement can resist for only a very short time because of the subsistence standard of living of its members. The economic situation of the workers also makes it impossible for them to control mass communications media and other resources necessary for the use of power.

In contrast, the use of violence is inexpensive, creates solidarity, and can be effectively used by a small group of laborers against isolated employers. Large-scale violence in the form of the general strike can also be used, but is generally less effective in underdeveloped countries. For a general strike to be effective, a large proportion of the population must be mobilized. To achieve this, in addition to drawing on the support of a numerically large labor movement, organized labor must control important mass communications media and have at its disposal large economic resources. All of these conditions are unlikely to be present in an underdeveloped country, and the general strike will be successful only if the government is very weak. The limited use of violence, however, can be effective under many circumstances. A good example is the sit-in strike, effectively used by American industrial unions in the 1930s to force employers to recognize them as bargaining agents. This tactic was also used by French workers during the Popular Front of Leon Blum to force French society to give a new deal to its laboring classes; and it has been an effective tactic in the struggle of the American Negro minority for equal rights.

In Colombia, the sit-in strike and its rural equivalent, land invasion, have been very effective labor tactics. They have been used frequently because of the inherent weakness of organized labor. In his report to Congress in 1935, Francisco José Chaux, the Minister of Industry, emphasized this relationship between labor violence and economically weak unions.

> Our labor organizations do not yet find themselves prepared to carry out long strikes or work stoppages, so a few days after a strike begins, the workers start to go without the bare necessities of subsistence and this causes the psychological reaction that leads the workers to material violence.[1]

Rural Organized Violence

In the late 1920s, the Colombian rural proletariat began to to have violent conflicts with landowners. The public works programs and the beginning of industrialization were creating a demand for wage labor outside of agriculture and causing price inflation and the emergence of an industrial and urban market for agricultural crops. These changes in economic conditions led to a revolution in the expectations of the landless peasant. He no longer depended exclusively on the large landowner. He could migrate and become a wage laborer in industry or public works, or if he became a small landowner he could subsist on the high prices brought about by economic growth. Also, because of improvements in the transportation network, he could sell on the market without having to rely on the monopsonistic demand of the local landlord. In fact, so many laborers migrated to the cities and took jobs in construction that agricultural output decreased and agricultural prices rose rapidly.[2] Those who remained on the land demanded more from the landlords, and conflict over tenant contracts became common.

1. *Memoria del Ministerio de Industrias y Trabajo, 1924.*

2. There is no question about the decrease in agricultural produce marketed and the increase in food imports, but because of lack of data it is difficult to show the magnitude of rural-urban migration.

The 1928 census is of very low quality, and neither the 1938 nor the

129

When in 1929 the great depression spread to Colombia, and the government's public works program abruptly stopped, the work gangs all returned to the countryside, where economic conditions were barely superior to those in the cities. The men who had been in contact with the anarchistic labor organizations in the oil fields, the banana zone, and among the railroad and dock workers refused to accept the archaic tenant-landlord relationship of the Colombian *latifundia*. With the help of communist agitators, the peasants formed leagues in Cundinamarca, Tolima, and Valle, and attempted to obtain the right to their own land. In some cases they invaded uncultivated haciendas, and defended their newly acquired land by force of arms. The most famous example of this tactic was the occupation of the Viotá estates. There the "revolutionary socialists," precursors of Colombian communism, convinced the peasants to invade the haciendas, and to create a defense organization to consolidate their right to the land. Aided by the difficult topography typical of Colombia's mountains, these squatters set up an independent communist republic of some five hundred square kilometres. They kept the central government at bay for over twenty years and were thus able to institutionalize the spontaneous land reform carried out at the time of the great depression.[3]

1918 census includes migration data. Furthermore, since it is thought that many of the migrants of the twenties returned to the rural sector during the great depression, the population movement of the twenties is hard to identify in the absence of good census material in 1928–29, the end of the period of prosperity. In the absence of quantitative data to confirm this "depopulation" of the countryside, we must fall back on secondary sources. For example, the Minister of Industry mentions the labor scarcity caused by the expansion of production in other sectors in his Report to Congress of 1928 (pp. 145–46). Also see Adan Arriaga Andrade, "El Liberalismo," pp. 246–47.

3. For a perceptive description of the Viotá experience see José Gutiérrez, *La rebeldía colombiana* (Bogotá, Tercer Mundo, 1962), pp. 83–96.

Another tactic used by the landless peasants was to pressure the landlords into letting them plant coffee trees on their rented land. Since according to Colombian law the owner had to pay for any improvements the tenant made on the land, this meant that the tenant obtained a right to his land—the landlord had to buy the tenant out instead of simply taking his land away. Furthermore, if the tenant's land was strategically located, the landlord had to pay high prices for the improvements (coffee trees), or initiate a long and expensive law suit.

Faced with the organized action of their tenants, the coffee growers of Cundinamarca and Tolima created an employers' association for mutual defense in order "to represent the landlords in their conflicts with their tenants, workers and squatters."[4] In May 1933 these landlords complained to the Minister of Industry and Labor in the following terms:

> Your excellency is not ignorant of the fact that the Peasant League of Tequendama, affiliated to the Central Committee of the Communist Party, has recently, as a strategy of aggression against landowners and the right to property, ordered its members, who include the majority of the workers on the coffee plantations, to plant coffee trees in their plots, in violation of the contract arrived at with the landowner . . . Permanent improvements on the land, such as the planting of coffee trees, if one is realistic, mean that the landowner cannot regain possession of his land . . ."[5]

In the coffee area of Cundinamarca, these tactics were very successful. Peasants got land, and kept it. Furthermore, conflict in the countryside was reaching such proportions that in time Congress passed the famous Law 200, known as the López land reform.

4. *Memoria del Ministro de Industrias, 1933.*
5. *Memoria del Ministerio de Industrias y Trabajo, 1934,* reply of the Union of Landowners to a letter from the minister concerning the social problems in the coffee plantations.

As was shown by the Viotá case, the government often did not have the resources to defend private property in the countryside, even if it wanted to. One solution to the problem was to buy the large haciendas, and sell them back to the squatters with long credit terms. The Caja Agraria, an agricultural credit bank set up in the early thirties, legalized the invasion of various haciendas in this way. Since the peasants could never have gotten credit to buy land if they had not first invaded that land, the effectiveness of organized violence was clear.

The invasion of uncultivated land and the often violent conflict between tenants and landlords changed the agrarian structure of the coffee area of Cundinamarca in the thirties, as can be seen in Table 8. In eight years the number of coffee farms doubled, largely

TABLE 8

Cundinamarca's Coffee Farms in 1932 and 1940

Year	Number of Farms	Production, in 60-kilo Sacks
1932	13,812	364,379
1940	30,270	370,018

Source: Ministerio del Trabajo, Seguridad social campesina (Bogotá, Editorial Cosmos, 1954).

because of the breakup of the large estates. This breakup took place partly through the invasions described above, but to a greater extent because of the destruction of the traditional relationship between the latifundia owner and his tenants. Organized violence and self-confidence created by association made it impossible for the landlords to sustain their traditional relationship with the rural labor force. This cultural change made the survival of coffee latifundia impossible, and the landlords therefore had to break up their estates.[6]

6. William McGreevey has correctly pointed out that the lack of any economies of scale in Colombian coffee technology facilitated the breakup of the large coffee estates.

Organized rural violence in the coffee areas of Cundinamarca and Tolima helped labor to achieve two important victories: the partial reform of an obsolete and unjust agrarian structure, and the passage of a land reform law. In Colombia, Congress tends to be a conservative institution, and it passes social reform laws only when it becomes clear that not doing so arouses serious social conflicts. Organized violence is the greatest pressure that can be brought to bear upon Congress, and, as was the case in the thirties when conflict in the countryside reached major proportions, this pressure may be effective and may lead to a radical change in the nation's legal and social structure.

The tactic of land invasions organized by rural unions is still practiced successfully. On the sparsely populated Atlantic coastal area, rural agrarian unions belonging to the Federación Agraria Nacional (FANAL), which is affiliated to the Unión de Trabajadores de Colombia (UTC), have organized land invasions which have given de facto property rights to thousands of peasants. In the report of the secretary general of UTC at the tenth congress of that labor body, it was reported that unions affiliated to FANAL had made 44,000 hectares of land available to landless peasants though invasion of "uncultivated" private and public lands. In some cases, the agrarian union forces the landowner to sell land to the peasants on credit; in other cases the Land Reform Institute intervenes and declares the invaded land a "land reform" area; and in other cases, the peasants keep their land through force.

It is important to remember that FANAL is a Catholic union, and that it has clerical moral advisers. These land invasions are often carried out with the approval of Church advisers and are often led by priests. Although such actions are approved by them only when they are morally justifiable, many of the advisers are progressive and reform-minded, and they will more often than not find a moral justification for the attempt of the peasants to obtain land.

In the countryside, where the influence of the Church is still very great, the role of the priest in the rural labor movement has remained very important. If it were not for the clerical support for community action boards and rural unions, it is likely that the Colombian peasant would be even less organized than he is today, and therefore less receptive to change. Community studies have shown that today the Catholic Church is one of the most effective agents of social change in rural Colombia.[7]

The fact that official agencies often carry out land reform in areas where there has been serious conflict between peasants and landowners suggests that one method by which the peasants can improve their condition is by invading private property and creating serious conflict. Faced with a touchy problem of public order or a land invasion, the government will often be moved to provide a solution by giving land or land rights to the peasants. For example, of the thirty land redistribution and colonization programs of Caja Agraria, twenty were carried out in zones where there had been *violencia* between 1949 and 1963.[8] In fact, there were some special government funds, called Fondos de Rehabilitación, given to Caja Agraria to carry out land redistribution in areas affected by rural violence. Caja Agraria distributed about 5,500 hectares of land with these funds in five areas affected by rural violence.

The first land reform program of INCORA, the Land Reform

7. See for example Eugene Havens, *Támesis: estructura y cambio* (Bogotá, Tercer Mundo, 1966); William Stuart, "Algunas instituciones variables en San Miguel de Sema" (unpublished manuscript, July 1962); Gustavo Jiménez Cadena, S.J., *Sacerdote y cambio social* (Bogotá, Tercer Mundo, 1967).

8. *Violencia* is the name given in Colombia to rural murders carried out for political or other social reasons. It is pure banditry at times and guerrilla warfare the rest of the time. To see the relation between violencia and land distribution projects, we mapped the areas of violencia and land reform, and although there was a high correlation, it could be spurious since the areas of violencia are also densely populated areas where land reform is technically logical. Nevertheless, according to Enrique Peñalosa, director of INCORA, very few land reform projects have been started in areas that have had no serious social conflicts.

Institute, was also in a zone that had been through a long period of rural violence. This was the Tolima 1 project in Cunday, Villarrica, and Icononzo. Cunday was one of the coffee areas where in the 1930s the peasants organized into Marxist peasant leagues in defense of their interests. The Sindicato Agrícola de Cunday dedicated itself to the "conquest" of land for its members, and soon other unions with different ideological backgrounds, such as the Sindicato de Oficios Varios and the Centro Agrícola, emerged.[9] The land invasions and militancy of the Sindicato Agrícola created serious conflict in the region, and in 1952 and 1955 several lives were lost. The rich landowners abandoned their haciendas, and large groups of workers fled to other zones or hid out in the woods. When relative peace returned to the region, the landlords did not return, and the large haciendas were left in a state of complete abandon. Toward 1961, from 500 to 600 families invaded and took possession of the large haciendas in the region. Because of the critical problems caused by the situation in Cunday, Villarrica, and Icononzo, the area was chosen as the first land reform project after INCORA was created. INCORA divided the abandoned estates, and by 1965 it had given 581 peasant families land in the Tolima 1 area. While in 1962, 10,600 hectares of land were owned by 47 landlords, by 1966 the area had been divided up among 606 peasant families.[10]

In summary, one of the most frequently used union tactics in the rural areas is land invasion, the equivalent of the industrial sit-in strike. These land invasions force the landowner to sell land to the peasants on credit, and often involve the government in land redistribution projects in which it buys the invaded land in order to sell it back with long credit terms to the squatters. In other cases, the government declares the invaded area national land, and gives the squatters legal title to it.

9. Victor Daniel Bonilla, "Tolima 1, primer proyecto de la reforma agraria," *Tierra, 1* (July–September, 1966), pp. 14–15.

10. Ibid., pp. 61–63.

In the cities, unions organized to carry out land invasions are also important. Colombian cities are growing extremely rapidly. While in 1951, 60.4 percent of the nation's population lived in rural areas, in 1964, 48 percent lived in the rural sector. The population of Bogotá grew during that same period at the incredible rate of 6.8 percent annually. This unprecedented urban growth has led to very serious shortages in urban housing and to high prices for urban land. In all of the major cities of the nation, unions of city dwellers have organized land invasions to solve this housing problem. During the night, hundreds of families invade idle land on the outskirts of the cities, or even in the central districts, and set up shanty towns in a matter of hours. Once established, these people cannot be moved out without risking a full-scale battle between the police and the organized invaders.

When on Good Friday, 1966, the Bogotá police attempted to stop an invasion of public lands in the center of town, the invaders and the police battled for various hours, and several lives were lost. Significantly, the purpose of the invasion was to expand the now well-established invasion neighborhood, the Policarpa Salavarrieta Barrio.

The Industrial Sit-in Strikes and Factory Invasions

Many of the trailblazing labor victories in Colombia have been obtained through the method of the factory invasion or sit-in strike. Probably the most famous case of this type in the last decade was the Ladrillos Moore strike. After the minimum wage went up in 1962, the factory was closed down because of supposed inability to pay the new legal minimum wage. After it had been closed for 52 days, 85 workers occupied the factory, started production, and named their own manager.[11] The Labor Minister and President Lleras upheld the workers' right to take over the factory on constitutional grounds.

11. UTC, "Informe del Comité Ejecutivo," IX Congreso Nacional, December 2–7, 1963 (UTC archives).

The real question in this struggle was whether capital has a social responsibility, as the constitution says it should.[12] The strike, as well as later court decisions, set the precedent that employers do not have the right to close a factory and fire all of its workers, unless there is truly no alternative. During the six months that one of its unions managed the Ladrillos Moore factory, the UTC proved that an enterprise supposedly unable to pay the minimum wage could function well and show profits when it was managed by the union. As an epilogue to this strike, after the factory had functioned for six months in the hands of the union, management signed an agreement giving employees a 40 percent wage increase, and continued operations with the manager named by the union.

This precedent has been followed by other invasions of factories and sweatshops. The latest incident, in early 1966, was the invasion of a sugar refinery by a union that had been on strike for several months. Once more, the union operated the factory efficiently and was able to show the employers and public opinion that the allegations of inability to pay on the part of management were unfounded.

In Colombia, the classical picket line with workers carrying placards is a very rare sight. In the 1940s it was a common labor tactic, since the state still protected the constitutional right of strikebreakers to work. At that time, the picket line was used to prevent uncommitted workers from going to their jobs, and it is still used in cases where only a small proportion of the workers go on strike. More commonly, when a strike is about to take place, the workers invade the factory and close it down. Occasionally they go as far as taking some high employees as hostages, and keeping them locked in the factory until a settlement is reached. Keeping these people until they are ransomed with a labor settlement clearly provides an added tactical advantage for a weak union.

12. Conversation with Belisario Betancour, Labor Minister at the time.

It was virtually impossible for the state to keep order during all of the strikes in which employers tried to break the unions by continuing production with the workers who did not respect the strike; for this reason the government has tacitly recognized since 1956 the right of unions to close down a factory during a strike. If a large number of workers go on strike, the state allows the union to take over the factory and to allow only work that is essential to avoid damage to the factory. This may involve keeping refrigeration plants and furnaces going, or preserving raw materials from spoilage.

Another labor tactic used frequently by weak unions is vandalism or the threat of vandalism. One illustration of the use of this method is given by the Andina Beer Company strike of September 1964.[13] During the strike, the union took over the factory by threatening sabotage unless the company handed over control. As the strike went on, the union started to pressure the company by withdrawing the personnel in charge of preserving raw materials. When the strike ended, the temperature in the raw materials cellars was found to be 18° C., instead of the 3° C. required. Thus approximately 400,000 pesos worth of raw materials were spoiled, and there could have been extensive loss of equipment as well. The union, therefore, had pressured the company to reach a settlement by threatening to destroy raw materials and installations worth millions of pesos. The company, which could not legally fire the union leaders, started legal proceedings against them for the "negligence" that caused this loss, but legal proceedings in Colombia are slow, and a year later there was as yet no verdict.

Another example of this type of tactic involved the striking workers of the Croydon Company in September 1965. After one month of strike, it seemed to the workers that they would have to give in and lose the strike. It appeared that only if the government intervened and pressured the employer to reach a settlement

13. Account based on personal interviews.

would the strike be won. So in desperation they decided to block one of the major roads to Bogotá in order to pressure the government to take action to solve a potentially dangerous conflict. The goverment sent mounted police, and traffic on the road was restored after half an hour. Several weeks later, the strike was still unresolved, and the union decided to carry out a sit-in strike in the offices of the Labor Minister until he named an arbitrator.

The Croydon strike, which is fairly typical, shows that as a rule Colombian strikes are relatively peaceful, especially if they are not declared illegal by the government. The strikers do not usually use violence, although they do use harassing tactics.

Union Tactics and Ideology in the Public and Private Sectors

The peacefulness of a strike depends to a large extent on whether the government intervenes in the conflict. The government of Guillermo León Valencia (1962–66) usually let labor and management settle their own differences, and used its police and legal powers very sparingly, in spite of the fact that the country passed the last months of the presidential term under a declared state of siege. Because of this attitude, strikes during the Valencia term were long, and usually peaceful.

As James Payne has pointed out in his study of unions in Peru,[14] vandalism, street disorders, and large-scale city-wide strikes are useful only in a situation where the government is weak and without true public support, and when it lets itself be blackmailed into intervening in favor of better conditions for the workers. In such a situation, the labor unions will use violence to achieve their economic ends. According to Payne, the alternative tactic, collective bargaining, will probably be less successful, since in Peru and Colombia unemployment is high and the economic situation does not present favorable conditions for an increase in wages.

14. James Payne, "Peru: the Politics of Structured Violence," *The Journal of Politics*, 27 (May 1965).

In Colombia this analysis is not generally valid. The elected governments are usually much more securely in power than they appear to be at first sight, and labor legislation has given unions the power to bargain effectively at the level of the individual enterprise, despite the existence of high levels of unemployment in the economy, by isolating the workers in well-established companies from the national or regional labor markets. The law made the survival of independent enterprise unions possible, regardless of their political power as shock groups, or their crucial "violence initiating" position.[15] For this reason, workers are usually reluctant to use violence. Since the government will not respond positively to this tactic, and there are alternative union tactics, violence is not frequent in industrial conflicts.

In the countryside there is often no alternative to the use of violence as a method of obtaining land and better economic conditions, so this tactic is used frequently by rural unions; but in the modern sector of the economy, there are institutionalized channels for bargaining and communication between employers and laborers. Society has created a legal structure where laborers are not at a complete disadvantage, and within which they can effectively obtain economic improvements. The net result is that Colombian labor-management relations in the modern industrial sector are relatively peaceful, at least in comparison with labor-management relations in other underdeveloped nations such as Peru, Chile, India, or the United States before the New Deal.[16]

15. According to Payne, the crucial "violence-initiating" position of the unions makes them the major tool of the opposition to the government, and therefore the government will usually "meet their demands rapidly with adequate concessions, so that violence will have little opportunity to build." Ibid.

16. In regard to violence in labor-management relations in India see Charles A. Myers, *Labor Problems in the Industrialization of India* (Cambridge, Mass., Harvard University Press, 1958), pp. 90–134. In Chile there has been a high degree of violence in labor-management relations; see James O. Morris, "The Labor Relations System in Chile" (New York State

Before the Liberal Party came to power in the thirties, violence in labor-management relations was not unknown. The nature of these relations and the bloody strikes in the first period of the history of the Colombian labor movement have been described. But even then, with the possible exception of the United Fruit strike of 1928, there have probably not been any large-scale and bloody repressions of labor unions and strikes in Colombian history. A progressive government came to power sufficiently early in the process of Colombian industrialization to avoid the bloody history that usually characterizes the early development of national labor movements.

The lack of violence that has characterized the Colombian labor movement probably has its roots in the early history of the movement in the thirties, when organization was relatively easy and the movement did not experience violent repression. In other nations of Latin America, the historical development of the labor movement was radically different. In Argentina and Chile, during the first decades of this century, when well-organized unions first began to emerge, violence between the police and the workers was common. Carlos M. Rama points out that in Argentina and Chile the fact that the labor movement was repressed periodically affected its ideology and its future development.[17] In particular, it made these labor movements antidemocratic and very politically oriented.

Today, in Colombia, most of the labor movement is deeply committed to democracy and collective bargaining. In addition to the historically positive relationship between the unions and the state, the existence of social mobility and universal suffrage have also been determinants of the type of ideology and tactics used by the labor movement. The existence of social mobility in

---

School of Industrial Relations, mimeographed). For the Peruvian case see the works of James Payne.

17. Carlos M. Rama, *Mouvements ouvriers et socialist de l'Amérique Latine* (Paris, Editions Ouvrières, 1959), pp. 122–31.

urban Colombia has been a crucial variable in the shaping of the labor movement. Labor will develop revolutionary ideologies if the working classes do not perceive the possibility of improving their economic and social position. In Colombia, however, labor leaders rise from the ranks of the proletariat and experience personally a substantial degree of social mobility. In addition to improving their economic condition, they rise in social status and are given much consideration by the society. Many of them are made elected officials (even congressmen), and they are consulted by the government at all levels of the decision-making process. Furthermore, the government and international organizations make available to them the two greatest marks of prestige in Colombian society: education and foreign travel. For example, all of the leaders of the UTC have had scholarships to study abroad, and the former secretary general of the UTC has a high prestige job at the ILO. Other labor leaders travel to various labor congresses, and the national education programs of the UTC and the CTC (Confederatión de Trabajadores de Colombia) are available to all promising union officers all over the country.

The results of a survey carried out among two groups of union leaders who participated in educational courses organized by the UTC are tabulated in Table 9. One of the courses was a political science seminar, and at a confrontation between university students and labor leaders during the seminar, the workers attacked the revolutionary ideas of the students and came out strongly for reform instead of revolution. Table 9 shows why. More than 50 percent of the state federation executives were homeowners; the great majority of the union leaders believed they had improved their standard of living since they joined the institutionalized labor movement and that they had as much or more influence on government decision making than the influential members of the middle class and the traditional elite. One man, the head of an industrial federation, asserted that he had more influence in decision making than all the people listed, including congressmen, the American ambassador, and bishops.

The values and the commitment to progress within the existing political framework, found in Colombia among a majority of the labor leaders, are not unexpected. In a survey carried out in Venezuela on a much broader scale, similar results were obtained.[18] In the Venezuelan case, it was found that 75 percent of the labor leaders questioned believed their standard of living would improve in the next five years, and more than 65 percent of them believed that the Venezuelan constitution and the political system were good or very good. The majority of the labor leaders also believed that there was considerable social mobility in Venezuela.

Unions and many of the workers who have worked for them have prospered in Colombia. The men involved understandably have some faith in the system. Not surprisingly, these labor leaders consider themselves members of the middle class, and are characterized by nonrevolutionary beliefs and ideologies. The Communist labor leaders are clearly different. The Communist unions are the only sector of the labor movement led by intellectuals. They, unlike their counterparts in UTC and CTC, have experienced downward mobility. This takes them close to the workers and makes possible their relations and communication with union members, but it also makes them revolutionary. Nevertheless, since the Communists control less than a third of the labor movement, the bulk of organized labor is still committed to democracy and to reforming without destroying the present structure of society.

One labor sector that does use violent tactics and is largely communist is that of the public service workers and government employees. This is because according to Colombian law public servants and government employees cannot go on strike. This makes collective bargaining ineffective, since the unions thereby lose much of their bargaining strength. Also, in these sectors the government has to intervene in labor–management relations,

18. Centro de Estudios del Desarrollo, *Estudio de conflictos y concenso, muestra de líderes sindicales,* Serie de resultados parciales 1 (Caracas, Editorial Arte, 1965)

TABLE 9

Results of Survey of UTC Union Leaders

	Group A[a]			Group B[b]		
	Yes	No	No Answer	Yes	No	No Answer
Believes that he has improved his standard of living since joining the labor movement	12	2	2	6	3	2
Homeowner	9	7	—	3	8	—
Believes himself to have equal or more influence in government decision making than:[c]						
University professor	5	4	1	2	4	—
State assemblyman	7	3	—	2	4	—
City councilman	8	2	—	2	4	—
Student leader	8	2	—	5	1	—

Employer of under 500 workers	10	—	—	6	—	—	—
Employer of over 500 workers	6	4	—	3	—	3	—
Parish priest	6	4	—	3	—	3	—
Bishop	5	5	—	2	—	4	—
Newspaper writer	9	1	—	4	—	2	—
Department head of Labor Ministry	6	4	—	1	—	5	—
Congressman	3	7	—	1	—	5	—
U.S. ambassador	3	7	—	3	—	3	—

a. Group A members were presidents of state federations, on the executive board of UTC, or of equivalent rank.

b. Group B members were high executives in local enterprise unions or employees of state federations.

c. Sixteen labor leaders answered this question.

Source: Results of a survey of UTC labor leaders who attended two short courses given by the author in the fields of economics and political science.

since they are regulated by arbitration in the public services and since in the public sector the government is the employer; and where the government intervenes political bargaining is more effective than collective bargaining.

Prices in the public services are often controlled to keep them from rising as rapidly as the general price level. Therefore enterprises defined as public services are usually in a difficult financial situation and will not give wage increases unless they can raise prices. Often the result is that the union and the employer get together and close down the industry. Since by definition the work stoppage is illegal, the police intervene from the start, and violence is used to try to obtain authorization from the government to increase prices. In return for their help in obtaining the price increase, the unions are rewarded by management with a wage increase. This has been the traditional procedure in the Colombian transportation sector.[19] The latest example of this tactic was the Bogotá bus strike of October 1965. A legal provision had raised the pay of laborers who worked on Sundays, and bus owners, who operated at a government regulated fare, claimed they could not pay the wage increase unless they were allowed to raise the bus fares. Workers and bus owners then joined in a stoppage, and to keep it effective they stoned taxis that went out on the streets and liberally sprinkled all roads and streets with nails. Since in Bogotá the number of cars per capita is very low, the transport strike paralyzed the city in its first few hours. With great wisdom, the government of Guillermo León Valencia did nothing about the strike, except arrest workers caught destroying property or throwing nails. Since road transport in Colombia is atomized and there are no large transport companies, the teamsters' unions are weak and usually exist only in name. After a few days of strike, people were somehow going to work and the drivers were beginning to go hungry since there were no strike

19. This was the case with the port workers' strike in October 1928. See *Memoria del Ministerio de Industrias, 1929.* Strikes with a similar cause have been frequent in transport since then.

funds available. After five days the strike was broken by the use of military trucks to transport people in the city, and the unions ordered the drivers to go back to work. Shortly afterwards, the government set up a committee to study bus fares, and on its recommendations, it later gave bus owners a subsidy instead of allowing fares to go up, which it considered too explosive politically.

In the public sector, the "violence-initiating" position of the unions is also exploited more than in the private sector because of the lack of effective institutional channels for the solution of labor demands. Government workers cannot strike legally, and the government is chronically short of funds. It will not, therefore, grant higher wages of its own accord. It becomes inevitable that the unions of government employees use the strike, despite the fact that it is illegal to do so. The result is that labor-management relations in the public sector are carried on outside the law, and for this reason the union's "violence-initiating" position is often exploited more frequently. Once outside the law, the unions have little to lose if they also get involved in other illegal actions, such as the use of violence to keep the strike effective.

A good example of the tactics used by government unions is provided by the powerful primary school teachers' union. In 1966 it sponsored two important labor protests. The first was a month-long strike in March, which happened to coincide with national elections for Congress.[20] These elections expected to be very close, were crucial since they indirectly determined the outcome of the presidential election. The strike, which affected some two million school-age children, clearly had important political repercussions. On March 22, the teachers organized mass rallies in all major cities in the nation, and in Pasto they invaded the governor's palace and destroyed some property. These mass meetings were fertile ground for agitators, but fortunately there

20. See *El Tiempo* (March 6–31, 1966). The elections took place on March 20, and the coalition in power lost ground.

was no violence. On March 23, the teachers issued an ultimatum, demanding that the government be made "responsible for any crisis that can occur in the country from now on."[21] They then proceeded to organize a nationwide citizens' strike against the state. On the 25th, agitators and unemployed youths stoned various buildings in Bogotá and sacked some shops. Although the teachers had not taken part in the vandalism, as one of its victims, El Tiempo newspaper, readily admitted, it was clear that "in the shade of a serious labor protest like that of the teachers, agitators begin to act."[22] The street agitation clearly pressured the government into reaching a settlement with the workers. In effect, a new tax was created to pay for the higher wages that the teachers demanded.

The other large-scale protest of the teachers' union in 1966 was a twenty-eight-day march from Santa Marta to Bogotá in October. The president of the union and some seventy teachers, including many women, walked the incredible distance of 1,600 kilometers in protest against the government's delay in paying the teachers of Magdalena their salaries. Needless to say, public opinion supported the marchers more and more every day, and the government was forced to find a solution to the problem. The "violence-initiating" potential of the teachers' union was again proved when after the mass meeting welcoming the marchers in Bogotá, agitators and delinquents stoned the windows of various shops in the central district and looted 30,000 pesos worth of merchandise from the Tia store.[23]

In summary, the fact that there are no effective institutionalized channels for the presentation of labor grievances and demands in the public sector has led to the deterioration of labor-management relations in that sector. The unions often obtain their demands only after threatening the government with large-scale social conflict or street disturbances that threaten its stability. In turn,

21. El Tiempo (March 24, 1966).
22. Editorial in El Tiempo (March 26, 1966).
23. El Espectador (October 22, 1966).

the government often and unexpectedly is firm toward these unions, and takes repressive measures. In a committee created by President Carlos Lleras to study the structure of the labor movement, both labor leaders and officials of the Labor Ministry, including the Labor Minister himself, agreed that the state was the worst employer in Colombia.[24] This has determined that the unions in the public sector identify themselves ideologically with the extreme left, and very few unions of government employees belong to the democratic federations CTC and UTC.

Another factor influencing the ideology and behavior of the unions of government employees is the historical development of wages in the public sector. While in the period before industrialization the government was the largest and highest paying employer, in the last two decades the salaries of public servants have increased much less than the salaries of workers in the private sector.

In general, therefore, although the strike is used as a "violence-initiating" tactic by certain labor groups to obtain economic concessions from central or local governments, this type of political bargaining is not very common in Colombia today, where labor-management differences are usually settled through institutionalized collective bargaining and where the ultimate weapon of the unions is the limited strike at the enterprise level.

24. From personal notes of these meetings, which took place during the week of September 12, 1966, at the Labor Ministry.

10

Labor Legislation and the Structure of the Labor Movement

The structure of the Colombian labor movement has been determined by two factors: the monopolistic structure of the product market, and the legal protection that the state has given labor unions throughout the industrialization process.

The structure of the product market in Colombia reflects in large part the heavily protectionist tariff policies that have been common since the early thirties, and the chronic shortage of investment capital in the country. These two factors have led to a highly monopolistic product market structure, where a single firm usually controls the production of a product or group of products.

Another factor that has led to monopoly production in Colombia is the combination of an imported technology and a limited consumer market. Technology imported from developed countries usually has large economies of scale, and efficient production with this technology requires a volume of production equal to or greater than the demand of the national Colombian market. The high transportation costs within Colombia also contribute to the problem of monopoly production. The high cost of transport, due to Colombia's mountainous terrain, limits the market for many products to a rather small region, thus leading to monopoly production in certain geographic areas. Therefore the existence of various firms in the nation producing the same product does not mean there is an oligopolistic market, since it only hides the fact that each firm monopolizes a certain geographical market.

Table 10 illustrates the nature of the product market in Colombia. Although the table refers only to corporations, it must be kept in mind that the largest firms in Colombia are corporations. The table also underestimates the degree of concentration in Colombia since within each sector there are various companies that monopolize the production of certain types of goods or monopolize sales in certain geographical regions. For example, although there are various companies producing beer, one company owns stock in most of the others.

The monopoly structure of the product market in Colombia has not encouraged the emergence of national unions or large-scale industrial unions. Industry-wide or nationwide unions develop in response to the threat of competition. It is clear that if in a competitive market a union manages to raise wages in an enterprise above the average for the labor market area, it will drive that enterprise out of business. The only way to maintain the union standard is therefore to unionize the whole industry or the whole trade. To be effective in obtaining higher wages in a competitive product market, the unions must control the whole labor market so that the high paying firms will not be driven to lowering wages because of the competition from low paying enterprises.

The lack of competition in the product market in Colombia has made it possible for the unions to be effective at the enterprise level, and has made the emergence of national craft unions or industrial unions unnecessary. The monopoly structure of the product market, encouraged by tariff protection, has therefore determined the importance of the enterprise union in Colombia and the slow development of industrial unions and national unions.

Another factor that has favored the development of enterprise unions is the level of skill of the Colombian workers. Since there has been no craft tradition in the nation and because the labor

TABLE 10

Industrial Concentration in Colombian Manufacturing Enterprises

Number of Corporations in the Group			Industrial Sector*	1959		1960		1961	
1959	1960	1961		Large Corporations as Percent of Total Controlled	Percent of Sales Controlled	Large Corporations as Percent of Total Controlled	Percent of Sales Controlled	Large Corporations as Percent of Total Controlled	Percent of Sales Controlled
—	5	9	Petroleum National	—	—	20.0	99.9	11.1	99.4
8	25	28	Foreign	37.5	98.4	12.0	93.1	10.7	89.2
6	4	5	Candy, biscuits, noodles, etc.	50.0	67.9	50.0	65.6	40.0	67.4
5	4	3	Chocolates	40.0	91.3	50.0	94.8	33.3	50.1
5	7	7	Sugar refineries	40.0	76.9	42.9	77.1	28.6	78.2
7	8	8	Beer	42.8	88.1	25.0	80.5	12.5	71.3
3	4	4	Tobacco	33.3	97.0	25.0	96.6	25.0	97.0
24	37	33	Textiles	37.5	86.7	16.2	67.3	12.1	70.1
8	8	6	Rubber	37.5	77.4	37.5	79.3	33.3	65.0

Oils and vegetables	6	6	6	50.0	97.4	50.0	89.8	33.3	65.1
Soap, chemical, and pharmaceutical laboratories	23	27	26						
National				30.7	69.3	15.2	85.4	15.0	55.4
Foreign				21.7	60.0	22.2	67.8	19.2	63.6
Cement and cement products	15	18	17	40.0	74.3	22.2	67.2	29.4	63.4
Iron and steel products									
National	35	22	33	26.5	76.0	14.8	56.8	15.1	65.3
Foreign	4	4	6	25.0	90.3	25.0	84.5	16.7	68.0
Manufacture of other metal products	—	21	20	—	—	23.8	72.6	25.0	65.7
Garments and ready-made clothes	13	8	9	38.5	75.5	37.5	70.3	3.3	65.3
Platinum, silver and gold mines (foreign)	8	9	8	25.0	91.7	22.2	90.7	25.0	89.5

*A company is classified as foreign when it is registered as such, but a company may be classified as national even if more than 50 percent of the shares are foreign owned.

Source: Data made available by the Departamento Administrativo de Planeación, and based on DANE statistics.

force available to industry is unskilled, industry has trained workers on the job. The workers have therefore very specific skills, useful only in a given enterprise. If such a laborer leaves an enterprise where he has learned a specific skill, he will either join the ranks of the unemployed or find work as an unskilled worker since in a monopolistic industrial structure no other enterprise will require the specific skill he has acquired. Therefore, the worker in Colombia is committed to the enterprise and not to a trade, and instead of practicing a trade he has various specific skills. This phenomenon tends to favor the development of enterprise unions and to hinder the growth of craft unions.

The prevalence of the enterprise union, however, has meant that the labor movement cannot grow very rapidly, and cannot encompass any important proportion of the labor force in Colombia. Since organizing unions in small enterprises is difficult and expensive, and there are few large enterprises in the nation, the labor movement remains small. According to Colombian law, the minimum size of a union is 25 workers, and there are only 23,711 nonagricultural enterprises with more than 10 workers in Colombia.[1] But since a union of fewer than 100 workers is unlikely to exist for very long or to be very strong financially, it is significant that in the manufacturing sector, where unions are traditionally strong, there were only 477 enterprises with more than 100 workers in 1963, and these enterprises employed only 149,361 workers.[2] Since the number of large enterprises in other sectors such as transport, trade, and services is also very small, it is clear that the area of potential influence of the enterprise union is limited.

1. Number of enterprises that contribute to Servicio Nacional de Aprendizaje (SENA). According to the law, all enterprises with ten or more employees must contribute, and evasion is small. The above statistic is for January 31, 1966, and was made available by SENA, Sección de Estadística, División de Recursos Humanos.

2. DANE, *Anuario general de estadística, 1963* (Bogotá, Multilith Estadinal, 1965), p. 612.

The Law and the Enterprise Union

The legal provisions regulating collective bargaining in Colombia since 1945 have also encouraged the growth of enterprise unionism. According to Law 6 of 1945, Article 39,

> enterprise unions are the basis of union organization . . . For this reason within any enterprise there cannot coexist two or more unions. If there are two or more unions, only the union with the greatest number of workers shall survive.[3]

Decree No. 1952 of 1961 clarified the privileged position of the enterprise union in the following terms:

> The enterprise union that includes the majority of the workers in a firm has exclusive bargaining rights. If the enterprise union has a minority of the workers, the workers shall be represented by all the unions within the firm. All the unions will create a bargaining committee, and agreements have to be approved by the general assemblies of all the unions.[4]

These legal provisions made the emergence of craft and industrial unions difficult, since the workers of a given craft are usually a minority within the enterprise. The enterprise union, however, is an inherently weak bargaining unit. Since it covers the whole plant or firm, any wage demand it makes is expensive to meet. The craft union, on the other hand, can obtain wage increases that are not very costly to the employer, since the workers involved are few; but it can carry out expensive and effective strikes, since craft workers often occupy strategic positions within the

3. República de Colombia, *Acto Legislativo y Leyes de 1945* (Bogotá, Imprenta Nacional, 1945).
4. *Código sustantivo del trabajo y código procesal del trabajo* (Colección "Codex Brevis," Bogotá).

enterprise. Furthermore, when a craft or industrial union goes on strike in a given plant, the strikers can be supported by the members of the union who are still working in other enterprises. The enterprise union, by contrast, can only depend on its own limited strike fund when it goes on strike, and given the monopoly structure of the Colombian product market, the defeat of an enterprise union usually does not affect the union standard in other firms. Thus the workers in other firms do not help the striking workers out of self-interest, but out of charity and brotherhood, sentiments which cannot always be counted on. For these reasons the enterprise union is usually financially weak, and it cannot easily weather a long strike.

Given the inherent weakness of the enterprise union, employers usually favor it over the industrial or craft union, and the law makes it possible for the employer to make the emergence of craft and industrial unions difficult by protecting the enterprise union which, if it retains the support of the majority of the workers, will have exclusive bargaining rights. In the last decade, various craft and industrial unions have been broken because of the advantage the law gives enterprise unions. In 1961, bank employees were not allowed by the Labor Ministry to present a unified collective bargaining front, and in the same year a strike by two craft unions of Avianca Airlines was broken and declared illegal by the government because of the existence of a parallel enterprise union.[5] The law concerning the bargaining unit has hindered not only the emergence of craft unions but also that of industrial unions. Since an industrial union is usually organized as a federation of enterprise or plant unions, in Colombia the employer can argue that each of these units is an enterprise union with exclusive bargaining rights, and the industrial union is therefore not allowed to present a united front.

5. For a discussion of this problem see Andrés Almarales and Marina Goenaga, *Las luchas obreras y la legislación laboral* (2d ed. Cali, Ediciones Bloque Sindical Independiente del Valle del Cauca, 1964), pp. 80, 90–93.

TABLE 11

Active and Inactive Unions in Colombia, 1939–59

Type of Union	1939	1940	1941	1942	1943	1947	1959 Urban Unions Active	Inactive	Rural Unions Active	Inactive
Enterprise unions	—	—	—	—	—	342	602	326	—	—
Craft unions	425	428	524	598	642	324	424	673	272	355
Industrial unions	77	114	142	130	131	181	85	73	—	—
Various trades	—	—	—	—	—	139	36	59	—	—
Employers' associations and mixed unions	11	12	13	14	15	—	—	—	—	—
Total number of unions	520*	554	679	742	788	986	1,147	1,154	272	355
Urban	—	395	479	527	563	—	—	—	—	—
Rural	—	159	200	215	225	—	—	—	—	—

*Does not add up, but the original source gives these figures.

Sources: José Joaquín Caicedo Castilla, *Memoria del Ministro del Trabajo, Higiene y Previsión Social de 1939;* José Joaquín Caicedo Castilla, *Memoria del Ministro del Trabajo, Higiene y Previsión Social de 1941;* Arcesio Londoño Palacio, *Memoria del Ministro del Trabajo, Higiene y Previsión Social de 1943;* Contraloría General de la República, *Primer censo sindical de Colombia, 1947* (Bogotá, Editorial Minerva, 1949); Otto Morales Benítez, *Memoria del Ministro del Trabajo al Congreso de 1959,* p. 33.

Before 1945, the law did not discriminate in favor of enterprise unions, and as Table 11 shows, craft and industrial unions were relatively more numerous then than in 1959; as is clear from the number of inactive craft unions in 1959, many craft unions died out in the intervening period. It seems therefore that legislation has been an important factor determining the structure of the labor movement. But the preponderance of the enterprise union is not only a function of Article 39 of Law 6. The whole of Colombia's legislation on unions as well as the general protection the state gives the labor movement have helped to determine the bargaining unit and the structure of the Colombian labor movement.

The History of Legal Protection of Unions

The first legislation protecting the right of workers to organize dates from 1931, but protection of the right to strike, which is probably more important to the unions than direct protection of the right to organize, dates from 1919 and 1920. Law 78 of 1919 provided that there would be no penal sanctions against abandoning work (breaking the work contract) as long as the work stoppage was peaceful. The same law, however, reserved to employers the right to break strikes and required the authorities to "protect those workers who freely want to continue to work, and those workers who offer their labor, or that are hired to replace those who have declared a strike."[6]

Law 21 of 1920 established some additional conditions for legal work stoppages. It instituted a compulsory conciliation period before a strike could take place, and made all strikes in the public services illegal. Law 21 also made all sudden strikes illegal by setting up a compulsory forty-eight-hour conciliation period,[7] and a maximum of seven days for the enterprise to answer a

6. Article 4, Law 78, 1919.
7. Conciliation was to be carried out by a third party named by common agreement or by two persons named by each of the parties.

workers' petition. By making all strikes in the public services illegal, Law 21 further limited the right to strike. The law defined the following activities as public services, and set up compulsory arbitration machinery for the settlement of disputes in these areas: (1) railroad, streetcar, and ship transport; (2) public water works; (3) public lighting; (4) street cleaning and garbage disposal; and (5) national mines. Since this list coincides with the activities that had the most developed labor organizations, it is clear that this law substantially limited the right to strike.

The next law regulating strikes and the activites of unions was Law 83 of 1931. As has been explained previously, the law officially recognized unions, set up penalties for employers who engaged in union persecution, and regulated the activities of unions. Article 18 of that law, however, confirmed the right to work provisions of the constitution and explicitly forbade unions to limit the right to work of nonmembers or to take any action to force workers to join the union. Although Law 83 was certainly an incentive to the growth of the labor movement and the emergence of new unions, it did not guarantee that these unions would be strong. On the contrary, the provisions against union persecution were such that an employer could easily get rid of any worker who tried to organize a union, and the provisions on strikes made it very difficult to carry out an effective walkout since the state remained committed to defending strikebreakers.

Faced by the weakness of its strike threat, the labor movement was able to obtain its demands only by bringing the state into the labor-management conflict, and having it pressure the employers for a settlement. Since in Colombia the government has been relatively secure in power, violence has not been used to threaten the government, according to the Payne model, but has been used against the employer, in the hope of forcing the government to intervene in the labor conflict. When the government intervened, it protected the employer's property, but only on the condition that it bargain with the workers. This forced employers to recognize unions and to make concessions.

159

Thus during the decade starting in 1934, the labor movement owed its effectiveness to the informal protection of the Liberal government. For this reason, the labor movement was very politically oriented and was, in particular, a defender of Alfonso López. President López' administration and his wing of the Liberal Party found their support among the urban workers and thus were ready to antagonize employers. Therefore, the intervention of the government in industrial conflict was usually favorable to labor.

Table 12 shows that government intervention was crucial for the settlement of disputes in the thirties. Of 218 labor-management disputes, only 44 seem to have been settled without government intervention. The table also shows that few strikes were declared illegal. Since other sources point out that most of the strikes during the period were in fact illegal, it is clear that the government tended to be benevolent toward labor, since declaring the strike illegal would have allowed the employers to break both the strike and the union. In a report to Congress in 1934, the head of the labor office stated that the lack of legal strikes necessitated a change in the legislation on strikes. Significantly, instead of recommending stringent measures against unions that broke the law, he suggested a greater degree of government intervention in industrial relations.[8]

Since the unions depended on the attitude of the government for their strength, it was very important to them that the López wing of the Liberal Party remain in power; the labor movement, therefore, went to great lengths to help this wing of the party win the elections for the 1938–42 presidential term. Unfortunately for labor, the left wing of the party lost the elections, and without the informal support of the government the labor movement lost a great deal of its strength during the Santos Presidency.

Before the establishment of the legal framework making the peaceful strike a really effective bargaining tactic, political bar-

8. *Memorias del Ministerio de Industrias y Trabajo, 1934,* pp. 307 ff.

gaining was the only labor tactic available. During this period it was clear that the unit of collective bargaining had to be large. Since the party in power helped the labor unions in industrial relations in order to obtain popularity, only large unions could obtain the help of the state. Thus before 1945 the federations were very important, as opposed to the small enterprise unions. This was the period in which the loosely knit CTC dominated the labor movement. Although it had no finances to speak of, and practically no power over the affiliated unions, it could speak in the name of thousands of workers and the government would listen. This was also the period when the large River Workers' Union and the Railroad Federation were very strong, and some industrial unions began to emerge. The nature of bargaining and the need for government intervention determined that the mass, loosely-knit unions prevail.

The unions continued to be politically oriented as long as no new labor legislation was passed giving labor protection from the unlimited supply of labor caused by high rates of population growth, rapid urbanization, and moderate rates of economic growth and industrialization. And since, as has usually been the case in Colombia, Congress was very conservative, no such legislation was forthcoming despite the efforts of the Liberal executive. The attempted coup d'état against López in 1944, however, radically changed the prospects for labor. After the coup, a state of siege was declared, and the executive proceeded to legislate by decree. Alfonso López had been paralyzed by Congress, but after the coup of July 10, 1944, he brought about a major social revolution by using all the power that the state of siege situation made available to the executive. His Decreto 2350 of 1944, which was passed a few months later in a somewhat watered down form as Law 6 of 1945, permanently transformed the nature of industrial relations in Colombia. The labor masses who had taken to the streets in defense of López and constitutional government on July 10, 1944, were thus generously rewarded.

Although Law 6 covered almost all aspects of labor-manage-

TABLE 12

Labor-Management Conflicts, June 1935 to May 1939

Fiscal Year	Total Number of Conflicts	Direct Settlement	Work Stoppages	Factory Occupation	Strikes Broken	Solidarity Strikes	Strikes Declared Illegal	Lockouts	Settlement by Arbitration	Settlement After Government Intervention*	Settlement After Conciliation
1935–36	21	4	7	1	—	1	3	—	1	11	4
1936–37	55	6	22	—	2	—	1	—	1	47	—
1937–38	72	12	24	—	—	1	—	2	1	57	—
1938–39	70	16	17	—	—	—	1	3	5	40	7
Total	218	38	70	1	2	2	5	5	8	155	11

*Columns 2 to 11 do not add up to the total in column 1 because strikes also appear in columns 10 and 11.

Source: Padilla Jorge, *Les Conflicts collectifs du travail en Colombie* (Bordeaux, Imprimerie E. Drouillard, 1941), p. 77.

ment relations, including the establishment of severance pay, pay for Sundays not worked, a minimum wage, new regulations on work accidents and nonoccupational illness, two-week paid vacations, and time-and-a-half for overtime and night work, the most important reforms for the labor movement were those regulating strikes and giving union leaders job security. Article 40 established absolute job security for up to ten officers of any local union, and for regional or national union leaders. This job security was also extended to all workers who decided to organize a union from the moment they informed the employer about their plans until three months later. Employers could fire such workers only by proving to a labor judge that the workers had broken work regulations. These provisions strengthened unions tremendously. They could no longer be broken by the employer, and the burden of proof for justifying the firing of union members was passed to the employer, thus making it much harder to engage in union persecution. Indirectly, these provisions also improved the finances of the labor movement, since employers had to pay the salary of workers who could dedicate most of their time to union activity. Before, union leaders were usually fired and had to survive by their own devices while they were engaged in labor activity. Article 42 further strengthened unions by making it illegal for an employer to change the proportion of union members within his firm through layoffs in any given year.

But the most important legislative change was in the provisions on strikes. Article 45 established that during a legal strike the employer could not make new work contracts, thus in effect outlawing the hiring of strikebreakers. The only requirements that the union had to meet in order to obtain state protection from strikebreakers were the following:

1. that the strike not be in a public service industry;
2. that its object be legal;
3. that the established procedures of conciliation be observed;

163

4. that the work stoppage be peaceful;
5. that the strike be declared by the majority of the workers in the enterprise or enterprises affected, or by the majority of the members of the union to which more than half of the workers of the enterprise belong.

The requirements for a legal strike established by Article 55 made it possible for 26 percent of the workers in an enterprise to call an effective strike which the employer could not legally break.[9] Once the state created such favorable conditions for carrying out a strike, the method of collective bargaining became a practical union bargaining tactic, and the structure of the labor movement changed.

As has been stated before, Law 6 of 1945 gave the enterprise union explicit preference over other bargaining units, but the provisions on strikes in the same law were an even more effective factor in the emergence of the enterprise union as the dominant bargaining unit. These provisions simplified the walkout at the enterprise level, and made the always difficult task of organizing multifirm unions unnecessary.

In a monopolistic product market, an enterprise union could be effective as long as the state defended the union from the competition of strikebreakers during a strike. If the enterprise union tried to raise wages above the market rate, the lack of competition in the product market did not pressure the employer to withstand a costly strike. Under these circumstances, the only thing that the union needed was to improve its finances so that it could withstand a long strike in case the enterprise wanted to hold out.

The law effectively protected the enterprise union from competition in the labor market, and thus made it effective at the enterprise level. But if the employer was not in a monopoly position, the union could easily drive the enterprise out of business if it exploited to the full its protected position by raising costs above

9. If 51 percent of the workers in the enterprise belonged to the union, and if 51 percent of the union members voted for a strike.

TABLE 13

Wage Differentials by Size of Establishment in Colombian Manufacturing

Size of Establishment (number of employees)	Average Yearly Wage* 1962	Index Country Average = 100	Average Yearly Wage Plus Fringe Benefits 1962	Index Country Average = 100
Under 5	P3,258.49	52	P3,478.35	44
5–9	3,627.52	58	3,993.11	51
10–14	4,255.34	68	4,761.07	61
15–19	4,334.40	69	4,947.67	63
20–24	4,543.34	73	5,234.31	67
25–49	5,166.56	83	6,097.86	78
50–74	5,702.26	91	6,942.11	88
75–99	6,280.02	101	7,807.71	99
100–199	6,928.63	111	8,513.88	108
200 or more	7,611.88	122	10,113.32	129
Total for country	6,245.99	100	7,863.82	100

*Wage bill for the year divided by number of wage and salary workers in the last pay period of November.

Source: DANE, Anuario general de estadística, 1962 (Bogotá, Multilith Estadinal, 1964), p. 760.

the competitive level. This, in fact, began to happen. In competitive sectors of the economy, unions did drive enterprises out of business; but in the larger companies, because of the limitations of the Colombian market, the unions usually dealt with employers who were in a monopoly position, with the result that wages could be raised substantially higher than the wages in the rest of the economy.

Table 13 shows the wage differentials between large and small firms in 1963, and Table 14 compares wage differentials by size of establishment in Colombia, Japan, West Germany, Sweden, and the United States. As can be seen from Table 14 the wage differential by size of establishment is much greater in Colombia than in the other countries, with the exception of Japan, where the enterprise union is also the dominant bargaining unit.[10] Table 13 also shows that the level of fringe benefits is higher in the larger establishments. This is in part due to the fact that by law larger firms have to pay some benefits that small firms do not have to pay, but it also reflects the fringe benefits obtained through collective bargaining in the larger firms.

There are many reasons why interfirm wage differentials should be wider in Colombia than in the other countries in Table 14. The relationships between wage differentials and the stage of economic development are now well established; the general proposition in this regard is that wage differentials of all kinds tend to be larger in the underdeveloped economies than in the developed.[11] More generally, income distribution is more unequal in the underdeveloped countries, a factor related in part to the very unequal distribution of education, skills, and labor productivity.

Thus, although the wide interfirm wage differentials observed for Colombia are due in part to the stage of economic develop-

10. In 1957, nearly 80 percent of all organized labor in Japan belonged to enterprise unions.

11. Koji Taira, "Japanese 'Enterprise Unionism' and Interfirm Wage Structure," *Industrial and Labor Relations Review, 15,* 1 (October 1961), pp. 46–47.

166

TABLE 14

Wage Differentials by Size of Establishment in Manufacturing in Various Countries
(largest enterprises=100)

Size of Establishment (number of employees)	Colombia 1965	Japan 1954	United States 1934	United States 1947	United States 1954	United Kingdom 1949	United Kingdom 1954	West Germany 1954	Sweden 1939	Sweden 1950
5–9	53	43[a]	—	74	69	—	—	82	85	87
10–19	63	48	73	86	74	84	80	88	88	93
20–49	66	51[b]	73	87	77	83	81			
50–99	77	57	73	88	80	84	82		94	95
100–199	81	63	75[c]	90[c]	82[c]	85	83			
200–299	86	69	—	—	—	85	83	92		
300–499	87	78	77[d]	92[d]	84[d]	87	87		95	97
500–999	101	87	83	96	90	89	90			
1000 or more	100	100	100	100	100	100	100	100	100	100

a. Establishments with 4 to 9 workers.
b. Average for establishments with 20 to 29 and 30 to 49 workers.
c. Establishments with 100 to 249 workers.
d. Establishments with 250 to 499 workers.

Sources: Colombia: tabulation from the original questionnaires received by DANE from a sample of more than 1,000 manufacturing firms; these questionnaires give payrolls and number of employees, and are returned monthly. This data is for one month in early 1965. Japan: Koji Taira, "Japanese 'Enterprise Unionism' and Interfirm Wage Structure," *Industrial and Labor Relations Review, 15*, no.1 (October 1961), Table 2. Other nations: Ibid., Table 6.

ment of the country, the union structure probably determines the wide dispersion of wages according to the size of the firm. Cross-national studies in Western Europe have shown that the greater the coverage of organized wage agreements, the smaller the wage differentials between firms. For example, in Sweden, which is the country where wage agreements have the greatest degree of coverage, interfirm differentials are lower than in other developed nations,[12] while Japan, where the enterprise union was until recently the predominant bargaining unit, shows much greater interfirm wage differentials. It is of interest to note that the wage dispersion between enterprises of different sizes is similar in Japan and Colombia and that both nations have an industrial relations system dominated by wage agreements limited to the enterprise unit. Although the data on interfirm wage differentials are not conclusive, they do suggest that enterprise unions have been effective in the larger firms and have made possible the survival of a wide interfirm wage structure.

12. Ibid., p. 48.

11

The CTC and the Period of Political Bargaining, 1935–1950

Before 1945, when legislation finally gave unions effective protection from the competition of the mass of unemployed and underemployed workers in the labor market, labor organizations found the tactic of political bargaining their most effective weapon. The unlimited supply of labor in the economy, and the commitment of the state to defend the right to work provisions of the constitutions, made collective bargaining and the use of the peaceful strike ineffective tactics for obtaining improved economic conditions.

In contrast, the political situation in the country made political bargaining a useful tool. The conflict between the Liberal executive and the owners of capital, especially during the López terms (1934–38 and 1941–45), created two conditions that favored the labor movement. First, the executive needed the support of labor to remain in power. The mass demonstrations of organized labor warned the army and the conservative elements in society against the possibility of a coup. Second, Alfonso López was ideologically committed to reform, and he could carry out such reform only if he minimized the political power of the owners of capital, whether industrial or agricultural. He could use organized labor to weaken the position of the capitalists, and at the same time obtain electoral support.

Under these circumstances, the best tactic for the labor movement to use was to get the executive branch of the government involved in all its conflicts. It is for this reason that almost all labor-management conflicts were solved only after the government intervened in them. But it was difficult for local union leaders to get the government to intervene in their conflicts with management. During the period of political bargaining the role of the national labor federation was therefore crucial, since it had effective channels of communication with the executive branch of the government.

The Creation of the CTC

The best way of studying the relationship between the labor movement and the Colombian political parties is to review the history of the Confederación de Trabajadores de Colombia (CTC) during its initial fifteen years. The history of the CTC also helps to illustrate to what extent the labor movement depended on the government for its growth and success.

In the euphoria that followed the election in 1935 of a Liberal Congress committed to passing the López reforms, the Colombian Confederation of Labor Unions (Confederación Sindical de Colombia), which some years later changed its name to Confederación de Trabajadores de Colombia, was created. The initiative for its founding came from the president of the *El Tiempo* union, Hernando Vega Escobar, who invited all of the unions in the nation to a congress to be held August 7, 1935, in Bogotá. But a few days before it was to meet, *El Tiempo* published a communication in which Vega Escobar announced the indefinite postponement of the congress. It appears that Eduardo Santos, the paper's director-owner, who was to be President three years later, had ordered Vega Escobar to postpone the meeting.[1]

1. Most of the information on this first congress has been obtained from an unpublished history of the CTC written by the labor leader Virgilio Conde Mantilla, and from documents found in *Acción Liberal*.

Santos' reasons for trying to postpone the congress are well illustrated by a letter sent to Hernando Vega Escobar by the secretary general of the Union Organization Committee of the National Liberal Directorate: "We would like to warn you of the dangers inherent in an invitation such as that which you issued to all unions in the nation. That invitation threatens the free and well intentioned labor movement, since it is more than likely that the Congress will fall into the hands of the so-called Communists."[2]

The postponement of the congress, however, came too late. The labor delegates who had come to Bogotá from other regions of the country walked the streets aimlessly until the anarcho-syndicalists of the union of the El Ruiz match factory decided to help organize the congress anyway. At this stage, some members of the Unión Izquierdista Revolucionaria (UNIR), the short-lived leftist party created by Jorge Eliécer Gaitán, also helped the old-time unionists to organize the congress. The delegates met on August 7, 1935, at an event organized by the El Ruiz union, and three days later the labor congress started to meet officially in the hall of the state legislature of Cundinamarca.

The delegates who attended were divided among Liberals, UNIR members, Communists, and anarcho-syndicalists, the last of whom were the closest there was to bread-and-butter unionists. Seventeen members were elected to the executive committee, one from each territorial division of the nation, and to avoid a division within the congress, it was also necessary to give each political tendency proportional representation on the executive committee. This policy, however, was not sufficient to create unity, and the election led to a break between the Communists and the independent unionists. The latter, who seemed to have been the chief organizers of the congress, included Socialist leaders of the twenties such as Juan de Dios Romero and Raul Eduardo Mahecha. Two executive committees emerged from the congress, one elected by the independents and the former members of the Socialist

2. *Acción Liberal* (August 1935), p 1254.

Party, and the other led by the Communists. The former group became the official labor confederation because the next morning they managed to register their mailing address first.

Thus, from the day it was officially founded, the Colombian Confederation of Labor Unions was divided along political lines. The structure of the labor movement, union dues, and centralism versus federalism—none of these matters were subjects of controversy or serious discussion. The real problem was which political group would obtain control of the organization which in the future would be able to speak for the wage-earning masses. This was logical, since given the weakness of the few unions that helped to create the confederation, it was clear that it could not dedicate itself to collective bargaining. Under those circumstances it was natural that the confederation should become a political pressure group.

The Popular Front

The political division within the labor movement did not, however, last long. A change of line imposed by the international communist movement made possible labor unity. By 1936, the Communists were committed to the popular front, and the division within the confederation was patched up. The independent unionists who had militated in the old Socialist Party of the twenties were excluded, and the Liberals and Communists divided the executive committee between them.

In August 1936, a unity congress was organized in Medellín by the Unidad Sindical de Antioquia (made up of twenty-three unions) and the Confederación Sindical de Colombia. At this congress the Communists defended "Union Unity," according to the tactics determined at the Seventh Congress of the Communist International,[3] and as a result of their efforts, a unified labor confederation emerged, with an executive committee made up

3. Comité Central del Partido Comunista de Colombia, *Treinta Años,* p. 34.

of representatives of all the different political factions. The congress took place in an atmosphere of violence. During the congress in Medellín, Liberals and union delegates clashed with the Conservatives during a Conservative-sponsored rally, with a toll of two dead and several wounded.[4]

It is significant that it was possible to hold the congress in Medellín thanks to the cash grant made by the government to pay the expenses of the delegates.[5] Needless to say, the government expected to be repaid for its kindness. Alberto Lleras, Minister of the Interior, made this clear in a speech on the last day of the congress when he stated that the government favored union organization, but that it was also determined to watch over that organization.[6] The congress, on its side, passed a resolution giving President López unconditional support, but at the same time it elected an executive committee in which the Communists were well represented.[7]

The government supported unionism in the hope of making the labor movement Liberal, while the Communists did everything in their power to retain their hold on an ever-expanding labor movement that was being promoted by the government.

Between August 1936 and January 1938, when the next congress of the Confederación Sindical de Colombia was held in Cali,

4. Montaña Cuéllar distorts this incident (Colombia, país formal, pp. 38–39). The antipopular front forces did not attack the congress. On the contrary, the shootings occurred during Conservative rallies, and the dead were Conservatives (See El Espectador [August 10, 11, 1936]).

5. El Espectador (August 6, 1936).

6. In fact, the government soon passed Decree No. 2342 of 1938 in which it gave the Labor Ministry wide regulatory power over unions. A division of union supervision was created within the Ministry, with the right to inspect unions' financial books and to regulate elections and other activities of the unions. Decree No. 2140 of 1937 regulated the organization of labor congresses.

7. The executive committee included eight Liberals, four Communists, three Socialists, and one anarcho-syndicalist (El Espectador [August 12, 1936]).

the labor movement grew rapidly. As can be seen in Table 1, in 1937 alone, more unions obtained legal recognition than in all the years of Conservative rule, and almost as many unions obtained recognition as in the previous three years. This made the labor congress important from a political point of view since whoever gained control of it could speak in the name of almost 80,000 workers.

The struggle at the congress was also of great significance because of the changes in the Colombian political situation in the previous months. In April 1937 the right wing of the Liberal Party won more seats in the House of Representatives than the López wing of the party. The result was that at the Liberal Party convention Eduardo Santos won the presidential nomination over Darío Echandía, López' Education Minister and the leader of the democratic Left.

In the face of the defeat at the polls of the partisans of the López reforms, and in view of the fact that the House was systematically voting against the projects presented by his administration, President López presented his resignation to Congress in May 1937.[8] Although it was not accepted, and Congress subsequently became more cooperative, it was clear from the elections that the left wing of the Liberal Party was electorally weak, and that a pause in the "Revolution on the March" was politically expedient. On paper, however, the change was not obvious. The programs of Santos and Echandía were similar, and Eduardo Santos clearly was not reactionary. However, many of his political friends and adherents were. Although Santos did not attack the López administration, his backers did.[9]

The labor congress met at a time when it appeared that the Liberal Party was backing away from the "Revolution on the March" of Alfonso López, and this political change was reflected in the conclusions of the congress. The day before the congress

8. "Mensaje de Alfonso López al Senado," *Acción Liberal* (May 31, 1937).

9. *Acción Liberal* (May 1937).

convened, the different political groups met to plan strategies; significantly, two groups of Liberals emerged, one of them comprising a substantial number of delegates "who did not militate in the ranks of the Communist, Socialist, or Liberal left parties."[10] These were clearly the Santistas among the delegates, who considered the Communists and Socialists as much their enemies as the Liberals of the López-Echandía faction. Each group named its committee of organization and propaganda, and it soon became clear that there were serious political divisions among the delegates. In an effort at conciliation, the executive offices of the congress were divided among the adherents of the different political groups, the Liberals getting the presidency and the secretary-generalship. But things were still in the firm control of the Left. In the coordinating committee responsible for nominating a slate of candidates for the election of the executive committee of the confederation, the Socialists were represented by Gerardo Molina, the Communists by Gilberto Vieira, and the outnumbered Liberals by Lázaro Restrepo.[11]

The election of the executive committee, however, reflected the Communist efforts to hold the congress together. A Liberal majority was elected to the executive committee, and the Communist and Socialist leaders contented themselves with creating an "advisory committee" of the confederation with a clear leftist majority. That committee was made up of Regueros Peralta, Gilberto Vieira, Augusto Durán, and Diego Montaña Cuéllar (all Communists), Gerardo Molina, Antonio García, Diego Luis Córdoba (Socialists), Armando Solano, Plinio Mendoza (Liberal Left), and José Umaña Bernal, the only moderate Liberal in the group.

The conclusions of the congress reflected the political division between moderate Liberals and the Left, as well as the predominantly political interests of the delegates. One of the major problems at the congress was a proposition to send greetings and good

10. *El Tiempo* (January 20, 1938). According to this newspaper, owned by Eduardo Santos, some 400 delegates were included in this group.
11. *El Tiempo* (January 25, 1938).

wishes to Eduardo Santos, the Liberal candidate for the Colombian Presidency. The Left, and especially the Socialist group, vetoed the proposition and the Liberal teamsters threatened to walk out because of the incident. On the other hand, one of the conclusions of the congress was "to thank the government party in the name of organized labor, for its support of unions. The Congress also hopes that the government party will continue this policy, by disarming its reactionary elements . . ."[12]

Although in retrospect it appears that this almost exclusive consideration of political problems hurt the labor movement, at the time it seemed to labor that political action was more effective than collective bargaining or any other conventional union tactic. For example, the first conclusion of the Cali congress was: "The Third Union Congress declares that labor organization should work tenaciously against the postulate of labor's political neutrality, *since it has been through politics that the workers have obtained the improved conditions that they enjoy today.*"[13]

Despite the efforts of the Communists to make the congress palatable to the various sectors of political opinion, the Liberal Party, now controlled by more moderate elements, reacted violently. The National Liberal Directorate condemned the antidemocratic politics of the Congress,[14] and formulated a policy of neutrality with respect to the labor movement.[15] This was a far cry from 1935, when the statutes of the party required that in all regional directorates, as well as in the national directorate of the party, one representative of the workers be included[16] and when the Casa Liberal Nacional provided free dental, medical, and legal services to the workers.[17]

12. *El Tiempo* (January 23, 1938).
13. Ibid. (Emphasis added).
14. *El Tiempo* (January 28, 1938).
15. Armando Solano, "El Deber del Partido Liberal ante los Sindicatos," *Acción Liberal* (February 1938).
16. Dionisio Ballesteros, "Conferencia Dictada en la Casa Liberal," *Acción Liberal* (June 1935).
17. "Acción Social del Partido," *Acción Liberal* (June 1935).

The Labor Movement During the Presidency of Eduardo Santos

The delegates at Cali had been right about what to expect from the new executive. The Santos administration did bring a pause in the reform process initiated by Alfonso López and created the conditions for a pause in the growth of union organization, but the labor leaders were partly responsible for the crisis. They had openly opposed Santos, probably overestimating their strength and influence, and the elections had shown that a majority of the Liberal Party desired a pause in the reform process or a "consolidation of past gains," as the new men in power liked to put it. The labor leaders gambled on Echandía and lost.

Quite naturally, Eduardo Santos was not particularly friendly to a labor movement that had opposed him politically. He explicitly recognized the right of association, but went on to say:

> The law on unions has established that they should not intervene in party politics . . . I have viewed with disquiet, made public various times, the fact that the Confederación Sindical de Colombia is directed by people who are in the majority enemies of Liberalism. I do not believe that it is indifferent to the interests of Liberalism, nor that it be innocent to the ends that union organization should seek, that at their heads should be prominent all, absolutely all, the leaders of Colombian Communism and Socialism; politicians who propagandize programs contrary to the principles of the Liberal Party, and who, although they do not belong to the working class, obtain the direction of unions for ends that one must be blind not to understand.[18]

The strained relationship between the government and the unions during the Santos Presidency is reflected in the statistics of the number of unions organized in these years. According to Table 1, it is clear that from 1938 to 1942, during the presi-

18. Quoted in Montaña Cuéllar, *Colombia, país formal,* p. 163.

dential term of Santos, there was a radical decrease in the number of new unions formed and legally recognized. This decline contrasts sharply with the obvious growth of the labor movement during the López administrations that immediately preceded and followed the term of office of Eduardo Santos.[19]

The decline of the labor movement during the Santos administration not only appears obvious now, but was also noticed by careful observers of the national scene at the time. In March 1939 the editors of *Acción Liberal* wrote of "The Ghost of Unionism." Commenting on the fact that in the elections of March 1939 there were no representatives of the workers on the party slates, the editors went on to say:

> Undoubtedly the eclipse of the labor movement in Colombia, its inertia in industrial and political life, its absence from Congress and state assemblies reflects an undoubted reality of today: there now exists nothing but the ghost of a labor movement. According to official statistics, only 167 unions in the country still exist, 391 having disappeared. And of those 167 we believe that only 17 are truly active, distributed among some large enterprises and the transportation sector.

Despite the government's lack of sympathy toward labor, the unions were still convinced that they could survive only with the support of the state. The strongest labor organizations were still in the public services, the sector where strikes were forbidden by law and where the state intervened most directly in collective bargaining. The faith of labor in the protection afforded by the state is well illustrated by the conclusions of the First National Con-

19. Strikes were also few and far between. This was logical since with a neutral administration it was more difficult to win strikes. In the congressional year 1938–39 there were only nine strikes, and in the fifteen months ending in March 1941, only two short strikes took place.

vention of Railroad Workers. At their convention in 1939, when the railroad workers were taking the first steps toward forming an effective national union, they declared themselves in favor of nationalization of railroad and river transport.[20] During the convention, the reason for this position was clarified. The railroad workers envied Fedenal, the federation of river and dock workers, which had obtained a closed shop in a pact sponsored by the government in July 1937. According to that pact, signed by the river unions and the ship owners, the employers could only hire workers belonging to unions affiliated with Fedenal, the federation of river workers' unions. Thus, with government help, the river unions had obtained the dream of any labor organization—the total monopoly of the labor market.

Before the fourth labor congress in 1940, the division between the Left and the moderate Liberals who supported President Santos within the Confederación Sindical de Colombia became official.[21] The German Soviet Pact of August 1939 contributed to the crystallization of the division in CTC. The confrontation between the moderate Liberals, who supported the government's sympathetic relations with the Allies, and the Communists, became more violent as a result of the pact. The Communists, who usually had a party member or fellow traveler in the strategic post of secretary general of the confederation, called a labor congress for December 6, 1940. Since the government had declared its neutrality toward the labor movement, it did not offer to finance this congress from public funds, as had previously been done. This gave the Communists, who were the only labor group with any finances to speak of, control of the congress. In November, about two weeks before the congress was to meet, only 50 of the 500 labor organizations belonging to the confederation had sent

20. *Acción Liberal* (February 1939).
21. Although in 1940 it was already usual to call the confederation CTC (Confederación de Trabajadores de Colombia), the name was not officially changed until the Bucaramanga Congress of 1943, and the Government approved the change of name two months later.

their credentials. To finance the congress, a contribution of five centavos had been levied on all workers belonging to unions affiliated with the confederation, and before the congress opened there were one hundred pesos in the confederation's coffers. The financial situation of the confederation guaranteed that the Communists who could pay their way to Barranquilla, where the congress was to be held, would control the assembly.[22]

The government and the Liberal majority in the CTC were not about to let the Communists get away with holding a congress at which they could speak against the government and its pro-American international policy in the name of more than 84,000 organized workers. Therefore, thirteen members of the executive committee passed a resolution postponing the Fourth Labor Congress.[23] An important group of labor leaders, however, decided not to obey the orders of the executive committee, and attended the Labor Congress of Barranquilla. As was to be expected, the government sided with those who opposed the Barranquilla meeting. It admitted that the meeting was not illegal, since it was protected by the constitutional right of freedom of assembly, but the labor office made it clear that the Barranquilla meeting was not a Labor Congress, since it had not met the requirements imposed by law for the convening of such an assembly. The labor office argued, for example, that it had not received copies of the minutes of the general assemblies in which the unions had elected delegates to the Barranquilla congress.[24] Like most regulations on unions, this one was a dead letter, but it could be revived by the government when it wanted to discourage a given labor attitude.

The labor meeting at Barranquilla was a melancholic affair, at

22. Augusto Durán, who was elected secretary-general of the party at its Fourth Congress, was an important labor leader in Barranquilla and many of the Barranquilla unions were controlled by the Communists.

23. *El Tiempo* (November 16–19, 1940).

24. *El Tiempo* (December 6, 1940). The legislation governing the convening of the labor congress was government Decree No. 2190 of 1937.

which a very small percentage of the nation's unions were represented. On December 10, the day after the Barranquilla meeting closed, the CTC members who had voted for the postponement of the fourth Labor Congress announced a "Great Labor Convention" scheduled to meet in Barrancabermeja with the object of naming a new executive committee of the CTC, in which the Communists, including the previous secretary general, would be excluded. When the Barrancabermeja meeting took place, the head of the labor office was present, and according to some sources he directed the proceedings.

The Second Popular Front

As had happened before, in 1941 the differences within the CTC were patched up because of a change in the international situation of the Soviet Union. On July 22, 1941, Nazi Germany attacked the Soviet Union. Forty days later the Colombian Communist Party held its so-called First Congress, "declared war on the agents of Nazi-Fascism," and called for a revival of the Popular Front and Union Unity.[25]

The impact of the second front in the European war on the Colombian labor movement was felt in the Fifth Congress of the CTC, held in Bogotá in the middle of December 1941. The event was labeled a Union Unity Congress, and it was called together by a coordinating committee of the two executive committees that had emerged from the Barranquilla and Barrancabermeja congresses of 1940. The president of the coordinating committee was the Congressman Carlos Arturo Aguirre, and the Labor Minister spoke in favor of union unity at the first session of the congress.

Labor unity, however, was not easy to achieve. During the deliberations the railroad workers and several other unions almost

---

25. Comité Central del Partido Comunista de Colombia, *Treinta Años*, pp. 55-57.

walked out. The major conflict within the congress was, as often before, the somewhat irrelevant question of the government's international relations. The Communists now contradicted their position of the previous year, and insisted on a greater government commitment to the Allied cause. The Liberals, on the other hand, wanted to continue their policy of support to the Allies, without a declaration of war.

Somehow, however, unity prevailed and the CTC elected a new Comité Confederal of thirty-three members on December 22, 1941. The makeup of the new executive body of CTC is interesting, since the number of representatives from each industrial sector gives an idea of the relative strength of the various unions. As Table 15 shows, in 1941 the labor movement was still essen-

TABLE 15

"Comité Confederal" of the CTC Elected in 1941

Unions	Number of Representatives in Committee	Unions	Number of Representatives in Committee
Railroad workers	3	Textiles	1
Teamsters	3	Communications	1
River and port workers	3	Printing trades	1
Employees	2	Miners	1
Peasants	2	Government workers	1
Construction	2	Food industry	1
Road construction	2	Beer	1
City employees	2	Movies and theaters	1
Tobacco workers	2	Banana workers	1
Coffee and lumber	1	Miscellaneous trades	1
		Cooperatives	1
		Total	33

Source: El Tiempo (December 23, 1941).

182

TABLE 16

Estimates of Union Membership in Colombia

Year	Union Membership	Year	Union Membership
1935	42,678[a]	1942	95,443[b]
1936	45,527[a]	1943	102,023[b]
1939	82,893[b]	1947	165,595[c]
1940	83,877[b]	1959	250,000 ± 50,000[d]
1941	94,190[b]	1965	700,000 ± 100,000[d]

Year	Number of Manufacturing Workers	Percent of Manufacturing Workers Unionized
1945	135,400[e]	23.6[e]
1961	254,179[f]	42.6[g]
1965	281,895[h]	64.4[i]

a. Antonio García, "La Economía Colombiana y el Movimiento Sindical," *Acción Liberal* (February 1937), pp. 55–69 (data for December 1935 and September 1936).

b. Estimates that appear in the *Memoria del Ministerio de Trabajo, Higiene y Previsión Social* for 1939, 1941, 1942, 1943. Figures are for the month of May.

c. Contraloría General de la República, *Primer censo sindical de Colombia, 1947* (Bogotá, Editorial Minerva, 1949). Data for July 1947.

d. Estimates made from union records and other sources. For the method used to arrive at these figures see the Statistical Appendix.

e. Contraloría General de la República, *Primer censo industrial de Colombia, 1945* (Bogotá, Imprenta Nacional, 1947).

f. DANE, *Anuario general de estadística, 1963* (Bogotá, Multilith Estadinal, 1965).

g. ANDI, unpublished survey of unionized workers.

h. Estimated from DANE data.

i. Survey of manufacturing industry; complete results in the Statistical Appendix.

tially controlled by the transport workers. The weakness of the textile workers, the largest group of manufacturing workers in the nation, and of the miners should be noted. The textile workers were Antioqueño women, and among them religious opposition to communism was an important barrier to organization. The miners, with the exception of the oil workers, were not organized because mining in Colombia took place on a small scale, and was scattered among small isolated rural communities.

In August 1942, Alfonso López again occupied the Presidency, and the labor movement started on a second period of rapid growth and development. From Table 1 we see that the number of unions recognized by the government increased from a low of 39 in the last year of Santos' term, to 79 in 1943, 180 in 1944, and 453 in the last year of López' second presidential term. Table 16 also shows the rapid increase in union membership during the second presidential term of Alfonso López, and Table 17 shows estimates of the population, labor force, and proportion of the labor force unionized in 1939, 1947, and 1964.[26]

TABLE 17

Percent of the Labor Force Unionized in Colombia, 1939, 1947, 1964

Year	Population[a]	Labor Force[b]	Percent of Labor Force Unionized[c]
1939	8,886,430	2,945,852	2.7
1947	10,544,670	3,495,558	4.7
1964	17,484,508	5,134,125	12–16

a. DANE, *Anuario general de estadística, 1947,* (Bogotá, Imprenta Nacional, 1950), *XIII censo nacional de población* (Bogotá, Imprenta Nacional, 1967).

b. For 1939 and 1947 the 1951 census participation rates were used because the 1938 census definition makes the data for that year useless. For 1964 the rate from that year's census was used.

c. From Table 16.

26. An explanation of the methodology for these calculations can be found in the Statistical Appendix.

The improved relationship between the government and the labor movement, resulting from labor's unanimous support of the candidacy of Alfonso López and from the international situation which allowed the Communists to support wholeheartedly the pro-Allied international politics of the government, meant that labor unity was viable; the labor congress convened on December 6, 1943, was one of the largest and most peaceful of the CTC's history. It seems that even unions led by Catholic and Conservative elements were present, and more than seven hundred delegates attended the meetings at Bucaramanga.

The opening speeches at the congress were made by Jorge Eliécer Gaitán, then Labor Minister, Guillermo Hernández Rodriguez, representative of the Liberal Party leadership and member of its union organization committee, and the Communist leaders Gilberto Vieira and Regueros Peralta. Vieira emphasized the need for labor to give full and unconditional support to the government.[27] Labor Minister Gaitán stated that the Colombian labor movement lacked revolutionary spirit and expressed surprise that in a country with close to 4,000,000 workers, only 92,000 were union members. As is clear from the quoted statements of Vieira and Gaitán, the popular front was a viable proposition in 1943.

The labor congress ended with the movement still united, when a mixed coordinating committee of Liberals and Communists put together a slate of candidates for the executive committee. This slate, which met no competition, included 19 Liberals and 13 Communists.

The months after the Bucaramanga congress were a period of rapid growth and consolidation of strength for the labor movement. As in the previous López administration, the executive branch fostered and helped the unions. This was also a period of serious political difficulties for President López, difficulties that culminated in the frustrated military coup of July 1944. On that occasion, the immediate reaction of organized labor against

27. *El Espectador* (December 7, 1943).

the attempt to impose military rule helped save the government and strengthened even further the ties between the administration and the labor movement. Out of this growing interdependence between the Liberal government and labor emerged the series of labor measures that culminated in the famous Law 6 of 1945.

This was also a period of close cooperation between the Liberal administration of López and the Communist Party. This guaranteed the political unity of the labor movement, a circumstance that could only strengthen the position of organized labor. A symbol of the understanding between the Communists and López was the presence of Labor Minister Adán Arriaga at the Second Communist Party Congress, as the President's official representative.[28] The campaign for the 1946 presidential election, however, broke both the Liberal Party and the labor movement.

The Presidential Campaign of 1946

Jorge Eliécer Gaitán had started his campaign while in the Labor Ministry by traveling to the Magdalena River, speaking to and informing himself about the plight of the politically strong but economically desperate river workers. (Erosion and road construction were making the river an uneconomical method of transport.) Once Alfonso López resigned from the Presidency late in 1945, Gaitán started his political campaign in earnest. A populist leader, he based his campaign on two slogans: the fight against the oligarchy of the Right and the Left, and the moral restoration of the Republic. The latter slogan coincided with the attacks against immorality and graft in the López government mounted from the editorial room of *El Siglo*, the mouthpiece of the Conservative leader Laureano Gómez.

As in the days of his debates over the Conservative massacre of banana workers in 1928, Gaitán thundered against immorality in the government. But this was the Liberal government of Alfonso

28. Comité Central del Partido Comunista de Colombia, *Treinta Años*, p. 64.

López, and he was fighting against the old Communist of the twenties, Gabriel Turbay, now the moderate and official candidate of the Liberal Party. Gaitán's criticism of López, the man who had brought the Liberal Party to power and the labor movement to life, destroyed party unity.

In order to win the election, Gaitán had to appeal to the masses over the heads of the Liberal Party hierarchy. He had to attack the record of his own party and of the democratic Left in Colombian politics, and yet his ideas were radically opposed to those of the Conservative leaders. He could, therefore, not hope to come to power within the existing political structure or by appealing to the traditional political sentiments of the Colombian voters. He appealed to the most basic belief of the thousands of immigrants who had flowed to the cities to become members of an industrial middle class. This was a population of individualists, who believed that by migrating and starting a new life they could obtain a new status. But after the euphoria of getting an urban salary twice as high as that obtainable in the countryside wore off, there was no economic or social advance in sight. Gaitán, playing on the deep-felt conviction of the possibility of social mobility and individual improvement of the new urban masses, blamed the lack of opportunities on a closed club which monopolized the state and, through it, all wealth. This club he labeled the oligarchy. In the speech launching his presidential campaign, Gaitán developed this theme.

> When in a country the political establishment turns its back on the serious interests of the nation, we can affirm without possibility of error that an oligarchic regime has been established . . . and necessarily shall come that deep putrefaction that hangs over Colombian life, to the great repugnance of its people. It is thus that the ethical concept has crumbled away. . . . What is the future of our children if they continue to live in the present state of affairs? Are you sure that they will progress because of their merit, their

capacity, their studies, or their efforts? No. If our children want progress, they will have to walk in the shade and by a back road, something we do not want for them. They will not get ahead because of hard work, or by being technicians, farmers, or engineers, knowledgeable 'in their professions, but by being vile and servile to the political bosses . . .[29]

Gaitán's populist campaign mobilized the urban masses away from the traditional Liberal Party leadership, while the Communists, who had committed themselves to the popular front with Alfonso López and had done so well under the López regimes, backed Gabriel Turbay. In the unions, as in the rest of Colombian society, a deep conflict emerged. The leadership and the institutional bureaucracy of the democratic Left and of the Communists backed the moderate and official candidate of the Liberal Party, while the rank and file of the unions and the urban workers committed themselves to Jorge Eliécer Gaitán. This conflict came to the surface at the Seventh Labor Congress convened in Bogotá on December 6, 1945.

At the opening of the labor congress, Parmenio Zapata, the influential leader of the road construction workers, announced that the assembly would not deal with any political matters, and that in particular there would be no discussion of the presidential campaign. Unfortunately, the labor movement was completely politically oriented. Political action had been more effective as a tactic than collective bargaining, and therefore the movement was unable to avoid the internal conflict and division that the disintegration of the Liberal Party was bringing upon the nation.

Before the opening addresses, two groups of workers had approached the congress, and to avoid conflict between them, the city had had to take all kinds of police precautions. One group of marchers obviously was Gaitanista; the other favored Turbay.

29. José María Córdoba, *Jorge Eliécer Gaitán* (Bogotá, Litografías Cor-Val), pp. 31–33.

188

The political tensions, symbolized by the two groups of marchers the first day, were soon brought out into the open. The labor congress broke up, and a group broke away from the CTC to found the CNT.

As soon as the delegates met, the Gaitanistas decided to create an independent federation, the Confederación Nacional de Trabajadores (CNT). Gaitán's private secretary had this to say about the creation of the CNT:

> Among the strategic victories which hurt the opposition the most, the decisive victory over the CTC should be singled out . . . It became necessary to use the stratagem of holding a Labor Congress simultaneous with and parallel to that of CTC, made up of the discontented elements that officially participated as delegates in the CTC convention. But since these members did not represent a sufficient number of unions it was decided to make up credentials and distribute them among the members of the city's political committees, to give the impression of having a greater number of delegates than the CTC Congress . . . When Dr. Gaitán found out about these tactics, he was justly annoyed, but soon he understood the logic of weakening the official leadership of CTC, which insisted on fiercely combating the popular wing of Liberalism, calling it fascist and totalitarian, despite the fact that the rank and file backed Gaitán all the way.[30]

While the delegates to the labor congress were gathered in Bogotá in December 1945, Colombian society was passing through a serious crisis. As had happened a century before, it was again becoming divided along class lines, and as in 1852, the reforming bourgeoisie were finding the company of the labor movement somewhat uncomfortable. The leadership of the movement was still loyal, but it was clear that the rank and file had

30. Ibid., pp. 43–44.

defected to the ranks of someone the elite considered a dangerous demagogue. In addition, the sector of the labor movement that was still loyal was not to be trusted. The Communists backed Turbay, but they also violently attacked President Lleras' foreign policy. The reform-minded bourgeoisie who were in the government, therefore, set out to destroy the power of a labor movement over which they had lost control. An editorial concerning the Seventh Labor Congress in the historically prolabor *El Espectador* marks the change of mood.

> The unions have turned their backs on the purpose for which they were created, which is that of bringing about the economic well-being of the workers, and they have dedicated themselves *exclusively* to politics, thus violating legal and constitutional provisions . . . They are thus in danger of losing all that they have gained and all that they have the right and duty of obtaining for their members in the field of better salaries, benefits, etc. . . . None of these ends has been mentioned in the two labor congresses now meeting, while there are already an uncountable number of statements backing one or the other presidential candidate.[31]

The mood of the editors of *El Espectador* was shared by President Alberto Lleras and a large sector of public opinion. Therefore when the Federation of River Workers declared an illegal strike a few days later, President Lleras set out to break the strongest labor union in the nation. This strike was a turning point in the history of the labor movement, since it marked the beginning of the end of the predominantly political orientation of the labor movement. The strike had many causes, but the two most often given at the time were an internal division within the Communist Party, which controlled the Federation, and retaliation of the Communists against Alberto Lleras for his attack on

31. *El Espectador* (December 20, 1945).

190

Molotov at the San Francisco meeting of the United Nations. On the economic side, the wartime and postwar periods were characterized by substantial inflation, and wages usually lagged behind prices.

Since legally the river workers could not call a strike but could settle with the employers only through arbitration, once the strike got under way, President Lleras went on the radio and gave Fedenal an ultimatum. He stated that the union had at no time wished to bargain or reach a settlement,[32] and explained to the nation that, as he saw it, the strike on the river implied a clear choice between a government by the Magdalena River workers or by the constitutional President. Lleras then went on to show to the nation that the labor movement was not as strong and unified as everyone believed. He declared the strike illegal, a measure which allowed Naviera Colombiana, for example, to fire all of its striking workers. Two days after the strike began, 2,000 workers were on the job, and the next day, 2,300 strikebreakers were keeping traffic on the river moving.[33] In addition, the railroad workers backed the government, and freight was moved from Buenaventura to the interior by railroad. The government also transported strikebreakers by airplane to ports where the strike was being successfully carried out.[34]

On December 28, the Liberal majority in the CTC declared that the strike should be terminated. It seems that the Liberal group had been in favor of turning to arbitration for some time, but had not been able to prevail because of the absence of two members of the confederation's executive council.[35] This incident demonstrates how the Communists were usually able to control the CTC, despite the fact that the Liberals had a nominal majority. The Fedenal strike also illustrates the degree to which the labor movement depended on the government's sympathy. Although this was far from the first illegal strike on the river,

32. Ibid. (December 20, 1945).
33. Ibid. (December 21, 1945).
34. Ibid. (December 24, 1945).
35. Ibid. (December 28, 1945)

it was the first in which the government had kept to the letter of the law. When the government gave strikebreakers their constitutional right to work and withdrew the legal protection given to striking workers and the injunction against firing labor leaders, the largest and strongest labor union in the nation was broken in a matter of a few days.

The day before his term ended, President Lleras withdrew the suspension of Fedenal and gave back to the union its legal personality, thus enabling it once again to deal with employers legally and to have the protection that the law affords unions. But it was too late, and Fedenal never recovered from the blow of December 1945.

The CTC Under the Conservative Government

The Conservative victory in the elections of 1946, caused by the Gaitán-Turbay division, was disastrous for the CTC. A few days after Mariano Ospina Pérez was inaugurated, the CTC again became officially divided at its Eighth Labor Congress. Two executive committees emerged from the Medellín gathering, one controlled by the Communists and the other by the Liberals. As often before, the Communists obtained control of the credentials committee, and through the largely mythical Communist agrarian unions, they had a majority of delegates. Thus when the congress became divided, the Liberals elected an executive committee with slightly less than 50 percent of the original 552 delegates to the labor congress participating, and the remaining delegates elected a Communist executive committee.

As it is often the case when serious conflict erupts within the labor movement, labor-management relations deteriorated seriously in the following months. There were frequent strikes, and the Liberals and Communists tried to outdo each other in militancy and demands. In October 1946, the Communists called out the oil workers to what turned out to be the longest large-scale industrial strike that the nation had ever experienced. The walkout of the oil workers led to violent strikes by Liberal teamsters in Bogotá, Cali, and other areas. These strikes gave President Ospina the excuse to declare, for the first time during his administration, a state of emergency.

Between the Medellín Labor Congress of August 1946 and the Ninth Labor Congress at Cali in December 1947, the labor movement continued to fall apart. Like many institutions in decline, the labor movement overestimated its power, and it continuously carried out actions that could only weaken it further. A case in point was the general strike organized by the CTC for May 13, 1947. Although ostensibly the strike was a protest against the high cost of living and against government persecution of unions, its real purpose was to cause a crisis of sufficient proportions to topple the government of President Mariano Ospina Pérez. The strike, however, was a complete failure and helped to bring the CTC into disrepute.

The general strike and the growing hostility of CTC toward the government elicited a response from those in power. The Labor Ministry began to be less complacent toward labor, and the government started to undermine the unions. The net result of this mutual hostility was a deterioration in labor-management relations and in the relations between the organized labor movement and the state. The division within the Communist Party also helped to deteriorate the relations between labor and the other sectors of society. While during the second López administration the Communist Party had obtained 27,000 votes in congressional elections, and had gotten its two most important officers elected to the Senate and the House, in the elections of March 1947, the party barely elected one man to the Cundinamarca state legislature. As a result of losing its popular electoral base, in part because of the mistake of not having backed Gaitán in the 1946 elections, there was a crisis and a change of line in the party. At a July 1947 congress of the party, Augusto Durán, the secretary general, was ousted and replaced by the intellectual Gilberto Vieira.

Actually, as usually happened at the CTC congresses, two factions emerged from the Fifth Communist Party Congress. One group, led by Durán, formed a new party, which included some important labor leaders, but this group did not prosper. The Communist Party under Vieira survived, but it never recovered any true mass support. The decline of the Communist Party and its internal conflict, however, were ultimately very harmful to the old CTC.

Less than two years after the Conservatives came to power, the political structure of Colombia was suddenly and radically changed. On April 9, 1948, during the Panamerican Conference and while General Marshall and all the foreign ministers of the American continent were in Bogotá, a fanatic shot and killed Jorge Eliécer Gaitán, as he left his office in the center of town.

For months the cost of living had been rising. In the last quarter of 1945, the cost of living index for Bogotá had stood at 152, and in the second quarter of 1948 it stood at 236. The wages of industrial workers had barely kept up with the increase in prices. There had been political murders in the countryside, caused by the change to a Conservative government, and the verbal and editorial violence between the parties and between different factions within the parties had reached incredible proportions. In this atmosphere of hatred and discontent, the murder of Gaitán was catastrophic. In a matter of hours, looting mobs controlled the city. Churches were sacked and burned.[36] The Conservative paper *El Siglo* was dynamited, and the presidential palace was attacked by angry mobs. On the evening of April 9, the police had gone over to the rebels' side, and the city was in flames. To make things worse, the CTC had called a general strike, and the deeply Gaitanista laboring masses had joined the stoppage. The nation

36. Benjamín Haddox explains the attack on the churches as caused by the traditional identification between the Catholic Church in Colombia and the Conservative party. Benjamín Haddox, *Sociedad y religión en Colombia* (Bogotá, Tercer Mundo, 1965), p. 159.

194

was paralyzed, but President Ospina remained at the presidential palace and refused to resign.

A new coalition government was formed between Ospina and Echandía, a former López minister and presidential candidate of the Liberal Left. Echandía went on the radio and spoke in the name of Gaitán, pleading with the unions to bring their people back to work. After a few days, troops brought in from the provinces had restored order in Bogotá. Being constantly on the brink of class war or revolution, however, is not compatible with democracy.

Although Colombia's democratic institutions survived the April days, they did not survive for long. When the Congress tried to impeach President Ospina in November 1949, he declared a state of siege and the dissolution of Congress for an indefinite term.[37] There followed a ten-year state of siege period, during which the government could legislate by decree, restrict the right of assembly, censor the press, and make arbitrary arrests. During those ten years, the labor movement regressed to the conditions of the 1920s. When democracy was restored in 1958 and the Liberal government of Alberto Lleras decided to give protection to labor again, CTC membership had been reduced to twenty-seven unions.[38]

The only CTC labor congress held after 1948 was the Congreso Obrero that took place in May 1950. As in the previous three years, in 1950 there were no May Day parades, since the state of siege provisions of the government did not allow mass meetings. The Tenth Labor Congress was therefore a working session in which the major problem, in the face of the disintegration of the Colombian labor movement, was with which world labor body the CTC should be affiliated.

A few days before the congress, the National Liberal Directorate ordered the Liberal Labor leadership to take the CTC out

37. Fluharty, *Dance of the Millions,* pp. 100–17.
38. CTC, "Informe de Actividades, Abril 1963–1965," *XIV Congreso Nacional del Trabajo* (Tipografía Portilla, 1965)

of the Communist-dominated Confederación de Trabajadores de America Latina (CTAL), and join the International Confederation of Free Trade Unions (ICFTU). The Liberal leadership had been frightened by the Communist activity in the April 1948 uprising, and as an opposition party it had to have more discipline and cohesion than as the party in power. These were some of the reasons for requiring the break with the Communists within the CTC, but the change in the cold war situation was also a powerful incentive. The National Liberal Directorate stated this explicitly to the Liberal labor leaders: "In the conflict of political tendencies that characterizes international life at present, the Liberal Party places itself unequivocally and without vacillation at the side of those who defend political democracy: the democratic government of the United States and the labor government of Great Britain."[39] The Liberal labor leaders obeyed their party, and insisted on taking the CTC out of CTAL. The result was a final break into two confederations, one Communist and the other Liberal. The vote on the CTAL question was 178 in favor of retiring from CTAL and 141 in favor of staying, thus showing once again the extent of Communist strength in the old CTC.

The expulsion of the Communists from the CTC occurred at a time when the cold war situation required the pro-American Liberal Party to break once and for all with its former allies among the Communist labor leadership. As had happened so often before, the international situation and Liberal Party electoral strategy determined CTC policy. For if the future of the labor movement had been the major consideration, 1950 would have been the worst possible time to create a division within the movement, since at that time organized labor was fighting for its very life.

The End of Political Bargaining

During the Liberal governments of Alfonso López, the strength of the CTC had depended on the fact that the executive branch

39. *Semana* (May 6, 1950).

needed labor support against the threat of a rightist military coup; furthermore, the government was ideologically committed to intervening in industrial conflicts in favor of labor. When the Conservative Party came to power, however, it became clear to labor that the political tactic of supporting the government in return for its intervention in collective bargaining was no longer useful, since the intervention of Conservatives was not likely to favor labor. The CTC tried to adapt itself to the new situation. Accustomed to political bargaining, it did not take advantage of the new conditions created by Law 6 of 1945, but instead tried to adopt the tactics of political bargaining described by Payne for Peru, i.e. the CTC attempted to become a threat to the Conservative government.

The Conservative government had been elected by a minority, only because the Liberal Party had become divided. The CTC leaders reasoned, therefore, that the Conservative regime could be easily threatened, since it could not feel securely in power. Working under this assumption, the CTC began systematically to threaten the government with mass uprisings if the government did not solve problems in the way the CTC desired. Having adopted this new tactic of becoming a political threat instead of a mobilizer of mass support for the government in power, the CTC began to use the weapon of the general strike with greater frequency.

While on May 15, 1944, the CTC had called a general strike in support of President López, in 1947 the CTC called a general strike that had as a purpose "the replacement of the national government."[40] But the CTC was less powerful than its leaders believed and the constitutional government of Mariano Ospina much more secure than the Liberals believed. The general strike was a failure, and public opinion approved Ospina's action of canceling the confederation's legal recognition. Instead of creating a crisis that would topple the government, the CTC strengthened it by

40. *Semana* (May 17, 1947).

demonstrating the weakness of the opposition. The CTC called a second general strike in April 1948, after Gaitán's assassination, but again the Conservative government survived. The CTC and the Liberal directorate called a third political general strike in September 1949, and a general strike in protest against the election of Laureano Gómez two months later, and these too were failures. By 1950, it was clear that the CTC could not be a threat to the Conservative government and that the period of labor's political bargaining was at an end.

Part IV

The Development of Collective Bargaining

12

Political Repression and the Emergence of the UTC

In the same way that the history of the CTC before 1950 provided a framework for the study of the period of political bargaining, the history of the UTC, the Catholic labor confederation, coincides with the emergence of peaceful collective bargaining in Colombia. The Union de Trabajadores de Colombia (UTC) was founded in June 1946, after Law 6 of 1945 had created the necessary conditions for the emergence of a labor movement oriented toward peaceful collective bargaining. But the incentive for the creation of the UTC was not the establishment of institutional conditions that favored a new type of unionism. The creation of the UTC was an attempt by the Catholic Church to counteract the growing influence of communism among the working classes.

As early as 1923, the Catholic Church of Colombia, under pressure from Rome, attempted to counteract communist and socialist influence among the workers by setting up unions and mutual benefit societies of workers under Church auspices. In May of that year, Monsignor Vicentini called together a group of prominent clergymen and Conservative politicians at the Palace of the Papal Nuncio, to organize the Acción Social Católica in Colombia. At that meeting, the Nuncio expounded the necessity, as an imperative of social justice and Christian charity, of trying to improve by practical means the living conditions of the workers. He finished by saying, "The coming battle between capital and labor will be terrible and destructive, if it is based on the misery in which presently live the majority of our people; it is therefore necessary to try to improve the economic situation of the people and this is the purpose of the *acción social católica.*"[1]

Even before this, however, some isolated priests had worked in the field of labor organization. The Círculo de Obreros, a mutual benefit society organized by Father Campoamor, S.J., was already a well established organization. The nature of the relations between Church and state, however, made the social work of the Church among the proletariat very difficult, since during the Conservative government of the first quarter of the century the Church and the state seemed to be completely dependent on each other. This relationship was best illustrated by the presidential campaign of 1930, when the candidacy of the Conservative Party hinged on the approval of the Archbishop of Bogotá. The unity between the Catholic Church and the Conservative Party also became public on each election day. There was usually a voting table for the clergy, and the published electoral return of the table must have been a thorn in the flesh of the Liberals. For example, in the elections of October 1921, in Bogotá, the vote of the clergy was 165 for the Conservatives and none for the Liberals.[2]

The alliance between the Church and the Conservative Party was a serious handicap for the churchmen trying to work with the proletariat, since most of the workers were Liberals and the Conservative government considered labor organizations both dangerous and undesirable. For these reasons, the Church was unable to prosper in its anticommunist campaign among workers throughout the first half of the twentieth century. In the 1930s, Monsignor Juan Manuel González and Dr. Murcia organized the Catholic Workers Youth Movement (JOC), which was a powerful youth

1. *El Espectador* (May 21, 1923).
2. *El Espectador* (October 3, 1921).

movement at the time in France and Italy, where it had some fascist overtones. This movement failed because of insufficient lay leadership and excessive Church intervention,[3] and because of Monsignor González' violent political conflict with the Liberal regime in power at the time.

TABLE 18

Nationally Federated Unions in 1939

	Total Number of Unions	Unions Federated to CTC	Catholic Unions*	Not Federated
Agriculture	153	42	48	63
Extractive industry	15	5	4	6
Manufacturing	147	66	11	70
Building	27	19	2	6
Transport	105	62	3	40
Commerce	44	12	1	31
Private service	31	8	4	19
Public service	49	10	—	39
Total	571	224	73	274

*Federated to Acción Católica Colombiana (ACC).

Source: Contraloría General de la República, *Anuario general de estadística, 1939* (Bogotá, Imprenta Nacional, 1940), p. 233.

By 1939, however, there were some Catholic unions in Colombia, most of them in the countryside. These unions belonged to what is today FANAL (Federación Agraria Nacional), the only important federation of agricultural workers. In Table 18 it is possible to compare the relative strength of the CTC and the Catholic unions in 1939. It is interesting to note that only in the Conservative countryside could the Catholic labor organizations prosper. In time, however, the constant fighting within the CTC,

3. Notes on union history by Manuel Recio, adviser to UTC (Archives of UTC).

the Communist domination of that confederation, and its preponderant concern with international power politics, robbed the CTC of support and favored the efforts of the Catholic Church to channel the energies of the proletariat away from that confederation.

Many of the workers in the large enterprise unions wanted to have nothing to do with political strikes. They were only interested in bread-and-butter issues. Furthermore, in 1946 the CTC did not back Gaitán, who was much more popular among the workers than Turbay. This explains why one of the chief officers of Gaitán's CNT wrote a form letter inviting the members of the old CNT to be present at the founding congress of the Catholic UTC. According to him, the new labor body would continue the job started by the Gaitanista CNT, i.e. "the salvation of the labor movement through the unification of the workers."[4] This unity was to be achieved by divorcing the Unión Nacional de Trabajadores (sic) from political partisanship and *caudillismo*.

The Founding of the UTC

The archives of the UTC make it possible to study the characteristics of the unions that decided to form the confederation. In the first place, the First Congress of the UTC was dominated numerically by the representatives from Antioquia, the most industrialized state in the nation and, at the same time, the area where the Catholic Church has traditionally been strongest and most influential. The unions from Antioquia that joined the UTC did not represent the transport or craft workers, which were the ones that had first organized in that state and the rest of the nation, but represented the industrial workers of the large factories around Medellín. Among the unions represented were those of the great textile companies such as Coltejer, El Hato, Vicuña, Rosellón, Indulana, and Alicachín.

4. Letter of Luis Angel Bunguero, *fiscal* of the CNT, to former members of CNT (Archives of UTC Founding Congress).

TABLE 19

Percentage Distribution of Unions by State

States	1965[a]	1947[b]	1942[b]	1939[b]
Antioquia	13.1	9.4	4.1	9.7
Atlántico	8.4	9.2	7.8	5.8
Bolivar	3.9	5.7	6.6	5.2
Boyacá	9.2	4.4	2.0	1.9
Caldas	7.8	7.9	9.5	7.1
Cauca	1.0	1.8	4.8	4.6
Córdoba	0.8	—	—	—
Cundinamarca	18.7	28.9	26.7	29.4
Chocó	0.3	—	—	—
Huila	1.1	0.9	1.8	2.7
Magdalena	3.7	3.1	9.1	7.1
Meta	1.8	—	—	—
Nariño	2.5	3.3	3.0	2.1
Norte de Santander	3.0	2.9	3.7	3.8
Santander	7.2	4.8	5.4	4.4
Tolima	2.0	5.7	6.0	6.1
Valle	15.2	10.4	9.5	10.1
Intendencias y Comisarias	0.3	1.6	—	—
Total	100	100	100	100

a. Since the statistics on unions include active and inactive unions, we used the statistics on the number of union executive committees approved by the state. Since union officers get job security if they obtain official approval, the number of executive committees approved should coincide with the number of active unions.

b. Data for active unions. In 1942 and 1939, it is not clear whether the reference is to active unions, but it appears to be so.

Sources: Ministerio del Trabajo, *Memoria al Congreso Nacional,* 1965; Contraloría General de la República, *Primer censo sindical de Colombia, 1947* (Bogotá, Editorial Minerva, 1949); Ministerio del Trabajo, Higiene y Previsión Social, *Memoria, 1939, 1942.*

This fact made the new confederation radically different from the CTC, since the politically oriented CTC had drawn its strength from the large mass unions of the transport workers, construction workers, and public service workers. The CTC could offer the government the support of large mass organizations in return for favorable state intervention in labor-management conflict, but neither the CTC nor the political parties had had any use for the small unions of manufacturing workers.

Political bargaining determined the distribution of strength within the labor movement. In 1941 there were 11,767 union members in manufacturing industry, 11,656 union members in the smaller public services sector, and 30,217 in the unions of the transportation sector. Political bargaining also determined the geographical concentration of the labor movement around Bogotá, the seat of the federal government. Thus in 1941 there were almost nine times as many union members in the manufacturing industry of Cundinamarca, where the Colombian capital is located, as in the manufacturing industry of Antioquia. And yet there were almost 40 percent more manufacturing blue-collar workers in Antioquia than in Cundinamarca.[5] The CTC was therefore not organizing the manufacturing workers, who were the largest reserve of potential union members in the country. Tables 19 and 20 show that before 1946, when the UTC was created, manufacturing workers were not well organized and the labor movement was losing ground in Antioquia, the most dynamic industrial state in the nation.[6]

When the Catholic Church started to organize a nonpolitical, economically oriented labor movement to counteract the leftist

5. Ospina Vásquez, *Industria, p. 499.* Figures for manufacturing workers by state from the Industrial Census of 1945.

6. According to the report of the Labor Minister to Congress in 1941, the labor movement in Antioquia was actually losing ground at that time (see *Memoria del Ministro de Trabajo y Previsión Social, 1941,* p. 44 and Table 18).

and political CTC, the manufacturing unions and the large masses of Catholic Antioquia joined gladly. The UTC philosophy was just what the manufacturing workers needed. By August 1946, the Catholic labor movement in Antioquia had had substantial success. During the CTC congress in Medellín in that month, UTRAN, the regional federation in Antioquia that helped create the UTC, made its presence felt. It had by then as much or more strength than the CTC unions of Antioquia.[7]

One of the major attractions of the UTC was that it avoided politics. This emerges very clearly from its archives and contradicts the generally held notion that the UTC was created by the Conservative government to neutralize the Liberal CTC.[8] In the documents pertaining to its founding congress, it is clear that although the UTC was formed on the initiative of the Catholic Church,[9] it explicitly rejected any political commitments. At that time, as now, many UTC leaders were Liberals, and some of the clerical moral advisers were also Liberals. One of the founders of the UTC was Eugenio Colorado, now a Liberal Congressman. Table 22 shows the political affiliations of a sample of UTC leaders. The top hierarchy of the confederation includes men who have been with UTC since its founding. As is clear from that table, the Conservatives are in a minority among the UTC leadership.

7. They claimed 30 unions and 12,000 members to CTC's 31 unions and 7,953 members in 1947. Although the UTRAN claim is probably inflated, it appears that the UTC and the CTC had about equal strength in Antioquia by 1947.

8. The belief that the UTC was a Conservative creation is almost universal in Colombia. It is an idea that up to a few years ago was a commonplace in the Liberal press (see *El Tiempo* [September 23, 1949], and *Semana* [January 31, 1955], p. 14). This same myth is supported by most authors who have written about the labor movement, including the following: Fluharty, *Dance of the Millions*, pp. 245–46; Montaña Cuéllar, *Colombia, pais formal*, p. 188; Almarales and Goenaga, *La luchas obreras*, p. 81.

9. Many of the credentials accrediting delegates to the founding congress were signed by parish priests (Archives of UTC).

TABLE 20

Number of Unions and Union Members in Colombia by State and Industrial Sector, 1942

State	Agriculture		Mining		Manufacturing		Construction		Transport and Communications	
	Unions	Union Members	Unions	Union Members	Unions	Union Members	Unions	Union Members	Unions	Union Members
Antioquia	9	2,734	3	861	5	445	1	50	9	3,327
Atlántico	9	812	—	—	12	2,866	3	666	23	5,903
Bolívar	9	1,384	1	145	5	237	3	250	20	2,513
Boyacá	7	1,311	—	—	3	374	1	133	3	593
Caldas	18	1,271	1	122	9	404	10	853	17	1,224
Cauca	18	2,055	1	305	5	220	6	461	3	212
Cundinamarca	61	10,075	15	1,241	39	3,886	17	1,031	26	7,330
Huila	5	159	—	—	2	53	6	300	—	—
Magdalena	41	2,852	1	25	6	590	8	550	7	1,080
Nariño	—	—	—	—	8	465	2	297	4	743
Norte de Santander	5	614	2	653	5	329	3	302	4	698
Santander	13	1,148	—	—	10	489	6	1,026	6	817
Tolima	28	1,828	—	—	3	176	3	150	7	956
Valle	14	1,121	1	35	13	1,233	6	901	17	4,821
Total	237	27,364	25	3,387	125	11,767	75	6,970	146	30,217

State	Commerce		Services		Public and Government Services		Total	
	Unions	Union Members	Unions	Union Members	Unions	Union Members	Unions	Union Members
Antioquia	3	348	3	62	—	—	33	7,827
Atlántico	8	651	1	44	7	408	63	11,350
Bolívar	3	732	3	189	9	1,708	53	7,158
Boyacá	—	—	—	—	2	69	16	2,480
Caldas	7	420	11	526	4	303	77	5,123
Cauca	2	357	3	64	1	84	39	3,758
Cundinamarca	20	1,580	15	2,286	23	4,534	216	31,963
Huila	—	—	1	42	1	73	15	627
Magdalena	1	30	3	180	7	568	74	5,875
Nariño	2	155	1	32	7	1,821	24	3,513
Norte de Santander	2	350	3	51	6	708	30	3,705
Santander	4	195	4	431	1	450	44	4,556
Tolima	3	271	5	166	—	—	49	3,547
Valle	11	917	6	583	8	930	76	10,541
Total	66	6,006	59	4,656	76	11,656	809	102,023

Source: Anuario general de estadística, 1942 (Bogotá, Imprenta Nacional, 1944).

TABLE 21

Number of Catholic and Non-Catholic Unions by State, December 31, 1939

| States | Unions Affiliated to a National Federation | | | | Not Affiliated | | Total | |
| | Catholic Unions[a] | | CTC[b] | | | | | |
	Unions	Union Members	Unions	Union Members	Unions	Union Members	Unions	Union Members
Antioquia	14	2,175	19	4,328	16	2,220	49	8,723
Atlántico	—	—	23	7,016	32	3,030	55	10,066
Bolívar	—	—	17	2,113	9	1,508	26	3,621
Boyacá	1	62	7	767	2	109	10	938
Caldas	—	173	14	803	21	1,921	36	2,897
Cauca	—	—	7	663	14	741	21	1,404
Cundinamarca	39	5,873	60	13,187	91	9,217	190	28,277
Huila	1	44	4	159	4	169	9	372
Magdalena	—	—	4	272	23	1,111	27	1,383
Nariño	2	125	4	440	8	641	14	1,206
Norte de Santander	5	924	10	1,432	7	1,003	22	3,359
Santander	4	810	16	1,421	3	184	23	2,415
Tolima	3	116	15	1,764	24	1,709	42	3,589
Valle	3	213	23	6,224	18	1,423	44	7,860
Intendencias y comisarias	1	—	1	50	2	134	3	184
Total	73	10,515	224	40,639	274	25,120	571	76,274

a. ACC: Catholic Social Action.
b. CTC: Confederation of Colombian Workers.

Source: Contraloría General de la República, *Anuario general de estadística, 1939* (Bogotá, Imprenta Nacional, 1940).

TABLE 22

Political Affiliations of UTC Leaders

	High Officials	Middle Rank Officials
Liberals	8	5
Conservatives	5	2
Christian Democrats	1	—
No political affiliation	1	2
No answer	1	2

Source: Special survey of two groups of UTC leaders.

But the most important thing about the UTC is that from the beginning there has never been political discrimination within its ranks. In the platform that was adopted when the UTC was created, the following statement is prominent: "It is the firm determination of this confederation not to permit itself to become a political force, at the service of groups, or persons . . . For this reason, it invites all Colombian workers to join its ranks . . ." In fact, workers of all political affiliations did join the UTC, since it chose to abandon the tactic of political bargaining.[10] The affiliated unions only engaged in collective bargaining, and the UTC dedicated itself to solving the economic problems of its members. The confederation's refusal to enter politics also helped it to remain united. It has not had any major division within its ranks in the twenty years since it was founded.

The UTC and the Political Parties

The philosophy behind the creation of the UTC determined to a large extent the structure of the new confederation. Article 3 of its statutes, approved by the founding congress on June 12, 1946, stated:

10. Tulio Cuevas, the present president, is a former Socialist, and Manuel Vélez Castilla, the secretary of organization, is a former Communist.

211

> The Confederation shall adopt as the fundamental basis for its struggle, the principles of Catholic Social Doctrine, as taught by the Popes. The Confederation shall inspire and orient its campaigns according to these doctrines, and within the law.

Since the papal encyclicals emphasize peaceful labor-management relations and reject the Marxist concepts of class war and the inevitable opposition of class interests, the UTC limited its action from the start to the tactic of peaceful collective bargaining, since political bargaining is based on the use of limited violence and illegal pressure. This dependence on collective bargaining also meant that the UTC could not enter the arena of partisan politics, since partisan politics inevitably create divisions within the unions, and such divisions can only harm the process of economic collective bargaining, a tactic that demands control of the labor market and union solidarity.

In general political scientists have found that the degree of cohesiveness within voluntary associations varies inversely with the universality of the goals of the association. Thus it is easier to achieve consensus if the association, in this case a union, is dedicated only to improving the economic conditions of its members, than if it attempts to take action in the political and social fields as well as in the economic field. The political neutrality of the UTC allowed it to develop without any serious internal conflicts, since laborers could usually agree on limited economic goals. In fact, the only serious crises within the UTC have developed when its leadership has become involved in politics. But up to 1966 these crises have always been solved by the expulsion of the leaders who have entered politics.[11]

11. At the end of the dictatorship of Rojas Pinilla, Tulio Cuevas, now president of the UTC, collaborated with the dictatorship and was expelled from the UTC for this. Being a bright, dynamic leader, he was reinstated a few years later.

This was the case in 1952, when the Fourth Labor Congress expelled Victor M. Duarte, president of the UTC, for his attacks on the leadership of the UTC and on the moral adviser of the confederation, the Jesuit Vicente Andrade Valderrama. The conflict between Duarte and the other members of the executive committee was caused by his political statements in favor of the Conservative government of the time. In the paper *El Nacional*, founded by the Conservative politican Gilberto Alzate Avendaño, Duarte had attacked the UTC in the following terms: "It is understood that the UTC is being run arbitrarily, and with a partisan concept, by the present Moral Adviser, who has shown signs of being an enemy of the government and of the Conservative Party."[12]

The executive committee of the UTC was particularly perturbed at the attempts of Duarte to put the confederation at the service of the Conservative Party, as the CTC had previously been put at the service of the Liberal Party. In April Duarte had stated to the press that the UTC was Conservative[13] and in August he and three other executives of the UTC published the following resolution:[14]

> That the UTC is being turned into an enemy of the Christian and rightist labor movement, and against the government of Laureano Gómez and the government party, to which the majority of the members of UTC are affiliated . . . We resolve, therefore, to congratulate President Laureano Gómez for the happy culmination of his first year in the government, during which the Colombian people and the working class in particular have been favored by his wise administration.

The Duarte incident illustrates the political posture of the UTC during the difficult years after 1949. Its relationship with the

12. *Eco Nacional* (May 15, 1951).
13. *El Siglo* (April 4, 1951).
14. *Eco Nacional* (August 11, 1951).

government was not unfriendly, but the confederation did not commit itself to any political party or group. The UTC has tried to maintain this policy, although of late it is being forced by the rank and file to enter politics in a more important way. In the presidential elections of 1966, the UTC did not back any candidates until they had made known their platform, and at its congress in December 1965, it presented the political parties with a minimum program to which they had to commit themselves in order to obtain the backing of UTC. The candidate of the National Front did attempt to please UTC by declaring his agreement with its program, and some of the leaders of the confederation were placed on the congressional slate of the National Front. Only after this did the UTC officially back the candidacy of Carlos Lleras. The CTC, on the other hand, backed Lleras before he officially declared his candidacy and before he proposed a political program.

The objective study of the development of the Unión de Trabajadores de Colombia (UTC) leads to the conclusion that the new Catholic confederation founded in 1946 was not the Conservative answer to CTC, as most authors have asserted, but was a labor federation based on principles radically different from those on which CTC was built, i.e. (1) the belief in the effectiveness of peaceful collective bargaining as a means of achieving improvements in the economic conditions of the workers; (2) a rejection of political bargaining and political partisanship on the part of the confederation; (3) the creation of economically sound unions that would use the strike to achieve limited economic objectives, and only when no other alternative was available.

The Structure of the UTC

Since the UTC was committed to collective bargaining, it could not have functioned had it adopted an extremely federalist structure similar to that of the CTC. From the start, the UTC became an organization dedicated to providing collective bargaining services. Since the level of education of the average Colombian worker is low, and labor legislation establishes rather complicated bargaining procedures, collective bargaining could not emerge without a specialized group of labor union officials dedicated to helping local unions in the process of bargaining with employers. The UTC and its state labor federations have provided this service. But since this is a service that costs money, the confederation insisted from the start on having a sound financial basis. At first it was helped financially by the Catholic Church, but in time it began to function with the support of the affiliated unions. This development is surprising in Latin America, where one of the trademarks of the labor movement is that union members do not pay dues.

TABLE 23

UTC Income and Its Sources

	Income	Dues as Per- cent of Income	Church Con- tribution as Per- cent of Income	Other Sources
Jan. 1952–Jan. 1954	P 87,193.86	21	n.a.	n.a.
Feb. 1954–June 1956	136,581.38	27	n.a.	n.a.
July 1956–June 1958	280,674.84	34	8	58[a]
July 1958–Dec. 1960	572,977.88	32	5	n.a.
Jan. 1961–Sept. 1963	830,899.70	58	4	38[b]

n.a.: not available

a. Net contribution from ORIT-ICFTU (the Organización Regional Interamericana de Trabajadores and the International Confederation of Free Trade Unions), 15 percent; government contribution for the Sixth Congress, 7 percent; building quota, 8 percent; advertisement in UTC newspaper, 10 percent; loans, 13 percent; and other minor sources of income.

b. Net contribution from ORIT-ICFTU, 8 percent; advertising in newspaper, 16 percent; union lottery and building rents, 10 percent.

Source: Informes del comité ejecutivo, 1954–63 (Archives of the UTC).

215

Before 1950, the CTC was never able to collect dues, and its leadership survived on donations from the Liberal and Communist parties. At present, the CTC finances are still far inferior to those of the UTC. Table 23 traces the development of UTC finances. Although the UTC has been able to collect dues, in the thirty-three months between January 1, 1961, and September 30, 1963, it appears that less than 54,000 workers paid their ten-centavo monthly dues regularly. At that time there were at least three or four times that number of workers nominally affiliated with the UTC.

Once the UTC and its state federations took on the job of carrying out negotiations for member unions, it became necessary for the confederation to become centralized and to have some control over whether unions should strike or not. Article 5 of the statutes approved at the founding congress covered this point: "Affiliated unions have the obligation of allowing the executive committee, through the state federations, to intervene in the solution of labor-management conflicts, and the union must obey the decisions made by the committee in these cases."

Since the UTC has never been able to amass a strike fund, its power over the affiliated unions remains one of persuasion, but its persuasive potential is substantial, since it can mobilize some solidarity funds when it has approved a given strike of conflict. At the present time, the UTC and its state federations are able to pay part of the wages of strikers in affiliated unions,[15] and this has made affiliation with the UTC very valuable and has enhanced the power of the federations over the individual enterprise unions. In a sense, the institutionalized solidarity contribution of unions to the state federations for the support of strikes of affiliated unions has been the equivalent of a strike fund.

The atomization of the Colombian labor movement, resulting from the prevalence of the enterprise union, and the growing

15. For example, during the *Alotero* strike, which lasted more than 70 days, 70 percent of the salaries of the workers were paid throughout the strike.

ability of the state federations to mobilize solidarity funds have made these state federations the most important part of the labor movement. These federations are now carrying on a substantial part of the collective bargaining for enterprise unions, with a group of full-time labor officers who have risen from the ranks of the proletariat; their power over the local unions has increased in proportion to the growing ability of the regional federations to provide financial support to striking unions which have been advised by federation officials.

The importance of the state federations, federations of diverse enteprise unions in a given state, has been determined by the structure of the labor movement. Since there are no national craft unions or industrial unions, the existing enterprise unions only require the services of bureaucrats who know the legal procedures for bargaining and who have access to the various local labor courts, local Labor Ministry officers, and state officials. Thus a local or state federation is able to provide the best collective bargaining services, since its officials are well equipped to deal with the collective bargaining problems of the enterprise union, and are close to the problems of all the unions in a certain area.

There are, however, some industrial sectors where the structure of the product market is competitive and where the enterprise union is therefore an inefficient bargaining unit. This is true, for example, of the restaurant and hotel workers. This is a competitive industry, characterized by easy entry and a large number of firms, and requiring relatively unskilled workers. Under these circumstances, the enterprise union cannot be effective, since increasing wages above the market rate may mean the ruin of an enterprise and unemployment for its workers. In this sector, probably the first national union in Colombia has emerged. FENALTHYS (the Federación de Trabajadores de la Industria Gastronómica Hotelera y Similares de Colombia) has attempted to organize all the hotel workers in the country, has helped to establish government sponsored courses to train hotel workers in the hope of making them harder to replace, has established a central strike fund, and bargains for all its members. It appears then that where there is competition in the product market, the national industrial union has replaced the unspecialized state federation as the bargaining agent.

Nevertheless, the state federations are still strong. In the early days of the labor movement they were strong because of their political position. Voting in Colombia takes place at the state level, and mayors are appointed by state officials. The natural political unit for the labor movement was therefore the state federation. These federations could also mobilize large masses of workers in support of the government or a political party, and they could organize mass demonstrations more easily than could a national federation. Once the enterprise unions dedicated to collective bargaining emerged, they strengthened the already existing state federations.

The traditional strength of the state federations has also had very important effects on the internal politics of the national confederations. The existence of these state federations, with more power than the national confederation at the local level, has been the source of a substantial degree of union democracy at the national level. The national confederation cannot survive if it does not give representation to the state federations. Thus to keep the national movement united, the executive posts within the national confederation have to be rotated. This is what happened in the UTC. For example, in the nine executive committees of the UTC between 1946 and 1965, the post of *fiscal,* one of the most important officers of the confederation and a member of the executive committee, was held by nine different persons. The post of secretary-general was held by three people, and that of president by seven. The office of first vice-president, also a major post in the confederation, was held by seven different persons. In 1965, the election of the executive committee of the UTC created a crisis because the post of secretary-general was not given to the powerful Cundinamarca state federation. The election, which was very close, showed the high degree of democracy within the UTC, a phenomenon made possible by the existence of powerful state federations that are to a substantial degree independent of the national organization.

Political Repression and the UTC

The above description of the structure and philosophy of the UTC has made it clear that the confederation created in 1946 embodied a new type of labor organization. The problem now is to explain why the new type of unionism was so successful during the same period in which the old CTC practically ceased to exist. Table 24 shows the success of UTC quantitatively. All the statistics in this table are based on documents of the UTC executive committee and may, therefore, exaggerate growth. Checking the figures against alternative sources and estimates, however, leads to the conclusion that the figures in the table are roughly correct and certainly reflect the right magnitude of growth of the Unión de Trabajadores de Colombia.

One of the major reasons for the success of the UTC was the rapid decline of the CTC after 1947. The old confederation was unable to adapt to the new conditions that arose with the change of the party in power. Accustomed to bargaining with government intervention, in the face of a hostile executive, it attempted to survive by toppling the government. The Conservative government, however, had the political and legal tools to destroy the CTC, and by 1950 there was only a shadow of the old confederation left.

The UTC, by contrast, was created as an apolitical labor movement and certainly as an anti-CTC movement. The Conservative government was therefore not hostile to the new confederation. On the contrary, the proclerical Conservative Party was glad to support a Catholic-inspired labor confederation. Since in Colombia the labor movement owes so much of its power to the legal support given to unions, the relative friendliness between the UTC and the Conservative government favored the new con-

TABLE 24

Growth of the Unión de Trabajadores de Colombia

Calendar Year	Number of Unions	Number of State and Industrial Federations	Strikes by affiliated Unions	Average Duration of Strikes (Days)[a]	Number of Collective Bargaining Agreements
1946	40	4	2	45	n.a.
1947	n.a.	n.a.	1	11	n.a.
1949	220	8	n.a.	n.a.	n.a.
1950[b]	315	10	n.a.	n.a.	n.a.
1952[c]	409	13	n.a.	n.a.	11
1954	450	15	1	17	27
1955			5	n.a.	57
1956	547	15			50
1957			3	28	69
1958	628	22	3	38	n.a.
Jan. 1959–May 1960	n.a.	n.a.	6	45	150
May 1960–May 1961[d]	764[e]	23	9	36	164
May 1961–Oct. 1963	902	n.a.	29	n.a.	700

n.a.: not available

a. Average of strikes for which there is data.

b. At the Third UTC Congress there were delegates from 50 enterprise unions, 98 agrarian unions, 23 craft unions, 64 mixed unions (city-wide unions, etc.), from 5 mining organizations, and from 8 state federations.

c. In 1952, the strength of the UTC was still in the countryside. It had 91 enterprise unions, 297 craft unions (the majority of which were peasant leagues), 4 industrial unions, and 17 mixed unions.

d. By 1961, agrarian unions were in the minority. Of the 764 unions claimed by UTC, only 140 were rural unions.

e. Since the claims of the confederations are usually exaggerated, we have tried to check them for consistency. Although the executive committee claimed that the UTC had 152 more unions in May 1961 than in September 1958 and that it had lost 16 unions between that date and March 1961, among the documents of the Eighth UTC Congress we found a report of the 18 major federations belonging to UTC claiming 812 unions. Thus there probably were at least 764 unions.

Source: Reports of the executive committees to the UTC Congress (Archives of the UTC).

federation and allowed it to obtain improved working conditions for its members. The war to the death between the CTC and the government, on the other hand, made the CTC rather ineffective. The net result was that many unions and workers found it more useful to belong to the UTC than to the CTC. But the effect of the peaceful relationship between the Conservative government and the UTC can be overestimated. It would be rash to assign this factor any more weight than is implied by Robert J. Alexander's statement that "although the leaders of the Unión de Trabajadores de Colombia refused to allow the Conservatives to control it, they could not help but benefit from the generally hostile attitude of the Ospina Pérez government to the Liberal-controlled CTC."[16]

Although it is true that part of the growth of the UTC was at the expense of the CTC, much of the growth of the new confederation was also the result of the organization of sectors that were previously unorganized or outside the CTC. It has already been pointed out that some Antioqueño industrial unions that had not previously belonged to the CTC helped to found the Unión de Trabajadores de Colombia. Another proof that the growth of the UTC was not simply at the expense of the CTC is the fact that by 1956 it had 547 unions compared with the CTC's 471 in 1947.[17]

The major factor contributing to the success of the new confederation was the legally instituted protection of the unions that resulted from Law 6 of 1945. As has been explained, before López left office he gave the labor movement its independence from the political parties by creating the conditions for the survival of economically oriented labor organizations. López substituted state protection of strikers for state protection of strike-

16. Alexander, *Organized Labor*, p. 137.
17. Data from Table 25 and from Contraloría General de la República, *Primer censo sindical de Colombia, 1947* (Bogotá, Editorial Minerva, 1949), p. 4.

breakers, and made it extremely difficult for employers to break a union by firing labor leaders.[18] These legal provisions strengthened the unions and made them more effective as collective bargaining agents. Shortly after this legislation was passed, the government began to crack down on political unions. The result was that the labor movement had to dedicate itself to peaceful collective bargaining.

In the early forties, legal strikes were the exception. The power of the unions depended on creating a problem of public order so that the state would intervene in labor-management conflicts. Once the Conservatives came to power, however, an illegal walkout immediately brought government retaliation. The government declared the strike illegal, thus allowing the employers to dismiss labor leaders without severance pay or any other legal benefits. The illegal strikes encouraged by the CTC therefore made it possible for employers to break up the existing unions.

The new political situation forced the unions to employ peaceful collective bargaining. If they did not keep strictly within the limits of the law, the state would allow employers to destroy the union, and in an economy with an infinite supply of labor, unions not protected by the state and the law could be eliminated easily. The combination of government repression of unions that did not keep strictly within the limits of the law, and new legislation on strikes and unions giving labor organizations that kept the law greater bargaining strength, led to the development of a new type of unionism. This new unionism, however, developed slowly. Under the government of Laureano Gómez (1950–53), and to a lesser extent under the dictatorship of Gustavo Rojas Pinilla, carrying out strikes was difficult. Permission had to be obtained from the government to hold union meetings, and representatives of the police or the army were frequently present.

18. The Conservative government of Gómez, and to a lesser extent the dictatorship of Rojas, allowed some employers to fire union leaders. This made possible the weakening of some major unions.

Because of the problem of organizing under the dictatorship, when Rojas Pinilla attempted to create a labor movement that would support his bid for permanent personal government in 1954–55, the majority of the UTC rejected the attempt.[19] In 1954 Rojas accorded juridical status to the Confederación Nacional de Trabajadores (CNT), which was affiliated with the Latin American Peronist labor movement ATLAS, by rather arbitrary methods. It appears that his Labor Minister even wrote the doctrinal aims and objectives of the group. The CNT however never became strong. Among other reasons, it ran into trouble with the Catholic Church[20] and the UTC. In January 1955, the CNT was attacked in a pastoral letter in Antioquia for being "Peronist and Anti-Catholic . . . and being opposed to the social teachings of the Church on questions of unionism."[21] Although it has been claimed that the opposition of the Church caused the downfall of the CNT, the fall of Perón in Argentina and the consequent drying up of foreign funds seems a more plausible reason.

Although some labor leaders cooperated with Rojas to the end, including Tulio Cuevas, current president of the UTC, most labor organizations participated in the general strike that brought down the Rojas dictatorship in May 1957. Seven years of more or less veiled dictatorship had taught the labor movement that democracy was superior to any dictatorial regime, even if the latter declared itself to be a friend of labor. The Colombian experience was in this way radically different from that of other Latin American nations. The labor movement chose the long, hard way of collective bargaining and democracy and rejected the attraction of improving the economic conditions of the proletariat through an alliance with a dictator.

19. The attitude of the moral advisers, especially Vicente Andrade, S.J., was influential in keeping the UTC away from Rojas.

20. It must be remembered that Perón was in trouble with the Church in Argentina.

21. Fluharty, *Dance of the Millions,* pp. 246–47.

The Use of the Strike

Although in the long run the choice made by the labor movement in 1957 has been very beneficial to the salaried classes, it was not an easy choice to make. Given the high population growth of the nation, the use of imported technology, and the structural problems leading to constant balance of payments problems, labor demand has grown slowly since 1957, and the development of collective bargaining has been difficult.

In Colombia the major weapon of collective bargaining, the strike, is very costly for labor. Given the monopolistic structure of the product market, a strike usually does not hurt the enterprise too much since it does not lead to the loss of markets or sales. In order to produce an effective threat, the labor movement has to be prepared to carry out long strikes which affect the enterprise because of the cost of maintaining idle capital in the form of raw materials, inventories, and machinery. Table 24 shows that from the beginning, the strikes carried out by the UTC have been of long duration. On the average they have lasted more than two weeks. Table 25 illustrates that at present the same is true for the labor movement as a whole.

Table 26 compares the duration of strikes in Colombia, the United States, and Peru. It will be observed that in Peru, where the method of political bargaining is still prevalent, strikes are

TABLE 25

Strikes and Their Duration in Colombia, 1962–65

	1962	1963	1964	1965
Number of strikes	36	69	75	84
Workers affected	48,800	110,000	118,000	171,000
Work days lost	325	1,200	2,200	1,976
Average duration of strikes (days)	9	17	29	24

Source: Documentos Políticos, no. 56 (January 1966), p. 90.

TABLE 26

Duration of Strikes in Colombia, the United States, and Peru

Colombia, 1965*		United States, 1960		Peru, 1957–58	
Duration (days)	Percent	Duration (days)	Percent	Duration (days)	Percent
1	17.5	1	12.3	1 or less	46
2–4	11.1	2–4	15.4		
4–7	14.3	4–7	14.0	2–3	25
7–15	15.9	7–15	21.3	4–10	18
15–30	15.9	15–30	15.4	Over 11	11
30–60	6.3	30–60	11.8		
60–90	7.9	60–90	3.9		
Over 90	11.1	Over 90	6.0		

*In *Documentos Políticos* there was no information on the duration of 19 of the 82 strikes recorded in pp. 90–93. Checking on the strikes without information we found some that were not short strikes, and therefore rejected the hypothesis that a lack of information always implied a short strike. For that reason it was decided to use the available data, ignoring the strikes for which there was no information.

Sources: Colombia: *Documentos Políticos,* no. 56 (January 1966), pp. 90–93; Peru and United States: James L. Payne, *Labor and Politics in Peru* (New Haven, Conn., Yale University Press, 1965), p. 266 and Tables 26 and 27.

much shorter than in Colombia. The greater similarity between duration of strikes in Colombia and the United States reflects the use of the strike as a collective bargaining weapon. Nevertheless, when the strike was used for political bargaining in Colombia, it was also short, as it is today in Peru. Between 1932 and 1939, there is data on the duration of thirty-seven strikes.[22] Of these, only two lasted more than four weeks.

Colombian unions have to pay a high cost for economic gains

22. Statistics obtained from the various *Memorias* of the Minister of Labor for these years.

obtained through the strike. For this reason, there are relatively few strikes in the country, a factor that makes unions less of a barrier to economic growth than if strikes were frequent and involved large masses of workers.

In the case of Colombia it is clear that collective bargaining, which implies that the unions must carry out long strikes to be effective, is less costly than the method of political bargaining, in which unions carry out short city-wide or industry-wide strikes in order to pressure the government to intervene in favor of labor. In 1965, for example, out of a total of some 2,555,300 man-days lost due to strikes,[23] 1,219,464 man-days were lost during the politically motivated and illegal public school teachers' strikes, and some 532,000 man-days were lost due to the illegal strikes in the Ministry of Justice, the Ministry of Labor, the official Telecommunications Company, and the Contraloría General de la República. This means that more than 65 percent of the man-days lost in strikes in 1965 were lost in strikes carried out by five groups of government employees interested in pressuring the government by illegal means. The rest of the man-days lost involved legal strikes by fifty-seven unions.

It is clear that when strikes cost a great deal to the workers and involve serious sacrifices for union members, the strike will be used sparingly. This guarantees to some extent that the economic disruptions caused by the labor movement will not be so great as to hinder economic development. The same cannot be said of a political labor movement, which will tend to carry out massive strikes precisely at the time that the government finds itself in difficult economic or political circumstances.

23. *Documentos Políticos*, no. 56 (January, 1966).

13

The Labor Movement and the Democratic State

An economically oriented labor movement has managed to grow in Colombia in the last two decades, in spite of high levels of unemployment and relatively low rates of industrial growth, largely because of the legal protection given labor organizations. Furthermore, by giving the unions real bargaining strength, the existing legal structure has made the labor movement independent of the political parties and the executive branch of the government.

Unlike the case of Argentina, where Perón greatly strengthened the labor movement as a political force, while the workers saw their real wages decrease 23 percent between 1948 and 1955,[1] the Colombian labor movement has not become more important politically since 1955, but real wages have more than doubled since that date.

Wages in the Colombian Economy

Colombian industrialization started in earnest around the time of the first world war; therefore the following analysis of wages

1. See Aldo Ferrer, *La economía argentina* (Mexico, Fondo de Cultura Económica, 1965), pp. 231–33. According to a study by Carlos Diaz-Alejandro, real wages per member of the economically active population rose by about 60 percent between 1935–36 and 1953–1955. The real wages of industrial workers, however, grew less rapidly.

228

will be limited to the period since 1914. In that year, the daily wages of unskilled construction workers in Bogotá averaged 41 centavos. In 1966, the daily wages of unskilled construction workers in Bogotá averaged roughly P18.30.[2] This increase in nominal wages, however, is not very meaningful. Unfortunately, there are no complete price indexes available to make possible the deflation of nominal wages for this period, and no satisfactory estimates of the movement of real wages can be made for the years before the second world war.

It was found worthwhile, however, to attempt to make some kind of estimate of real wages during the last forty years, as background material for a more serious discussion of wages for the period 1938–65. As a deflator for money wages in construction I used the price of a basket of construction materials. I took as the basket the expenses on materials incurred in the construction of the Justice Department building during a week in September 1923.[3] In order to justify the deflation of construction wages by the price of construction materials, it was assumed that the prices of construction materials move parallel to the general price level. This assumption seems to be justified by historical experience in Colombia.[4]

2. Table 6 and June 1966 unemployment survey of Bogotá carried out by CEDE, Universidad de los Andes.

3. The basket of materials used, as it appeared in the records of the Public Works Ministry was as follows:

    5,000 bricks *(Ladrillos toletes)*
    5 quintals of round iron of ¼"
    50 regular boards
    5 m³ of washed sand
    1 arroba of nails

4. The assumption that the prices of materials move parallel to the general price level might lead to overestimating the rise in real wages, since the prices of construction materials may rise more slowly than the cost of living. For example, between 1938 and 1949, the price of construction materials in Bogotá increased 6 percent less than the cost of living index for manual workers in Bogotá. Between 1949 and 1950, the cost of living increased 21 percent while the price of materials for con

Using the basket of construction materials, a price rise of 1,339 percent is obtained between 1923 and 1966.[5] The basic wage of unskilled construction workers, on the other hand, increased from P0.53 per day to P18.30 per day, or 3,353 percent. In prices of 1923, therefore, wages increased from P0.53 to P1.27 a day, an increase of 140 percent in the real wage. In 1923, however, there were no legal fringe benefits. If we correct the 1966 wage for legal fringe benefits (severance pay, health insurance, etc.) we obtain an average wage plus benefits for unskilled construction workers in 1966 of P25.60 per day,[6] which implies an increase of 233 percent in real wages and fringe benefits for construction workers between 1923 and 1966. Using the various price series that exist for the period 1923–66, the increase in real wages and benefits appears to be about 135 percent, a figure that seems more plausible.[7]

---

struction increased only 7 percent. After that the two indexes move fairly closely. For the whole period 1938–1962, the prices of construction materials in Bogotá increased 8 percent less than the cost of living index for manual workers in Bogotá. Thus, in general, the prices of construction materials do not seem to be a bad proxy for rises in the cost of living. For the comparison of the two price series see Arvids Kalnins, *Análisis de la moneda y de la política monetaria colombiana* (Bogotá, Tercer Mundo, 1963), Table 8.

5. Using the various price indexes that exist for the years 1923 to 1966 we obtain an increase in prices of 1,947 percent, in contrast to the 1,339 percent increase in the price of construction materials. This confirms the results of the comparison between the cost of living index and the construction price index in footnote 4, where it appears that construction prices have tended to rise more slowly than the general price level.

6. It has been calculated that in Colombia legal fringe benefits amount to 40 percent of the basic wage.

7. The increase in the value of real wages and fringe benefits is about 135 percent if we deflate by the price series for 1923–66. This figure seems more plausible than that obtained when we deflate by the construction index, since it is unlikely that real wages should have increased sufficiently between 1930 and 1938 to offset the stagnation in 1923–30 and 1938–55 (see Tables 6 and 27).

TABLE 27

Index of Real Wages of Manufacturing Workers
in Bogotá, 1938–54

Quarter		Average Quarterly Index of Real Wages	Quarter		Average Quarterly Index of Real Wages
1938			1947		
	September	111.0		March	107.2
	December	114.0		June	101.0
1939				September	105.0
	March	108.6		December	112.0
	June	108.5	1948		
	September	110.8		March	105.0
	December	113.5		June	106.0
1940				September	107.0
	March	113.0		December	109.0
	June	110.0	1949		
	September	115.0		March	115.0
	December	118.0		June	116.0
1941				September	120.0
	March	118.0		December	129.0
	June	109.0	1950		
	September	115.0		March	141.0
	December	117.0		June	130.0
1942				September	120.0
	March	117.3		December	127.0
	June	113.0	1951		
	September	115.0		March	—
	December	112.0		June	—
1943				September	127.2*
	March	110.0		December	—
	June	109.6	1952		
	September	115.0		March	106.0
	December	113.0		June	103.0
1944				September	110.0
	March	108.0		December	117.0
	June	98.0	1953		
	September	103.0		March	106.0
	December	106.0		June	105.0
1945				September	101.0
	March	96.0		December	104.0
	June	94.0	1954		
	September	103.0		March	—
	December	109.0		June	—
1946				September	102.7*
	March	101.0		December	—
	June	104.0			
	September	105.0			
	December	107.0			

*Average for the year.

Source: Anuario general de estadística, various years.

Nevertheless, construction workers probably have not experienced the greatest improvement in wages. Since this is a relatively unorganized trade in Colombia, and the supply of unskilled construction workers seems to be completely elastic, it is probable that wages in manufacturing and other trades increased more rapidly, or in the worst of cases, as rapidly as in construction.

In Tables 27 and 28 the trend of real wages in manufacturing can be observed. It appears that between 1938 and 1954, the basic real wage in manufacturing did not increase. Between 1955 and 1965, on the other hand, the real wages of manual workers in manufacturing almost doubled. These tables, however, must be accepted with reservations, since the data used to put them together are not of the best quality, especially for the period prior to 1955.

The wage data for 1938-54 come from a sample of manufacturing industries in Bogotá and the surrounding area. The sample was probably arbitrary, since the first Colombian manufacturing census took place in 1945, several years after this sample of firms was obtained. There is therefore no assurance that the firms sampled are representative of Bogotá's industry. In general, however, the sample of manufacturing firms seems to be fairly inclusive.[8] The wage data for the period 1955–62 come from a much better sample of manufacturing firms. The sample was based on the 1953 manufacturing census, and it is stratified by size of the firms.[9]

The only major problem with the sample of manufacturing firms used by the Departamento Administrativo de Estadística (DANE) before 1962 was that it was static, i.e. no new firms were incorporated into the sample. Since many of the new firms established in the country after 1955 tended to be in new and techno-

8. The most complete results of this sample were published in the *Anuario general de estadística, 1939* (Bogotá, Imprenta Nacional, 1940).

9. The method followed by DANE to obtain this index can be found in DANE, *Boletín mensual de estadística,* no. 69 (December 1956).

TABLE 28

Index of Real Wages in Manufacturing Industry in Colombia,
1955–65

| | Index of Real Wages | | | Index of Real Wages | |
| | White-Collar | Manual | | White-Collar | Manual |
Quarter	Workers	Workers	Quarter	Workers	Workers
1955			1961		
March	100	100	March	96	141
June	104	103	June	96	137
September	105	106	September	98	143
December	107	105	December	100	149
1956			1962		
March	104	107	March	101	151
June	105	106	June	*	*
September	98	109	September	125	181
December	98	112	December	128	188
1957			1963		
March	92	120	March	126	197
June	91	116	June	123	197
September	94	125	September	123	195
December	92	125	December	122	193
1958			1964		
March	92	124	March	121	191
June	92	121	June	120	185
September	94	121	September	121	188
December	94	122	December	124	196
1959			1965		
March	94	120	March	124	196
June	94	121	June	126	194
September	95	123	September	127	197
December	97	128	December	125	195
1960					
March	96	127			
June	97	127			
September	98	140			
December	98	141			

*Date of the reform in the sample of manufacturing firms surveyed by DANE.

Source: DANE, Boletín mensual de estadística, 1956–66.

logically advanced industries, which in general pay higher wages because of the level of skill of their labor force, the sample tended to underestimate the level of wages in manufacturing as time went on. In 1962, the sample was changed and new firms were added to the old sample. The result was that in the new index, wages were much higher than in the index based on the previous sample. In fact, the sample change led to an increase of 22 percent in the average wage of white-collar workers. Thus most of the increase in wages observed in Table 28 between the first and fourth quarters of 1962 is due to the change in the sample from which wage data was taken. This increase should be spread out evenly over the previous years. Thus, although the year-to-year movements of wages may not be accurately portrayed in Table 28, the general wage rise for the whole period shown in the table probably does reflect the reality of wage movements accurately.

The deflators used in both of the wage series presented here were cost of living indexes. The first index used for the 1938–54 wage series was the cost of living index for Bogotá workers. This index was based on a consumer survey of workers' families. However, the original survey, used to determine the consumer basket that would serve as the basis for the index, left much to be desired. It only covered the family's expenses for one month, and the sample used was somewhat arbitrary.[10]

The cost of living index used to deflate the 1955–65 wage series is of much better quality. The consumer baskets used to build this index were determined after a very thorough and well-conceived consumer survey in 1953.[11] The only problem with this index is that the consumer basket may have become to some extent obsolete because of changes in consumption patterns be-

10. For the methodology used to build the cost of living index between 1938 and 1954, see *Anales de Economía y Estadística, 1,* nos. 1, 4 (1939); *3,* no. 4 (1940).

11. Rafael Bernal Salamanca y Carlos Quintero Ferro, "Nuevas Bases para los Indices de Costo de la Vida," *Anales de Economía y Estadística,* iv Epoca, *11,* no. 81 (1955); and *14,* no. 85 (1958).

tween 1953 and 1965. This problem, however, is to a large degree unavoidable, and it would be absurd to think of correcting the consumer basket too frequently because of the very high cost of national consumer surveys.

Thus, although the real wage index for 1938–54 is to some extent unreliable, the statistics used for the real wage index after 1955 are of good quality, and the resulting index can be considered a good approximation of the real wage movement in this period. Keeping in mind the limitations of the data, the increase in real wages in the last decade is very impressive. A 95 percent increase in real wages for manual workers in manufacturing was recorded, without including changes in fringe benefits. If fringe benefits are included in the wage index, total real wages increased 19 percent more in the period 1955–63 than if fringe benefits are excluded, which means that the total wages and benefits of blue-collar workers more than doubled between 1955 and 1963.[12]

Some economists in Colombia, however, have asserted that the rapid increase in real wages in the manufacturing sector in the last decade have been at the expense of other sectors of the population. To test this hypothesis, historical wage data were obtained for workers in industrial sectors other than manufacturing. Unfortunately, the only wage data in existence for nonmanufacturing workers are those found in the *Anuario general de estadística* of 1939 and the wage data available from the quarterly unemployment survey in Bogotá, carried out since 1963. Based on these two sources, the growth in wage rates between 1939

12. Real wages plus benefits increased by 113 percent in 1955–63. To arrive at this estimate we corrected basic wages by the percentage of basic wage paid in the form of fringe benefits by employers in manufacturing in the two end years. Since in 1955 fringe benefits were 13 percent of the basic wage, and in 1963 they amounted to 28 percent of the basic wage in manufacturing, the wage plus benefits index rose from 100 to 213 between the two end years. The data on fringe benefits were obtained from the 1956 and 1963 *Anuarios generales de estadística*.

TABLE 29

Wages of Manual Workers, 1939–65

Economic Activities	Women Average Yearly Growth Rate of Wage	Men Average Yearly Growth Rate of Wage
Manufacturing sector	(percent)	(percent)
Printing	—	8.63
Paper and cardboard products	—	11.89
Wood	11.29	10.17
Clothing	8.73	—
Textiles	13.98	11.27
Alcoholic beverages	—	—
Beer	—	10.12
Soft drinks	—	10.71
Tobacco	—	—
Tanneries	—	10.02
Chocolates	12.70	15.46*
Mills (flour)	—	—
Biscuits	12.15	—
Nonmetallic minerals	14.70	10.77
Candles	—	—
Matches	—	—
Laboratories	13.98	10.27
Metal products	—	11.23
Soap	—	—
Nonmanufacturing sectors		
Land transport	—	13.14
Air transport	—	13.85
Taxi service	—	13.08
Electricity	13.71	11.89
Shoe making and leather making	7.17	7.83
Hotels and restaurants	14.28	13.94
Mail and telegraph services	14.96	11.23
Telephone service	—	10.77
Theater service	8.61	11.27
Bar and coffee shop service	10.77	—
Public works	—	12.44
Construction	—	11.27

*In the sector labeled chocolates, only one man was found in the 1965 sample, and he earned the high wage of P50 to P51 a day. The wage increase among men in the chocolate sector is therefore probably not representative of actual wage movements.

Sources: Contraloría General de la República, *Anuario general de estadística, 1939* (Bogotá, Imprenta Nacional, 1940); CEDE, "Unemployment Survey of Bogotá" (unpublished).

and 1965 was calculated for both manufacturing and nonmanu-facturing activities.[13]

The results of the comparison between wages in 1939 and 1965 appears in Tables 29 and 30. As can be seen from Table 29, the 1939 data covered 19 manufacturing industrial classifications and 12 nonmanufacturing classifications. For 4 manufacturing classifications, however, a comparison of wages was impossible due to a lack of wage data for those classifications in the unemployment survey. Since this survey covers only 500 households and 1,202 members of the labor force, it is not surprising that some activities should not be represented. Table 30 shows that wages in the nonindustrial sector increased more rapidly than wages in the industrial sector for both men and women. This is true, however, only if the 1965 wages of the sectors existing in 1939 are the only wages considered for the calculation of average wages in 1965.

This is a valid procedure only if the measurement of wage changes in a given set of industrial sectors is desired. But if the purpose is to measure wage changes in the whole manufacturing sector through time, it is incorrect not to include new industries and industrial sectors in the calculation of the 1965 average wage of manual workers in manufacturing. In row 2 of Table 30, the reader will find the average wage for manufacturing workers in the 19 industrial classifications of Table 29. This wage is well below the wage recorded in row 6 of Table 30. The average wage found in row 6 refers to the whole manufacturing industry, and is higher than the average wage for the limited number of sectors in 1939, because new and high-paying industries such as the rubber, chemical, and machine tool industries were established after that date.[14]

13. Since the unemployment survey is not tabulated on a two-digit in-dustry breakdown, a special tabulation of one survey had to be carried out, and the 1965 average wages refer only to the month of September and not to an average for the year.

14. The unemployment survey may underestimate wages to some ex-tent, since it is a household survey. But in general, the wage data from

TABLE 30

Changes in Manufacturing and Nonmanufacturing Wages in Bogotá, 1939–65

Industrial Classification	Year	Number of Workers		Average Daily Wages per Worker (manual workers)					
		Men	Women	Men		Women		Men and Women	
				Wage	Index	Wage	Index	Wage	Index
Industrial wages	1939	2,195	987	P 1.37– 1.62	100	P 0.91– 1.16	100	P 1.23– 1.48	100
(according to Table 29)[a]	1965	66	32	22.25–23.25	1,435–1,624	17.00	1,466–1,868	20.52–21.19	1,432–1,668
Nonindustrial wages	1939	3,183	296	1.10– 1.35	100	0.87– 1.04	100	1.08– 1.33	100
(according to Table 29)	1965	155	28	22.00–23.00	1,704–2,000	16.00	1,538–1,839	21.10–21.95	1,650–1,954
Industrial wages	1939[b]	n.a.	n.a.	n.a.	n.a.	n.a.	n.a.	1.23– 1.48	100
(according to DANE)	1965[c]	n.a.	n.a.	n.a.	n.a.	n.a.	n.a.	29.00	1,959–2,358

a. Industrial wages in the activities recorded in Table 29.

b. Daily wage of manufacturing manual workers according to the *Anuario general de estadística, 1939*, pp. 258–60; refers to the last pay period of October 1939.

c. Daily wage of manufacturing manual workers in Cundinamarca in September 1965, as published by DANE. Since DANE publishes the hourly wage paid, we assumed an eight-hour day to transform the data into daily wages. Since there is a difference between hours paid and hours worked, the estimate of daily wage may be on the low side, because in Colombia Sunday rest is paid for. Another problem with this wage figure is that it refers to Cundinamarca, and not to Bogotá. But since almost all manufacturing industry in Cundinamarca is centered in the greater Bogotá metropolitan area, this does not seem to be a serious problem.

Sources: Anuario general de estadística, 1939; CEDE, "Unemployment" (September 1965); DANE, *Boletín mensual de estadística*, no. 183 (June 1966).

Thus wages in the nonmanufacturing sector of Bogotá rose faster than wages in the traditional and less technologically advanced sectors of manufacturing industry, but they rose somewhat more slowly than wages in the whole manufacturing industry. In either case, it appears that in Bogotá manufacturing and nonmanufacturing wages rose by a similar percentage between 1939 and 1965, and since real wages in manufacturing doubled in this period, real wages in the city as a whole roughly doubled.

The evidence of rapidly rising real wages in urban Colombia[15] contrasts radically with the record of real wages in other Latin American nations. As has been mentioned, real wages in Argentina seem to have decreased or stagnated,[16] and the same seems to have been true in Chile. In Chile, it seems that real wages have not increased in the economy as a whole in the last decades, and that real wages have decreased in some sectors of the economy.[17] In the public sector, it appears that real wages in Chile have not increased at all in the last one hundred years.[18] This situation compares very unfavorably with the Colombian case, where real wages in the urban sector have more than doubled since 1930.[19]

---

the survey are surprisingly good. According to the survey, the average wage in manufacturing for manual workers in September 1965 was P26.60 a day. According to the DANE survey of firms, the average wage was P29.00 on the same date. Thus the unemployment survey underestimated manufacturing wages by only 8 percent.

15. There is no reason to believe that real wage rates rose more slowly in cities other than Bogotá in this period. On the contrary, wages in Cali probably rose faster. Thus we have assumed that the rise in real wages in Bogotá is typical of the rise in real wages in the whole urban sector of the country, defining the urban sector as cities of over 50,000 inhabitants.

16. See n. 1, this chapter.

17. Tom E. Davis, "Capital y Salarios Reales en la economía Chilena," *Cuadernos de Economía,* year 3, no. 8 (January-April 1966), p. 85.

18. Ibid., p. 88.

19. Real wage series in the agricultural sector have been developed by Albert Berry of the Yale University Economic Growth Center. He has also

Unions and the Wage Rate

Even in the United States, where there is a wealth of statistical material on the subject, there is no agreement on the magnitude of the effect that unions have had on wages. The comparison of wages in union and nonunion firms is far from conclusive, since nonunion firms may pay high wages in order to keep their workers from organizing. Another problem with comparisons of wages paid in union and nonunion firms is that often there is a positive correlation between size of firm and wages paid, and a positive correlation between unionism and size of firm. Given these relationships, it is possible that the higher wages observed in unionized companies may reflect the fact that larger companies pay high wages and also tend to have unions, but there may be no causal relationship between the existence of unions in the firm and high wages.

Despite all these problems, it was decided that it would be worthwhile to attempt to measure the impact of unions on wages. To do this it became necessary to obtain some data that were not available in Colombia directly from a sample of manufacturing firms. The details of this survey are to be found in the Statistical Appendix, but they will be summarized here.

In the survey it turned out that most manufacturing firms with more than one hundred employees had unions, and the major concentration of nonunion firms was in very small manufacturing enterprises. Although the evidence does not allow us to make any very strong assertion concerning union and nonunion wage differentials, it appears that wages are significantly higher in union firms, even when union and nonunion wages are compared among firms of similar size.

---

developed real wage series for government employees. According to his series, the real wages of government employees increased about 40 percent between 1939 and 1961, and the real wages of agricultural workers remained about constant.

Among the firms investigated, wages for blue-collar workers are on the average 30 percent higher in firms with unions than in nonunion firms. If the size of the firm is held constant, however, the wage differential turns out to be only about 20 percent. The conclusion arrived at in the Statistical Appendix is that unions have created a wage differential of between 18 and 23 percent in favor of unionized workers, a differential not substantially different from that found by H. G. Lewis for the United States.[20]

This result is not unexpected. Although there has been much statistical debate in the more advanced countries concerning the effect of unions on wages, it is hard to believe that unions could survive if they did not in fact improve the economic position of their members. In Colombia, the rapid growth of the labor movement since 1955, especially of the dues-paying membership, can only be explained by the growing success of unions in obtaining better wages and benefits for their members. During the last decade, the rank and file worker has begun to perceive that his union dues are an investment with a high return. Indeed, where unions have not been able to function, such as in the public sector, real wages have decreased or remained constant during the inflation of the last decade.

The Sources of Union Strength in Colombia

In theory, for a union to obtain wages higher than those prevalent in the absence of a union, it is necessary that it should be able to restrict the supply of workers or to control the wage rate directly by (1) preventing existing employers from undercutting the union rate, and (2) preventing the entry of new employers who would do so.[21]

20. H. G. Lewis, *Unionism and Relative Wages in the United States* (Chicago, University of Chicago Press, 1963), pp. 4–5.
21. Lloyd Ulman, "Marshall and Friedman on Union Strength," *Review of Economics and Statistics, 37,* no. 4 (November 1955), 393.

In Colombia, direct control over the wage rate is achieved through what Milton Friedman calls "political assistance."[22] Concretely, labor legislation has been passed which makes the use of the strike threat a very efficient method of raising wages. As Ulman points out,[23] the strike and the threat of a strike are the means by which a union keeps the employer from exploiting the existence of an excess supply of labor by hiring nonunion labor at a lower wage. By threatening the employer with a strike, the union confronts the employer with an alternative to which the extra cost involved in paying the union wage might be preferable.

As has been explained previously, Colombian law forbids an employer to hire any new workers during a strike and makes mass and individual layoffs at any time either impossible or very expensive. Furthermore, since the Peldar strike in 1955 when Minister of Labor Castor Jaramillo Arrubla allowed the workers to blockade the factory and to keep raw materials from entering and finished goods from leaving the plant, the state has in effect allowed workers to force the shutdown of striking factories. As has happened often before in Colombian labor relations, after this informal practice had come to be accepted by a large sector of employers, it was passed into law in the labor reform of September 4, 1965. The relevant article of the decree states: "While the majority of the workers in the enterprise are on strike, the authorities guarantee the exercise of this right and will not authorize or encourage the entrance into the factory of groups of workers belonging to the minority, even if these laborers express the desire to work."

The law not only gives the union a strong bargaining position by making it capable of carrying out a strike that will be costly to the employer; it also makes it difficult for the employer to undermine the union rate slowly by firing high paid workers in

22. Milton Friedman, "Some Comments on the Significance of Labor Unions for Economic Policy," in David McCord Wright, ed., *The Impact of the Union* (New York, 1951).
23. Ulman, "Marshall and Friedman," p. 393.

order to replace them with lower paid workers out of the large reserve of unemployed and underemployed in the labor market. In addition to legal provisions requiring equal pay for equal work, a company must obtain approval from the Labor Ministry for any mass layoffs. This requirement was made into law on October 18, 1963, and since then the Labor Ministry has made the process of obtaining permission for mass layoffs both time consuming and expensive. Even after all the inspections by labor officers and the study of the financial position and profitability of a firm have been carried out, less than half of the requests for layoffs are accepted. For example, in the first seven months of 1965, a period of contraction of industry due to the lack of foreign reserves needed for the purchase of raw materials, requests for the laying off of 7,099 workers reached the ministry, and only 3,926 workers were allowed to be put out of work.[24]

Because the cost of obtaining permission for mass layoffs and the reluctance of many firms to have their books and profits examined by the Labor Ministry before the layoff is allowed, few requests for layoffs reach the ministry. The more common method is to buy the resignation of the worker. Since the late fifties, many firms have negotiated tables of dismissal pay with their unions. By law, all workers dismissed had to be paid in addition to the *cesantía,* or one month's pay for every year worked, the equivalent of 45 days of pay.[25] The additional tables of dismissal pay obtained from companies by individual unions varied, but they typically gave workers who had been with the company two years more than 60 days dismissal pay, and workers with a seven-year record 145 days or more in dismissal pay.

As often before, this private practice which was developed by the companies that refused to give complete job security to their workers, as some of the major companies had done, was

24. Ministerio del Trabajo, *Memoria al Congreso Nacional, 1965.*
25. The alternative was to give the workers 45 days' notice of his dismissal. This was seldom done, since the productivity of the worker in those 45 days was often negative, and there was the threat of sabotage.

passed into law in the labor reform of 1965. In that reform it was further established that workers who had been with a company more than 10 years would have to be paid 205 days pay plus 30 days pay for every year over 10 in the employ of the company. Thus the cost of layoffs in Colombia is extremely high. If in addition to this the employer has to cover the cost of breaking in an entirely new work force on the job, a cost that is substantial due to the unavailability of skilled workers, it is clear that the cost of undercutting the union rate is extremely high.

Thus, because of the unavailability of workers accustomed to industrial life and possessing the minimum skills needed to use modern technology, and because of the legal provisions which create job security and allow unions to carry out effective strikes, the alternative costs to the employer of undercutting the union wage or not giving a union the wage increases demanded are the following: (1) incurring a strike, or (2) breaking the union. In the first case, since interest rates in Colombia are on the order of 14 percent or more, the cost of a complete shutdown is higher than in more highly developed countries. In the second case the employer has to lay off part of his work force and replace it by new workers; this entails a double cost—the training of low quality labor for the jobs vacated and very high outlays for dismissal pay.

The proof that more often than not the employers offer higher wages rather than incur the high cost of undercutting the union wage by replacing its workers is the statistic on turnover rates. As is shown in the Statistical Appendix, turnover rates in Colombia are less than a third of those in the United States during years of prosperity, and almost a half of United States separation rates during years of relatively high unemployment. The statistics on turnover rates also suggest that union wages are probably higher than nonunion wages since turnover in union firms is lower.

Given the fact that legal provisions make it possible for the enterprise union to carry out strikes that will be costly to employers, and given the structure of Colombian manufacturing

244

industry, enterprise unions can obtain large wage increases above the free market rate. The structure of Colombian manufacturing industry gives enterprise unions bargaining strength because it is characterized by (1) difficult entry, a reflection not only of high interest rates and the lack of capital, but also of the government's tariff policy and development loans which often favor established firms, and (2) monopoly production, created by the small size of the market and the economies of scale of modern technology.

But although monopolists can raise prices substantially in order to pay for the higher wages demanded by the unions, they cannot do this indefinitely. Although entrance into an industry is difficult, it is not impossible, and the demand for most products is not completely inelastic. There are always possible substitutes. Thus, there is always a price level above which even a monopolist cannot go without having the profitability of the business decline. In some Colombian enterprises it appears that unions have pushed wages too high, and to meet higher wage costs the enterprise has raised prices too much to remain profitable. At present, therefore, many large monopolistic companies are being forced to take a hard line position toward union wage demands. This tough industrial relations policy has coincided with a period of high unemployment,[26] a fact that has weakened the bargaining position of the unions. The result is that unions will probably find it harder to obtain economic concessions in the next few years than they have in the recent past.

Thus, economic conditions plus a growing awareness on the part of employers of the dangers of giving in too easily to the unions have made the task of labor officials more difficult. Gains in job security and wages are beginning to be hard to obtain, and this has inevitably lowered the prestige of unions and their growth potential. Furthermore, the labor movement has gone as far as it could go within the framework of enterprise unionism.

26. Unemployment in Bogotá averaged 8.9 percent in 1965 and 10.1 percent in 1966. For Cali and Medellín the level of unemployment has been even higher.

Most of the firms of any size have been unionized, and the marginal cost of unionizing additional workers within the enterprise union structure is growing rapidly.

With manufacturing industry largely organized[27] the confederations must now attempt to organize the atomized road transport, mining, commerce, and service industries. And because entry is easy and competition is thus severe, enterprise unionism in these industries cannot be effective. Many unions will have to follow the lead of the restaurant and hotel workers, and organize national industrial unions. But the transformation of the structure of the labor movement will not be easy. It will create internal conflict, and structural change will proceed slowly. It is therefore doubtful that in the near future the paying membership of unions will increase radically.

27. About three-quarters of all workers in manufacturing are in firms with unions, according to the survey of firms described in the Statistical Appendix.

The Role of the Labor Movement in Colombian Political and Economic Development

After World War I, when the first unions organized and the first strikes took place in Colombia, intellectuals and politicians initiated a debate in the Bogotá press concerning the labor movement. The question under discussion was whether labor organizations could contribute to economic progress or whether, on the contrary, they made such progress more difficult.

At that time, the progressive Liberals and the Socialists vigorously defended on both constitutional and economic grounds the right of workers to organize. Leftist theoreticians like José Mar argued that labor organizations would help Colombia avoid many of the social evils that uncontrolled capitalism had brought to the industrialized countries, and that only a strong labor movement could insure an equitable distribution of the fruits of economic progress under capitalism. Furthermore, the Liberals argued that unless a mechanism such as organized labor forced employers to pay good wages, Colombian industry would stagnate because of an insufficient market for mass-produced goods.

The Conservatives countered these arguments by pointing out that labor unions could make it difficult for capitalists to save for reinvestment. They further contended that although workers should have the right to organize and go on strike, employers should also have the right to choose freely their labor force. In other words, they did not want to limit the freedom of workers to organize, but they did want to limit the degree of protection given by the state to organized workers.

In this first round of the debate, the Colombian Left clearly won out. It was very difficult to argue against those who wanted to redistribute income from the capitalists to the workers. Forty-five years later, however, the terms of reference for the debate on the role of unions in economic development had changed radically, and for that reason in 1965 the Colombian Left could be found on the side of those who believe that unions are harmful to economic development. In contrast, the major defender of organized labor at present is the Catholic Church.

The reason for the change of opinion of the Colombian Left is that in the forty-five years that elapsed between the first strikes in the ports of Barranquilla and Cartagena, and the government of Guillermo León Valencia, the real income of organized laborers increased by substantially more than 100 percent, and in 1963–65 it was clear that union members were no longer in the lower half of the income scale. The Colombian Left has now become convinced that the gains achieved by the labor movement have not been at the expense of the capitalists but at the expense of the large mass of poor consumers who have been forced to pay higher prices for industrial goods. Thus the intellectuals of the Movimiento Revolucionario Liberal coined the phrase "the blue-collar oligarchy" to designate the labor movement.

The Colombian Left, appealing to the ideal of income redistribution, changed sides in the debate and in the 1960s has been the major defender of attempts to curb the power of unions. Progressive liberals argue for the control of unions on the following grounds:[1]

1. See for example Alberto Lleras, "La Puerta Estrecha," *Visión* (July 9, 1965), and Lauchlin Currie, *Ideas básicas sobre la aceleración del desarrollo* (Bogotá, 1965).

1. The demands of unions for a higher real income for their members will endanger the economy's efforts to increase the rate of investment.
2. Unions are a threat to price stability. In some cases they may be instrumental in initiating an inflationary spiral, but more often they will provide the mechanism for the survival of an inflationary process initiated by balance of payments problems, short-run scarcities, or budgetary deficits.
3. Labor unions, in collaboration with a generally monopolistic manufacturing industry, have caused a redistributtion of income in favor of organized workers, at the expense of farm workers and nonunionized workers in the cities.

These propositions, if true, would lead to the conclusion that unions should be destroyed or at least controlled in the interest of achieving more rapid economic development. At first sight, the economic arguments favoring the repression or control of unions seem truly overwhelming. For example, in an environment in which the government is politically weak and the unions politically influential, consumption-oriented unions may indeed delay the process of capital formation. In many underdeveloped nations, and in Latin America in particular, the unions have been able to force weak governments to give periodic wage increases in state enterprises and to carry out periodic upward revisions of minimum wage legislation. At the same time, unions have pressured for price control of public utilities, transportation, house rents, and basic necessities. Thus while prices are controlled, wages go up and profits are squeezed. This profit squeeze may be particularly harmful to the strategic export sector, since in that area higher costs cannot be met by a rise in prices.

In general, however, profit rates cannot be squeezed and the effect of price controls is simply a misallocation of resources, accompanied by a cost-push inflation. In protected economies, where import substitution has proceeded to an important degree, union-obtained wage increases are translated into higher internal prices in unionized industries. These increases in prices lead in turn to other price increases, and inflation is the result. Furthermore, the deficits in state enterprises, due to stable prices and rising wages, become a major source of deficit financing by the government and a major cause for inflation.[2]

Politically, however, the strongest argument against unions is that they have caused unemployment and greater inequality in the distribution of income. It has been suggested that by forcing wages in manufacturing industry above the marginal productivity of labor in the economy, unions have led employers to substitute capital for labor in that sector, thus decreasing the opportunity for employment of the vast mass of underemployed and unemployed in developing economies. Furthermore, it is claimed that since the rate of return on capital is not squeezed by union action, union-obtained wage increases are translated into higher prices, and that therefore union wages are financed, in economies with any degree of tariff protection, by consumers whose real income is lower than that of manufacturing workers. The net result is then that the distribution of income becomes more unequal. In Colombia, Indalecio Lievano Aguirre has suggested that unions are responsible for a worsening in the terms of trade between the rural and urban sectors, a phenomenon that has led to an increasingly unequal distribution of income.

Finally, it is often pointed out that there is a strong historical argument in favor of weak unions. It is argued that some of the pioneer countries in the process of industrialization, such as England, France, the United States, the North German Confederation, and Japan, succeeded in delaying the emergence of effective unions for some time by legislative, administrative, or

2. In Brazil, for example, the deficits produced by the state railroads have been a major reason for government deficits.

judicial devices. Thus the repression of labor unions in presently developing nations would have much historical precedent. And although no one argues that growth is a function of union repression, a plausible argument can be made for the notion that the lack of strong unions was a positive factor in the development of the now industrialized nations. Indeed, historical analysis has suggested to some authors that the existence of unions may be one of the major disadvantages of the nations that are latecomers to the process of industrialization.

Considering these arguments, John Dunlop, an economist who has always looked with sympathy upon labor, has gone so far as to suggest that countries in the process of development should not have any trade unions, at least for a time, or should have controlled unions.[3]

It seems, however, that much of the debate on the role of unions in economic development has been based on the erroneous assumption that in backward nations economic and political problems can be isolated. In fact, it is unrealistic to discuss the problem of unions simply from an economic point of view. The labor movement in developing nations is often more political than economic in nature, and although its destruction may make sense from an economic point of view, it may have political repercussions which will make planning and economic development more difficult.

The study of the historical development of the Colombian labor movement suggests the hypothesis that unions in developing economies are not naturally strong, and that as a rule, without the direct or indirect support of the state, they could not be effective in bringing about changes in work conditions. In Colombia, as in most backward nations, high rates of population

3. Paul Fisher, "Unions in the Less-Developed Countries: A Reappraisal of Their Economic Role," in Everett M. Kassalow, *National Labor Movements in the Postwar World* (Evanston, Ill., Northwestern University Press, 1963), p. 104.

growth and low overall levels of literacy determine that most private and public organizations face a labor market in which the supply of labor is unlimited, and any group of workers faced by virtually infinite competition for their jobs cannot effectively demand and obtain higher wages unless there is some noneconomic restraint on that competition.

Thus the very existence and certainly the bargaining strength of labor organizations depend on the restraints on competition in the labor market imposed by legislation, administrative practice, and day-to-day politics. Not surprisingly then, Colombian unions, just as those in other developing nations of Latin America, often engage in political action rather than in collective bargaining. In the early stages of the development of the labor movement in Colombia, the prosperity of the labor movement depended on the political strength of the government in power. If the progressive Liberal governments of López were seriously threatened from the Right, they would protect and help the labor movement in return for its political support. Moderate governments, however, were relatively secure from any threat from the Right or Left; they did not need the support of the unions and would therefore not help them out in labor-management conflicts. In these circumstances the unions had no hope of success since they could not act effectively within the established economic order.

The strength of the early Colombian labor movement therefore lay in the political weakness of the various governments in power during the process of industrialization, a weakness which made it possible for the unions to pressure the state into protecting certain labor groups from the ravages of competition in the labor market. In Colombia, political bargaining was the only effective tactic until the government institutionalized state protection of unions by law. Once legal protection became effective, the unions became independent from the political parties and from the government, and only then was the labor movement able to use the tactic of collective bargaining.

The protection obtained by the Colombian unions, which has

given them bargaining strength in the face of an unlimited labor supply, is complete job security. Labor leaders cannot be fired or layed off under any circumstances, and the rest of a firm's personnel is also virtually permanent. Except on grounds of bad behavior, firing a Colombian worker is very costly. Since the firm cannot replace personnel and is forbidden to break a legal strike, the union at the enterprise level effectively controls the supply of labor and therefore has substantial bargaining strength. For this reason collective bargaining has become important despite very high rates of unemployment and underemployment in the country.

Statistics show that the greatest gains in real wages in manufacturing industry have been achieved since 1955, or during the period of collective bargaining. In the twenty years before that, when unions were essentially political organizations and political bargaining was the most common union tactic, real wages in manufacturing did not increase and only some workers in state enterprises benefited from union action. During the period of political bargaining the workers did not improve their economic position, but labor organization did cause some degree of political instabilty, inflation, and economic waste.

Since violence is a necessary ingredient in political bargaining, the labor movement contributed to the atmosphere of violence and to the increasing rejection of peaceful democratic processes that led to the closing down of the Congress and the dictatorship of the early fifties. The general strikes aimed at overthrowing Mariano Ospina attempted by the CTC were the first large-scale efforts at overthrowing the legal order and thus contributed to the violence and lawlessness of the decade that followed. In this sense the politically oriented labor movement of the forties hindered economic growth by helping to retard political development and the establishment of political stability.

In the economic field, the political labor movement also produced many of the harmful effects described by the advocates of weak unions in developing nations. The short but widespread political strikes were just as disruptive of production processes as the longer but limited strikes due to collective bargaining, and politically obtained wage concessions in the public services were certainly inflationary. Since it must be supposed that the government did not produce monopoly profits in state enterprises, all politically obtained wage increases in these enterprises no doubt led to increases in prices or deficits financed by inflationary monetary policies. Furthermore, price increases in the public services, the sector where political bargaining was most successful, were much publicized, affected the costs of many firms, and therefore were particularly inflationary.

The study of the development of the Colombian labor movement leads to the conclusion that from an economic point of view political bargaining is not less harmful than collective bargaining, but that, on the contrary, it may be a greater barrier to political development and stability, which are in turn prerequisites for economic development. Since the Colombian experience also suggests that in an environment with a minimum of freedom some kind of union activity is inevitable, the question is not whether union activity should be allowed, but what kind of union bargaining tactics would be most desirable in a developing nation.

Since in the absence of legal protection for unions, labor market conditions in developing nations force the labor movement to adopt the tactic of political bargaining, and since this type of union tactic is no less harmful to economic development than is collective bargaining, a very good political case can be made for maintaining a certain degree of legal protection for unions. In addition to this general consideration, in the case of Colombia there is a further argument for the continued state protection of unions: the state could not now change its policy toward labor even if it wanted to. The present political system rests on the tacit acceptance by a majority of the people of an established legal order, and a major component of that legal order is protective labor legislation. Any attempt to withdraw the state's legal support for unions would imply a radical change in the nation's political structure, a change inevitably involving some kind of repression. In any case, the price to be paid would be the elimination of the limited degree of democracy that has developed in the country.

Furthermore, although the labor movement in Colombia may have constituted in some cases a barrier to development, it has also had some beneficial effects. For example, collective bargaining has given many industrial workers a standard of living equivalent to that of government employees and other traditional members of the middle class, and in this way has strengthened that class in the country. This growing middle class is a force that contributes to political stability since its members have improved their standard of living within the existing social structure. In other nations of Latin America, where the standard of living of the middle class has not improved and where there have been few new entrants into that class, the middle sectors of society have not become a force committed to political stability.

At present, the labor movement is the greatest threat to any revolution from the Right or the Left. The anticommunism of the two largest labor federations is well known, but they have also consistently rejected populist or rightist political solutions. The army, for one, is keenly aware of this and considers the labor movement one of the major forces it would have to contend with in any bid for power.

But the labor movement is not simply a force for moderation. It has also contributed to the gradual transformation of the social structure of the nation. Although the labor movement has done well within the present social and political structure, it wants to do better. It has become a dynamic pressure group in the campaign for expansion of credit for the poor, workers' housing, and increased investment in education. For example, it was the widespread teachers' strike of 1966 that forced the government to commit a larger proportion of its resources to education.[4]

4. *El Tiempo, El Espectador, El Siglo* (March 6–31, 1966).

In these ways the labor movement has effectively contributed to making Colombia a more democratic and open society. Furthermore, it has also improved the nature of politics. The labor federations have required politicians to state their programs and to work for them once elected. Although not always successful, the labor movement is the only organized spokesman for the lower classes that can bring pressure to bear on the politicians. Also, the labor movement has helped to renovate the political class in the country. From the ranks of the labor movement many men have risen to positions of power within the state and in the political apparatus. For example, three labor leaders were elected to the House of Representatives in 1966. Various other labor leaders won elections to city councils and state assemblies.

In the area of income distribution, the effect of the labor movement has also been less negative than the Colombian Left claims. Statistics on prices suggest that the terms of trade between the industrial and agricultural sectors have not deteriorated at the expense of the latter, thus implying that the unions have not been directly responsible for the stagnation in the standard of living of the rural population. If anything, the unions have improved the real income of blue-collar workers at the expense of white-collar workers. This redistribution of income, however, does not seem undesirable since before the emergence of collective bargaining in the fifties the wage differential between white- and blue-collar workers was abnormally high. If in fact the labor movement has had this redistributive effect, it would be difficult to criticize it on equity grounds.

In conclusion, it seems that in Colombia the positive contribution of unionism may far outweigh its negative impact on economic growth. It must be remembered that capital is not the only strategic factor affecting the rate of economic progress. It has now become far clearer than before that economic development cannot proceed without a favorable economic, social, and political climate. A study of the Colombian labor movement confirms the thesis of Paul Fisher that "it is in this environmental area that the major economic significance of the union lies . . . Union experience fosters substitution of reform for revolt. Union membership with its implied offer of democratic expression contributes to that political and social stability which is one of the basic ingredients of the climate in which peaceful economic development can proceed."[5]

5. Fisher, pp. 109, 113.

Statistical Appendix

To obtain some statistics that would make possible a discussion of the impact of unions on wages in Colombia, a survey of a sample of manufacturing firms was made by the author. Because of budgetary difficulties, the survey was carried out by mail, a circumstance that detracts from the results since the percentage of nonrespondents turned out to be very high.

The questionnaire was made on the basis of the experience obtained in twenty interviews with industrial relations directors and presidents of companies in Bogotá and Medellín, and it covered four major topics: turnover rates, whether the firm was or was not unionized, what federation the union belonged to, and the average wage of manual workers.

The sample of firms surveyed was taken at random from the directory of firms made available by the government statistical institute. The directory presumably includes all manufacturing firms of more than fifteen employees, so a random sample from the list of all firms of this size is theoretically representative of manufacturing firms. Unfortunately, as has been noted, the proportion of nonrespondents to the mail survey was very high.

For example, of the 302 questionnaires first sent out in November 1965, only 64 usable questionnaires came back. The total number of questionnaires returned with some usable data was 186. Unfortunately not all of the questionnaires sent back were

TABLE A-1

Distribution of the Sample by Size of Firm

Size of Firm (total number of workers)	Percentage Distribution in the 1963 *Anuario*	Percentage Distribution in the Sample from the 1964 *Directory of Firms*	Size of Firm (number of blue-collar workers)	Percentage Distribution of Responses
15–19	19	19	15–19 or less	25
20–24	14	14	20–24	8
25–49	31	31	25–49	24
50–74	12	13	50–74	13
75–99	6	6	75–99	7
100–199	10	9	100–199	12
200 or more	8	8	200 or more	11

completed, and in other cases the answers were obviously incorrect. For example, only 144 questionnaires were returned with usable wage data. Virtually all questionnaires had data on whether the firm had a union or not, and there were 146 questionnaires with usable data on turnover rates.

Although it is possible that the low response rate could have introduced a bias in the results, it appears that the firms that responded constituted a representative sample of manufacturing firms. In the first place, as Table A–1 shows, the distribution of firms by size in all manufacturing industry in the sample and among the respondents is very similar. Thus it appears that there was no bias such that larger than average firms are overrepresented in our survey.

Another possibility of bias was that on the average the better paying firms should have been more cooperative, and that therefore the results of the sample should have represented the situation in that kind of firm and not in manufacturing industry in general. It seems that this bias was not present either since according to DANE the average weekly salary in manufacturing for blue-

TABLE A–2

Wage Differentials by Size of Firm—DANE and Author's Samples
(average wage in largest grouping equal to 100)

Number of Workers in the Enterprise	DANE Sample 1964*	Author's Sample 1965
20–49	66	65
50–99	77	83
100–199	81	89
200–299	86	86
300–499	87	99
500–999	101	98
1,000 or more	100	100

*Special tabulation of the DANE wage sample for one month of 1964.

collar workers in November 1965 was P191.50, a figure very similar to the P204.54 average salary obtained in our sample.

Finally, it is possible that even if the average salary in the sample is similar to the average salary obtained by DANE, the firms of various sizes in our sample should not be representative of firms of similar size in the universe. But when a comparison is made between wage differentials for firms of different size in the DANE and the author's sample, we find once again a substantial similarity which suggests that the mail sample has not produced biased results. This comparison appears in Table A–2.

Thus, it was decided that the sample of union and nonunion firms is not biased because of the low rate of response and that its results can be used with some confidence.

Union-Nonunion Wage Differentials

Table A–3 shows the percentage of firms that had unions, and the percentage of workers in firms that had unions. Table A–4 shows the relative strength of the various national confederations.

TABLE A–3

Degree of Unionization in Manufacturing Firms

	Number of Firms	Workers in Union and Nonunion Firms (by percent)	Union and Nonunion Firms (by percent)
Union	65	78	38
Nonunion	105	22	62

From Table A–3 it is clear that unions are rare in small firms and common in large firms. Thus, although only 38 percent of the firms surveyed had unions, 78 percent of the workers in the firms surveyed worked in enterprises where labor was organized.

The average daily wage in enterprises without unions was P21.44, while the average wage* in enterprises with unions turned out to be P27.63. The question is, however, whether this difference is statistically significant or not.

TABLE A-4

Unions and Workers Affiliated to the Various Federations

Federation	Percent of Workers in Firms with Unions Belonging to:	Percent of Firms with Unions Belonging to:	Percent of All Manufacturing Workers Belonging to:
UTC	41	48	28
CTC	34	21	20
CSTCª	13	11	8
Independentᵇ	10	12	7
Other	2	8	2

a. CSTC is the official communist federation, although it has not been legally recognized by the government.

b. This includes leftist unions of various tendencies and some truly independent unions.

There was sufficient wage data for 87 firms without unions and for 57 firms with unions. To determine whether there was independence between union organization and wage levels, a chi-square test was used. At a 0.01 level of significance, and with one degree of freedom, the chi-square table gives a value of 6.64. The following null hypothesis was tested: that there is independence between average wages paid by firms, and the existence of unions in those firms. The X_0^2 value obtained from a contingency table was 15.64, which is significantly greater than 6.64 and therefore indicates that the differential between union and nonunion wages is statistically significant.

*The average was calculated as $\sum\limits^{i} \dfrac{\overline{W}_i}{n}$ where $\overline{W}_i$ is the average wage in enterprise i.

To determine whether the difference between the average wage in unionized and nonunionized firms is statistically significant, the test for the difference between two means was also used and the result was:

$$\frac{(\bar{x} - \bar{y}) - (\mu_x - \mu_y)}{\left(\dfrac{S_x^2}{N_x} + \dfrac{S_y^2}{N_y}\right)^{\frac{1}{2}}} = 3.71$$

This means that the wage differential is statistically significant at a 95 percent level of significance.

Although the above tests suggest that union firms pay significantly higher wages than nonunion firms, it is necessary to test whether this differential is due to labor organization or to some other factors. It is therefore necessary to test whether the union-nonunion differential is significant when other variables are held constant. First, the size of the firm must be held constant. In Table A–5 the average wages in union and nonunion firms

TABLE A–5

Average Union and Nonunion Wages of Workers in Firms of Different Sizes*

Size of Firm (number of blue-collar workers)	Firms with Unions		Firms without Unions	
	Number of Firms	Average Wage	Number of Firms	Average Wage
15–49	9	P23.26	68	P20.17
50–99	15	28.92	15	23.53
100–199	17	27.10	2	35.43
200 or more	17	31.12	1	27.15

*In contrast to other averages discussed in this appendix, where $\bar{X} = \dfrac{\overset{i}{\Sigma}\bar{W}_i}{n}$, in this table $\bar{X} = \dfrac{\Sigma\bar{W}L}{\Sigma L}$, where $\bar{W}$ is the average wage of workers in a firm and L is the total number of workers in that firm. The number of firms is n.

264

of different sizes are recorded. Since there were very few non-union firms with more than 100 workers, we tested the significance of the wage differentials only for firms smaller than this. The null hypothesis that there is independence between average wages paid by firms and the existence of unions in those firms was tested for all firms with fewer than 100 workers, and the estimated X_0^2 was 6.80, which is greater than the 6.64 obtained from the chi-square table. Thus when the size of the firm was held constant, a significant relationship was found between wages and the existence of a union in the enterprise. Using the test for the difference between two means in small samples we obtained a t value of 1.276 for firms with 15 to 49 workers and a t value of 1.345 for enterprises with 50 to 90 workers. In the first case the t value demonstrates a significant difference between the means at a 0.15 level of significance and the second case at a 0.10 level. This confirms the finding that there is a statistical relationship between the level of wages and unionization in firms of similar size.

Finally, it was decided to attempt to hold the level of skill of the labor force constant. To do this, the union and nonunion wages were compared in the following group of industries: food products, beverages, tobacco, shoe making, wood, leather products, pharmaceutical products, and clothing. The null hypothesis of independence between the level of wages and unionization was again tested, and at the 0.01 significance level, that hypothesis was again rejected. In this case, the calculated X_0^2 was 12.45, which is substantially above the theoretical 6.64 obtained from the chi-square table.

Methodologically, the major problem in the measurement of wage differentials between union and nonunion firms is the influence that unions may have on wages paid in nonunion firms. It may be that nonunion firms pay high wages in order to avoid unionization. This influence of unions on nonunion wages will lead to an underestimation of the impact of unions on wages if a simple comparison is made between firms that have been organized and those that have not.

In Table A–5 it can be observed that the wage differentials between union and nonunion firms of fewer than 100 workers fluctuates between 18 and 23 percent. Given the structure of the labor movement in Colombia the influence of organized labor on the wages of nonunion workers in small enterprises is probably small. This would determine that the measured wage differentials give a fairly good idea of the impact of unions on the level of wages of their members.

The most important characteristic of the Colombian labor movement is the size of the typical union. There are very few industrial or craft unions in the country, and the enterprise union is the prevalent form of organization. Given this union structure, when a firm is small and therefore capable of avoiding government control, it can pay a wage determined by the infinitely elastic supply of labor common in a high unemployment economy, since in these enterprises the cost of avoiding unionization and strikes is low. Therefore among small firms it is unlikely that unions will influence the level of wages in sectors without labor organization. Furthermore, collective bargaining in the large enterprises probably does not affect the level of wages in the rest of the economy, because the enterprise union is not an effective transmitter of wage gains in union firms.

Due to the structure of the labor movement and the existence of high levels of unemployment, in Colombia the salaries paid by small enterprises without unions are probably not influenced by collective bargaining in other sectors of the economy. Because of these institutional factors, it is reasonable to suppose that the labor movement is responsible for no more than the 18 to 23 percent increase in wages in the small- and medium-sized enterprises shown in Table A–5.

That table, however, does not allow us to calculate the impact of unions on the wages paid by large enterprises, since very few large enterprises are not unionized. Furthermore, even if some large enterprises do not have unions, it is clear that they can avoid unionization only by paying high salaries. This is the case of

Carvajal, the best-known nonunionized large company. That enterprise pays salaries and wages significantly above the average for the industry.

TABLE A–6

Wage Differentials Between Manufacturing Establishments of
Various Sizes

Size of the Enterprise (number of workers)	1956[a]	1958[b]	1963[c]	1965[d]
20–49	65	65	68	67
50–99	77	73	80	85
100–199	82	81	94	91
200 or more	100	100	100	100

a. DANE, *Anuario general de estadística, 1957* (Bogotá, Multilith Estadinal, 1958).

b. DANE, *Cifras estadisticas de la industria manufacturera nacional, 1958* (Bogotá, Multilith Estadinal, 1961), pp. 112–15.

c. DANE, *Anuario general de estadística, 1963* (Bogotá, Multilith Estadinal, 1965).

d. CEDE, "Muestra industrial, 1965" (unpublished data).

Many observers of the Colombian economy believe that unions have raised wages substantially in large enterprises at the expense of the consumer. This conclusion, however, does not seem to be supported by the data on wage differentials. Table A–6 shows that the wage differentials between large and small manufacturing enterprises have not increased in the last decade, the period of rapid increase in the real wages of manufacturing workers. For this reason, we estimate that unions have also been responsible for only an 18 to 23 percent increase in the wages of large manufacturing establishments over the level that would have prevailed in the absence of unions.

Turnover Rates

As far as is known, this survey provides the first data on turnover rates for Colombian industry. As can be seen from Table A–7, separation rates are very low in Colombia, and they seem to be substantially and significantly lower in union firms than in nonunion firms. A chi-square test was used to determine whether there was independence between turnover rates and the existence of a union in an enterprise. The X_0^2 value found was 11.69 which once again led to the rejection of the null hypothesis of independence. But since in the questionnaire the separation rates were divided into voluntary and involuntary separations, the chi-square test could be tried out for involuntary separations only. In this case, $X_0^2 = 1.59$. Since 1.59 is less than 6.63, the null hypothesis of independence between involuntary separations and the existence of unions could not be rejected.

TABLE A–7

Average Monthly Turnover Rates (Separation Rates) in Three Countries

	Colombia[a] 1965	United States[b] 1945	United States[b] 1958	India 1952	(Bombay 1953	Textiles)[c] 1954
Union	1.51%	—	—	—	—	—
Nonunion	3.42%	—	—	—	—	—
Total	2.57%	9.6%	4.1%	1.23%	1.03%	0.98%

a. Turnover rates were calculated in the following way: average number of workers per month who left the firm voluntarily and involuntarily during 1965, divided by the number of workers in the firm at the end of the year.

b. Data were chosen for years prior to 1959 because, starting in January 1959, published turnover rates refer to both blue- and white-collar workers. Previous data, limited to blue-collar workers, are more comparable with the Colombian data. U.S. Bureau of Labor Statistics, *Employment and Earnings Statistics for the United States, 1909–64* (Washington, D.C., G.P.O., 1964).

c. Charles A. Myers, *Labor Problems in the Industrialization of India* (Cambridge, Mass., Harvard University Press, 1958).

This result is consistent with the explanation that job security in Colombia is a result of legal protection. Since legal protection of workers covers both union and nonunion firms, there is no reason why involuntary separations should be related to the existence of unions. On the other hand, if wages in union firms are higher than wages in nonunion firms, it is logical that voluntary separations should be higher in nonunion firms than in union firms.

Estimates of Union Strength in 1965

Any estimate of the size of the labor movement should logically have as a basis the data published by the Ministry of Labor. Unfortunately, the union listings of the Ministry are never up to date and include many inactive unions. According to the Guia Sindical, there were 3,781 unions in 1965, of which 590 were rural unions. These figures, however, can be considered as an upper limit in view of the problem of inactive unions included in the listings. For example, a careful study in 1967 by the Labor Ministry determined that there were 556 rural unions instead of the 590 in the listings in 1965.

To estimate the maximum number of union members in the country we can multiply the 3,781 unions in the ministry files by 183, which is the average number of union members per union according to the 1947 union census. This gives us a total of 692,000 union members for 1965. But since the unions of today are probably larger on the average than those of 1947, it is necessary to correct the estimate for the average membership per union. The method used for such a correction was to assume that unions grew parallel to the growth in the average labor force per manufacturing enterprise.

Since in 1945 there was an average of 15 workers per establishment and in 1963 the average had increased to 25, it was assumed that the average union grew 67 percent between 1947 and 1965. The average urban union is therefore assumed to have 311 workers, which gives a maximum of some 992,000 union members in the urban sector. According to the 1967 *Memoria del Ministro de Trabajo,* the number of rural union members is 27,000, which means there was a maximum of 1,019,000 union members in 1965.

We can arrive at a more realistic estimate of union membership if we use the data presented at the Tenth Labor Congress of the UTC in 1965. Based on the reports of the regional federations of the UTC it can be estimated that the confederation had in December 1965 some 1,300 affiliated unions and 270,000 members. This gives an average of 208 members per union, a fairly plausible figure given the structure of the Colombian labor movement. If we multiply this average by the total number of unions in the Labor Ministry listings, we obtain an estimate of 786,000 union members for the country.

The sample of manufacturing firms described in this appendix also makes possible the distribution of union membership among the major confederations. Table A–4 shows that the UTC is clearly the strongest national labor confederation. The data of the survey give a distribution of membership very similar to that estimated by the communist writers N. Buenaventura, C. D. Cruz, and A. Paredes in the October-December 1964 issue of *Documentos Políticos.* In their article they estimate UTC strength at 350,000 members, and estimate total union membership in 1964 to be in the neighborhood of 666,000.

In summary, various independent estimates put total union membership in Colombia in 1965 at roughly 700,000 workers, of which somewhat less than a half belonged to the UTC.

270

Bibliography

General Reference Works

Alexander, Robert J., *Communism in Latin America,* New Brunswick, N.J., Rutgers University Press, 1957.

——, "The Jacobin Left and the Future of the Communists in Latin America," in *The Realities of World Communism,* ed. W. Petersen, Englewood Cliffs, N.J., Prentice-Hall, 1963.

——, *Labor Parties of Latin America,* New York, League for Industrial Democracy, 1942.

——, *Organized Labor in Latin America,* New York, Macmillan (The Free Press), 1965.

——, "Unions in Latin America and the Caribean Area," in *International Labor Directory and Handbook,* New York, Praeger, 1955.

Arcos, Juan, *El sindicalismo en américa latina,* Estudios sociológicos Latinoamericanos, no. 12, Madrid, Sucesores de Rivadeneyra, 1964.

Caplow, Theodore, *The Sociology of Work,* New York, McGraw, 1954.

Consejo Interamericano Económico y Social, *Informe final de la segunda reunión de la comisión especial del CIES sobre asuntos laborales,* Washington, D.C., Unión Panamericana, 1964.

——, *Resumen de los informes nacionales sobre la situación laboral en el continente,* Washington, Unión Panamericana, 1964.

Di Tella, Torcuato S., *El sistema político argentino y la clase obrera,* Buenos Aires, Eudeba, 1964.

Form, William, and Albert A. Blum, *Industrial Relations and Social*

Change in Latin America, Gainesville, University of Florida Press, 1965.

Friedman, G., and P. Naville, *Tratado de sociología del trabajo,* 2 vols. Mexico City, Fondo de Cultura Económica, 1963.

Friedman, Milton, "Some Comments on the Significance of Labor Unions for Economic Policy," in *The Impact of the Union,* ed. McCord Wright, New York, 1951.

Gavin, Miles E., *Unionism in Latin America,* New York State School of Industrial and Labor Relations, Bulletin 45, Ithaca, N.Y., Cornell University Press, 1962.

Guillen Martínez, Fernando, *Raíz y futuro de la revolución,* Bogotá, Tercer Mundo, 1963.

Hicks, J. R., *The Theory of Wages,* London, Macmillan, 1932.

International Labor Organization, *The Role of Labor Ministries in the Improvement of Labor Relations in Latin America,* Labor Management Relations Series, no. 20, Geneva, 1964.

———, *Some Aspects of Labor Management Relations in the American Region,* Labor Management Relations Series, nos. 11 and 11A, Montevideo, 1960.

Launterbach, A., "Government and Development: Managerial Attitudes in Latin America," *Journal of Inter-American Studies, 7* (April 1965).

Mehta, Asoka, "The Mediating Role of the Trade Union in Underdeveloped Countries," *Economic Development and Cultural Change, 6* (October 1957).

Poblete Troncoso, Moisés, *El movimiento obrero latinoamericano,* Mexico City, Fondo de Cultura Económica, 1946.

Poblete Troncoso, Moisés, and B. G. Burnett, *The Rise of the Latin American Labor Movement,* New York, Bookman Associates, 1960.

Rama, Carlos M., *Mouvements ouvriers et socialistes: l'Amérique Latine,* Paris, Editions Ouvrières, 1959.

Romualdi, Serafino, "Labor and Democracy in Latin America," *Foreign Affairs, 25* (April 1947).

Simon, Fanny S., "Anarquismo y Anarco-Sindicalismo en América del Sur," *Mundo Libre, 4,* 54 (July 1946).

Sturmthal, A., and D. Felix, "Latin American Labor Unions," *Monthly Labor Review, 83* (June 1960).

Sturmthal, Adolf, "Unions and Economic Development," *Economic Development and Cultural Change, 8* (January 1960).

Sufrin, Sidney S., *Unions in Emerging Societies,* Syracuse, N.Y., Syracuse University Press, 1964.

Ulman, Lloyd, "Marshall and Friedman on Union Strength," *Review of Economics and Statistics, 37* (November 1955).

Webb, Sidney and Beatrice, *Industrial Democracy,* London, Longman's Green, 1902.

Nineteenth Century

Political and Economic History

Bushnell, David, *El régimen de Santander en la gran Colombia,* Bogotá, Tercer Mundo, 1966.

Camacho Roldán, Salvador, *Acusación i denuncio contra el ciudadano presidente de la república i los secretarios de gobierno i de guerra por la responsabilidad en que han incurrido por consequencia de la traición i rebeldía consumadas el 17 de abril,* Bogotá, Imprenta de Echeverri Hermanos, 1845.

Cárdenas Acosta, Pablo E., *La restauración constitucional de 1867,* Tunja, Colombia, Galería de Autores Boyacenses, 1966.

Cordovez Moure, José María, *Reminiscencias de Santafé y Bogotá,* Bogotá, Biblioteca Popular de Cultura Colombiana, 1945.

Cuervo, Angel, and Rufino José Cuervo, *Vida de Rufino Cuervo y noticias de su epoca,* Bogotá, Biblioteca Popular de Cultura Colombiana, 1946.

Le Moyne, Augusto, *Viajes y estancias en América del Sur: la Nueva Granada, Santiago de Cuba, y el Istmo de Panamá,* Bogotá, Biblioteca Popular de Cultura Colombiana, 1945.

Liévano Aguirre, Indalecio, *Los grandes conflictos sociales y económicos de nuestra historia,* Bogotá, Ediciones Nueva Prensa, 1962.

———, *El proceso de Mosquera ante el Senado,* Bogotá, Italgraf, 1966.

Mantoux, Paul, *The Industrial Revolution in the Eighteenth Century,* New York, Harper Torchbooks, 1962.

Mollien, Gaspard T., *Voyage dans la republique de Colombie en 1823,* Bogotá, Biblioteca Popular de Cultura Colombiana, 1949.

Nieto Arteta, Luis Eduardo, *El café en la sociedad colombiana,* Bogotá, Breviarios de Orientación Colombiana, 1958.

Ospina Vásquez, Luis, *Industria y protección en Colombia, 1810–1930,* Medellín, E.S.F., 1955.

———, *Plan agrícola,* Medellín, Editorial Granamérica, 1963.

Parsons, James J., "Antioqueño Colonization in Western Colombia," *Ibero-Americana, 32* (1949)

Pérez Aguirre, Antonio, *25 Años de historia colombiana, 1835 a 1878. Del centralismo a la federación,* Bogotá, Editorial Sucre, 1959.

Reseña histórica de los principales acontecimientos políticos de la ciudad de Cali, desde el año de 1848 hasta el de 1855 inclusive, Bogotá, Imprenta de Echeverri Hermanos, 1856.

Restrepo, José Manuel, *Historia de la Nueva Granada, 1832–1845,* Bogotá, Editorial Cromos, 1952.

———, *Historia de la Nueva Granada, 1845–1854,* Bogotá, Editorial El Catolicismo, 1963.

Rivas, Medardo, *Los trabajadores de tierra caliente,* Bogotá, Biblioteca de Cultura Colombiana, 1946.

Robertson, Priscilla, *Revolutions of 1848—A Social History,* New York, Harper Torchbooks, 1960.

Safford, Frank, "Foreign and National Enterprise in Nineteenth Century Colombia," *The Business History Review, 39* (Winter 1965).

Samper Bernal, Gustavo, *Breve historia constitucional y política de Colombia,* Bogotá, Litografía Colombia S.A., 1957.

Thompson, David, *Europe Since Napoleon,* New York, Knopf, 1958.

Intellectual History

Colmenares, Germán, "El Conservatismo y sus Fuentes," *Eco, 12* (November 1965).

———, "Florentino González, El Mentor," *Revista del Colegio Mayor de Nuestra Señora del Rosario, 59* (November-December 1965).

———, "Formas de la Conciencia de Clase en la Nueva Granada de 1848," *Boletín Cultural y Bibliográfico, 2, 3* (1966).

———, "Formas de la Conciencia de Clase en la Nueva Granada— Las Cuestiones que se Debatían," *Boletín Cultural y Bibliográfico, 2, 4* (1966).

Gilmore, Robert Louis, "Nueva Granada's Socialist Mirage," *The Hispanic American Historical Review, 36* (May 1956).

Jaramillo Uribe, Jaime, *El pensamiento colombiano en el siglo xix,* Bogotá, Editorial Temis, 1964.

Manuel, Frank N., *The Prophets of Paris,* Cambridge, Mass., Harvard University Press, 1962.

Nieto Arteta, Luis Eduardo, *Economía y cultura en la historia de Colombia,* Bogotá, Tercer Mundo, 1962.

Wilson, Edmund, *To the Finland Station,* Garden City, N.Y., Doubleday Anchor Books, 1940.

Labor History

Estatutos de la Sociedad de Artesanos de Manizales fundada en abril de 1910, Manizales, Imprenta "El Renacimiento," 1911.

Estatutos de la Sociedad de Mutuo Auxilio de Barranquilla, Barranquilla, 1899.

Estatutos de la Sociedad Cooperativa Fraternal de Ocaña, Santander, December 1895.

Estatutos de la Sociedad de Socorros Mutuos de Manizales, Bogotá, Imprenta de Zalamea Hnos, 1889.

Estatutos y escritura de asociación de la Sociedad de Socorros Mutuos de Cali, Cali, 1898.

Heredia, Emeterio, *Contestación al cuaderno titulado "El desengaño o confidencias de Ambrosio López, etc." por el presidente que fué de la Sociedad de Artesanos el 7 de marzo de 1849,* Bogotá, Imprenta de Morales, 1851.

Informe de la Sociedad de Mutuo Auxilio de Bucaramanga (December 1892).

López, Ambrosio, *El desengaño o confidencias de Ambrosio López primer director de la Sociedad de Artesanos de Bogotá denominada hoi "Sociedad Democrática,"* Bogotá, Imprenta de Espinosa, 1851.

————, *Invitación a la fiesta de la Santísima Trinidad,* Bogotá, Focion Mantilla, 1865.

————, *El triunfo sobre la serpiente Roja cuyo asunto es del dominio de la nación,* Bogotá, Imprenta de Espinosa, 1851.

Reglamento de la Sociedad de Artesanos, Bogotá, Imprenta de Nicolás Gómez, 1847.

Reglamento de la Sociedad de Mutuo Auxilio y Beneficencia en Girardota, Medellin, Imprenta Oficial, 1906.

Reglamento para la instrucción de la Sociedad de Artesanos de Bogotá, Bogotá, Imprenta de Nicolás Gómez, 1849.

Sociedad de Socorros Mutuos—acta de la sección solemne verificada el 6 de agosto de 1890, Bucaramanga, Imprenta de Silva y Plata, 1890.

Triana y Antorveza, Humberto, "El Aspecto religioso en los Gremios Neogranadinos," *Boletín Cultural y Bibliográfico, 9,* 2 (1966).

————, "Exámenes, Licencias, Fianzas y Elecciones Artesanales," *Boletín Cultural y Bibliográfico, 9,* 1 (1966).

————, "Extranjeros y Grupos Etnicos en los Gremios Neogranadinos," *Boletín Cultural y Bibliográfico, 8,* 1 (1965).

————, "La Protección Social en los Gremios de Artesanos Neogranadinos," *Boletín Cultural y Bibliográfico, 9,* 3 (1966).

Twentieth Century

Political, Intellectual, and Economic History of Colombia

Comisión Económica para América Latina, *El desarrollo económico de Colombia,* Mexico City, Naciones Unidas, 1957.

Comité Central del Partido Comunista de Colombia, *Treinta años de lucha del Partido Comunista de Colombia,* Bogotá, Editorial Paz y Socialismo, 1960.

Córdoba, José María, *Jorge Eliécer Gaitán,* Bogotá, Litografías Cor-Val, n.d.

Cuéllar Vargas, Enrique, *13 Años de violencia,* Bogotá, Ediciones Cultura Social Colombiana, 1960.

Fluharty, Vernon Lee, *Dance of the Millions: Military Rule and the Social Revolution in Colombia, 1930–1956,* Pittsburgh, University of Pittsburgh Press, 1957.

Gaitán, Jorge Eliécer, *Las ideas socialistas en Colombia,* Bogotá, Editorial América Libre, 1963.

García, Antonio, *Gaitán y el problema de la revolución colombiana,* Bogotá, Cooperativa Nacional de Artes Gráficas, 1955.

Guillén Martinez, F., et al., "Existe en Colombia una oligarquía?" *Acción Liberal, 3* (February-March 1966).

Gutierrez, José, *De la pseudo-aristocracia a la autenticidad,* Bogotá, Tercer Mundo, 1961.

Guzmán, Mons. Germán, O. Fals Borda, and E. Umaña Luna, *La violencia en Colombia,* 2 vols. Bogotá, Tercer Mundo, 1962–1964.

Hagen, E. E., *El cambio social en Colombia,* Bogotá, Tercer Mundo, 1963.

———, *On the Theory of Social Change,* Homewood, Ill., The Dorsey Press, 1962.

Kalnins, Arvids, *Análisis de la moneda y de la política monetaria colombiana,* Bogotá, Tercer Mundo, 1963.

Latorre Cabal, Hugo, *Mi novela: apuntes autobiográficos de Alfonso López,* Bogotá, Ediciones Mito, 1961.

Latorre Rueda, Mario, "Radiografía de dos Elecciones," *Acción Liberal, 2* (October-November 1965).

Lleras Restrepo, Carlos, *De la república a la dictadura,* Bogotá, Argra, 1955.

López de Mesa, Luis, *Escrutinio sociológico de la historia colombiana,* Bogotá, Biblioteca Eduardo Santos, 1956.

López Pumarejo, Alfonso, "Conferencia en el Teatro Municipal, noviembre 30, 1936," *Acción Liberal,* no. 42 (December 1936).

Mendoza Neira, Plinio, and Alberto Camacho Angarita, *El liberalismo en el gobierno,* 3 vols. Bogotá, Prag, 1946.

Montaña Cuéllar, Diego, *Colombia, país formal y país real,* Buenos Aires, Editorial Platina, 1963.

Morales Benítez, Otto, *Revolución y caudillos,* Medellín, Horizonte, 1957.

Nieto Rojas, José María, *La batalla contra el comunismo en Colombia,* Bogotá, Empresa Nacional de Publicaciones, 1956.

Parra Sandoval, Rodrigo, *El caso de la candelaria: la estructura social y el cambio en la tecnología agrícola,* Bogotá, Tercer Mundo, 1966.

Puentes, Milton, *Historia del Partido Liberal colombiano,* Bogotá, prag, 1965.

Santa, Eduardo, *Sociología política de Colombia,* Bogotá, Tercer Mundo, 1964.

Torres García, Guillermo, *Historia de la moneda en Colombia,* Bogotá, Imprenta del Banco de República, 1945.

Documents on Colombian Labor

Almarales, A., and M. Goenaga, *Las luchas obreras y la legislación laboral,* Cali, Ediciones Bloque Sindical Independiente del Valle del Cauca, 1964.

Barbieri, William M., S.J., "Latin America's 'New Breed,'" *The Sign,* 44 (April 1965).

Bonilla, Victor Daniel, "Tolima 1, Primer proyecto de la reforma agraria," *Tierra, 1* (July-September 1966).

Braum, Kurt, *Labor in Colombia,* U.S. Department of Labor, Bureau of Labor Statistics Report no. 222 (March 1962).

Buenaventura, N., C. D. Cruz, and A. Paredes, "Es la clase obrera vanguardia revolucionaria en Colombia?" *Documentos Políticos,* no. 45 (October-December 1964).

Caballero Calderón, E., *Siervo sin tierra,* Medellín, Bedout, n.d.

Caicedo, Edgar, "Vida y Pasión del Sindicalismo Colombiano," *Cromos, 88* (May 4, 1959).

Castrillón, Alberto, *Ciento veinte dias bajo el terror militar o la huelga de las bananeras,* Bogotá, Tallerres de la Revista Universidad, 1929.

Confederación de Trabajadores de Colombia, *xii Congreso nacional del trabajo de la Confederación de Trabajadores de Colombia,* Bogotá, Tip. Portilla, 1963.

————, *Informe de actividades: abril 1963–abril 1965*, Bogotá, Tip. Portilla, 1965.

Cortés Vargas, Carlos, *Los sucesos de las bananeras*, Bogotá, Imprenta de "La Luz," 1929.

Cuevas, Tulio, et al., "La Política Laboral," *Acción Liberal, 3* (February-March 1965).

Donado Salcedo, Ricardo, *Salario mínimo*, Bogotá, Universidad Javeriana, 1958.

Durán, Augusto, "Colombia Faces the Imperialist Offensive," *The Communist, 20* (July 1941).

Espinosa, Justiniano, *La contratación colectiva*, Bogotá, Editorial Justicia, 1962.

————, *Manual sindical*, Bogotá, Instituto de Fomento Gremial, 1964.

————, *El sindicalismo*, 2d ed., Bogotá, Editorial Justicia, n. d.

————, *Los sindicatos y su papel en la construcción de un mundo mejor*, Bogotá, Editorial Justicia, 1956.

Fals Borda, Orlando, *El hombre y la tierra en Boyacá*, Bogotá, Antares, 1957.

Grant, J. A. C., "Colombia Tackles Dual Unionism," *Inter-American Economic Affairs, 2* (Spring 1949).

Gutiérrez, José, *La rebeldía colombiana*, Bogotá, Tercer Mundo, 1962.

Gutiérrez Navarro, Issac, *La luz de una vida*, Bogotá, Editorial ABC, 1949.

Haddox, Benjamín E., *Sociedad y religión en Colombia*, Bogotá, Tercer Mundo, 1965.

Havens, E., and M. Romieux, *Barrancabermeja, conflictos sociales en torno a un centro petrolero*, Bogotá, Tercer Mundo, 1966.

Havens, Eugene A., *Támesis, estructura y cambio*, Bogotá, Tercer Mundo, 1966.

ICFTU, "Activities of the UTC in 1955," *Free Labor World, 67* (January 1956).

Instituto de Educación y Capacitación Sindical de la Confederación de Trabajadores de Colombia, *Manual de educación sindical*, Bogotá, Tip. Portilla, 1963.

Jiménez Cadena, Gustavo, *Sacerdote y cambio social*, Bogotá, Tercer Mundo, 1967.

Lipman, Aaron, *El empresario colombiano*, Bogotá, Tercer Mundo, 1966.

Mock, James R., and Eugene D. Owen, "Employment Situation in Latin America," *Monthly Labor Review, 62* (May 1946).

Morales Benítez, Otto, *Planteamientos sociales*, Bogotá, Imprenta Nacional, 1960.

————, *Reforma del código del trabajo*, Bogotá, Imprenta Nacional, 1960.

"El Movimiento Huelguístico en 1965," *Documentos Políticos*, no. 56 (January 1966).

Muñoz Vila, Cecilia, *El nivel de vida de los trabajadores ferroviarios*, Bogotá, Universidad Nacional, 1963.

Oficina Internacional del Trabajo, *Informe al gobierno de Colombia sobre la política a seguir en la retribución del trabajo*, Geneva, International Labour Office, 1963.

Organización Regional Interamericana de Trabajadores, *15 años de sindicalismo libre interamericano*, Mexico City, Impresiones Modernas, 1963.

————, *Informe al sexto congreso continental* Mexico City, 1965.

Osorio, Roso, "El Congreso Sindical," *Documentos Políticos*, no. 61 (August 1956).

Padilla, Jorge, *Les Conflicts collectifs du travail en Colombie*, Bordeaux, Imprimerie Drouillard, 1941.

Palacio Mejía, Hugo, "Los Grupos de Presión en Colombia y el Paro de Enero," *Universitas, 3* (July 1965).

Puentes Vanegas, Ventura, *Curso elemental de educación sindical*, Bogotá, Editorial Suramericana, 1965.

Restrepo Hoyos, Jorge, *Aspectos económicos de la seguridad social en Colombia*, Bogotá, Cromos, 1960.

Rincón, Victor M., *La rebelión popular*, Imprenta Osmar, 1965.

Rippy, J. Fred, *The Capitalists and Colombia*, New York, The Vanguard Press, 1931.

Robles, Nelson, "La Lucha en el Movimiento Sindical," *Documentos Políticos*, no. 60 (June-July 1966).

Ruiz, H., "La Situación de la Clase Obrera en Antioquia y el Movimiento Sindical," *Documentos Políticos*, no. 45 (October-December 1964).

Santa, Eduardo, *Rafael Uribe Uribe*, Bogotá, Ediciones Triángulo, 1962.

Sindicato Nacional de Trabajadores de Bavaria, S.A., *Estatutos*, Bogotá, 1965.

Sindicato Nacional de Trabajadores del Consorcio de Cervecerías Bavaria, S.A. *Estatutos*, Bogotá, 1952.

Sociedad Obrera de Fenicia, *Estatutos*, Bogotá, 1934.

Tovar Mozo, Efraín, *Zig zag en las bananeras*, Bogotá, Offset de Colombia, 1964.

Unión de Trabajadores de Colombia, *Estatutos,* Bogotá, 1962.

Unión de Trabajadores de Cundinamarca, *Qué es y qué ha hecho?* Bogotá, Editorial Justicia, 1961.

Urrutia, M., and L. Castellanos, *Estudio económico social de la población de bogotá,* Bogotá, C.A.R., 1962.

Urrutia, M., *Estudio económico social de los centros urbanos secundarios de la C.A.R.,* Bogotá, C.A.R., 1963.

————, "La Viabilidad de una Política de Salarios en Colombia," *La Nueva Economía, 4,* 1 (May, 1966).

United States Department of Labor, Bureau of Labor Statistics, *Labor Law and Practice in Colombia,* BLS Report no. 217, Washington, D.C., 1962.

Villegas, Guillermo, S.J., *Doctrina social católica,* Bogotá, Instituto de Fomento Gremial.

————, *Etica sindical,* Bogotá, Instituto de Fomento Gremial, 1963.

Yepes Zuluaga, Horacio, "El Movimiento Sindical Colombiano," *Estudios de Derecho, 55* (February-March 1959).

Zuleta Holguín, Francisco, "Paralelismo Sindical," *La Segunda República,* Bogotá, Editorial Nuevo Signo, 1956.

Comparative Works

Abegglen, J. C., *The Japanese Factory,* Glencoe, Ill., The Free Press, 1958.

Alexander, J., *Labor Relations in Argentina, Brazil and Chile,* Cambridge, Mass., Harvard University Press, 1962.

Commons, John R., et al., *History of Labor in the United States,* New York, Macmillan, 1961.

Davis, Tom E., "Capital y Salarios Reales en la Economía Chilena," *Cuadernos de Economía, 3,* 8 (January-April 1966).

Dudra, Michael, "Approaches to Union Security in Switzerland, Canada and Colombia," *Monthly Labor Review, 86* (February 1963).

Ferrer, Aldo, *La economía argentina,* Mexico City, Fondo de Cultura Económica, 1965.

Fillol, Tomás Roberto, *Social Factors in Economic Development: The Argentina Case,* Cambridge, Mass., M.I.T. Press, 1961.

Galenson, Walter, ed. *Comparative Labor Movement,* New York, Prentice Hall, 1955.

————, *The Danish System of Labor Relations,* Cambridge, Mass., Harvard University Press, 1952.

————, *Labor and Economic Development,* New York, Wiley, 1959.

————, *Labor in Developing Economies,* Berkeley, University of California Press, 1963.

Hotani, R., and H. Takashi, "The Evolution of Wage Structure in Japan," *Industrial and Labor Relations Review, 15* (October 1961).

Kassalow, Everett M. ed., *National Labor Movements in the Postwar World,* Evanston, Ill., Northwestern University Press, 1963.

Levine, Solomon B., *Industrial Relations in Postwar Japan,* Urbana, Ill., University of Illinois Press, 1958.

Myers, Charles A., *Labor Problems in the Industrialization of India,* Cambridge, Mass., Harvard University Press, 1958.

Payne, James, *Labor and Politics in Peru: The System of Political Bargaining,* New Haven, Conn., Yale University Press, 1965.

———,"Peru: The Politics of Structured Violence," *The Journal of Politics, 27* (May 1965).

Taira, Koji, "The Characteristics of Japanese Labor Markets," *Economic Development and Cultural Change, 10* (January 1962).

———, "The Dynamics of Wage Differentials in Japanese Economic Development, 1880–1940," Western Economic Association, *Proceedings of the Thirty-Fifth Annual Conference,* 1960.

———, "Japanese 'Enterprise Unionism' and Interfirm Wage Structure," *Industrial and Labor Relations Review, 15* (October 1961).

———, "Market Forces and Public Power in Wage Determination: Early Japanese Experience," *Social Research, 30* (Winter 1963).

Ulman, Lloyd, *American Trade Unionism, Past and Present,* Berkeley, Cal., Institute of Industrial Relations, Reprint no. 157, 1961.

Universidad Central de Venezuela, Centro de Estudios del Desarollo (CENDES), *Estudio de conflictos y consenso, muestra de líderes sindicales,* Caracas, Editorial Arte, 1965.

Government Documents and Statistical Sources

Anuario general de estadística (1916–); has been published by various agencies, including Ministerio de Hacienda, Contraloría de la República, and DANE.

Asociación Nacional de Industriales, "Survey of Manufacturing firms," 1961 (mimeographed).

Banco de la República, "Cuentas nacionales" (mimeographed).

Centro de Estudios sobre Desarrollo Economico (CEDE), *Demand Projections for Agricultural Products in Colombia,* Bogotá, University of Los Andes, 1966.

———, "Encuestas sobre Desempleo en Bogotá," Bogotá, 1966 (mimeographed).

Código sustantivo del trabajo y código procesal del trabajo, Bogotá, Colección "Codex Brevis," 1966.

Comisión Operativa del Ingreso y la Cooperación Social, *Conclusiones,* Bogotá, Ministerio del Trabajo, 1966.

Consejo Nacional del Trabajo, *Para una política de empleo,* Bogotá, Ministerio del Trabajo, 1966.

Contraloría General de la República, *Primer censo industrial de Colombia, 1945,* Bogotá, Imprenta Nacional, 1947.

————, *Primer censo sindical de Colombia, 1947,* Bogotá, Editorial Minerva, 1949.

Departamento Administrativo Nacional de Estadística, *XII Censo de población,* Bogotá, DANE, 1965.

————, *Cifras estadísticas de la industria manufacturera nacional,* Bogotá, DANE, 1961.

————, Estadísticas Laborales, raw data of the manufacturing industry sample, used to obtain wages by size of firm.

Incora, *Informes de actividades,* Bogotá, Incora, 1962–64.

Ministerio de Gobierno, Departamento de Justicia, *Reseña del movimiento sindical, 1909–1937,* Bogotá, Imprenta Nacional, 1937.

Ministerio de Industrias, *Memoria presentada al Congreso,* 1924–38, Bogotá, Imprenta Nacional, same date as in title.

Ministerio de Trabajo, *Caldas: memoria explicativa del "atlas" socioeconómico del departamento,* Bogotá, Empresa Nacional de publicaciones, 1957.

————, "Cuadro Histórico del Salario Mínimo en el País a Partir del año 1949" (unpublished).

————, "Encuesta de Salarios Mínimos en el Sector Público, 1963" (unpublished).

————, "Guía Sindical," 1965 (unpublished).

————, *Memoria del Ministro de Trabajo al Congreso,* 1947–48, 1959–66, Bogotá, Imprenta Nacional, same date as in title. The latest *Memorias* have been published directly by the Ministry.

————, *Seguridad social campesina,* Bogotá, Editorial Cosmos, 1954.

Ministerio de Trabajo, Higiene y Previsión Social, *Memoria del Ministro de Trabajo, Higiene y Previsión Social,* 1939–46, Bogotá, Imprenta Nacional, same date as in title. In 1936–38 the *Memoria* was published by Editorial "El Grafico"; the 1946 *Memoria* was published in 1947.

Ministerio de Trabajo, Sección Económica Laboral, "Convenciones Colectivas y Pactos entre Junio 1958 y Febrero 1965" (unpublished).

SENA, División de Recursos Humanos, "Aportantes al SENA por Seccionales y Actividades Económicas," July 1966 (unpublished).

————, "Empresas del Sector no Agropecuario que Aportaron al SENA—Estimativo a 1966" (unpublished).

United States Department of Labor, Bureau of Labor Statistics, *Employment and Earnings Statistics for the United States, 1909–1962,* Bulletin 1312–1, Washington, D.C., G.P.O., 1963.

UTC, "Lista de Sindicatos Afiliados a U.T.C. en Junio, 1965" (unpublished).

Other Unpublished Material

Andrade Valderrama, Vicente, "Panorama del Movimiento Sindical en Colombia," January 1963–, (author's possession).

ANDI, "Algunos Comentarios al Resumen de 53 Convenciones Colectivas Vigentes en Cuanto a Estabilidad en el Empleo," May 1965.

———, "La Reforma Laboral del Decreto 2351 de Septiembre 4, 1965" (mimeographed).

Camacho, Armando, "Informe Acerca de la Confederación de Trabajadores de Colombia (CTC)," July 1957.

Colmenares, Germán, "Los Artesanos" (author's possession).

Conde Mantilla, Virgilio, "El Movimiento Sindical en Colombia" (author's possession).

Coordinación Nacional de Acción Social Católica, "Actividad Sindical Cristiana en Colombia" (mimeographed).

Duque, S., and J. F. Ocampo, "Situación Laboral en Manizales," 1965 (author's possession).

"Estatutos para la Coordinación de Acción Social de la Arquidiocesis de Medellín" (mimeographed).

Garzón, Pablo Jaime, "Apuntes de Historia Sindical," Bogotá, Instituto de Fomento Gremial, 1966 (mimeographed).

———, "Reseña Histórica del Movimiento Sindical," Bogotá, Fomento Gremial, 1962 (rough draft).

Hadley, George, "Some Characteristics of Colombian Industry," Bogotá, CEDE, 1965.

McGreevey, William Paul, "Economic Development of Colombia," doctoral dissertation, M.I.T., 1965.

Morris, James O., "The Labor Relations System of Chile," New York State School of Industrial and Labor Relations (mimeographed).

Newton, June, "The Labor Movement in Colombia," master's thesis, University of Chicago, 1945.

Recio, Manuel, "Algo sobre el VIII Congreso Sindical," UTC Archives, 1946.

"Reunión de Coordinadores de Acción Social, Conclusiones," February 1965.

Safford, Frank R., "Commerce and Enterprise in Central Colombia, 1821–1870," doctoral dissertation, Columbia University, 1965.
Savage, Charles H., "Social Organization in a Developing Economy," doctoral dissertation, Harvard Business School, 1962.
Stuart, William, et al., "Un Análisis Regional Preliminar de San Miguel de Sema, Boyacá," Bogotá, C.A.R., 1962.
UTC, Archives, 1946–65.
Villegas, Guillermo, S.J., "El Sindicalismo Colombiano en los Ultimos Años," UTC Archives, 1955.

Newspapers and Periodicals

Acción Liberal, 1934–39, 1965–.
Banco de la República, *Revista del Banco de la República,* 1927–.
El Bolchevique, 1934–35.
CTC, 1959–60.
Departamento Administrativo Nacional de Estadística, *Boletín Mensual de Estadística,* 1952–.
Diario Oficial, 1946–.
Dirigentes Agrarios, 1965.
Documentos Políticos, 1964–.
Ediciones Laborales, 1965– (Medellín).
El Espectador, 1918– (Bogotá).
Gaceta Oficial, 1851–54.
Gaceta Republicana, 1918–19.
El Hotelero, 1966– (Bogotá).
Justicia Social, 1946–(Bogotá).
Semana, 1946–61 (Bogotá).
El Siglo, 1936–53, 1957–.
El Tiempo, 1918–55, 1957–.
UTRACUN, 1955–.
Voz Proletaria, 1955–.

Index

285